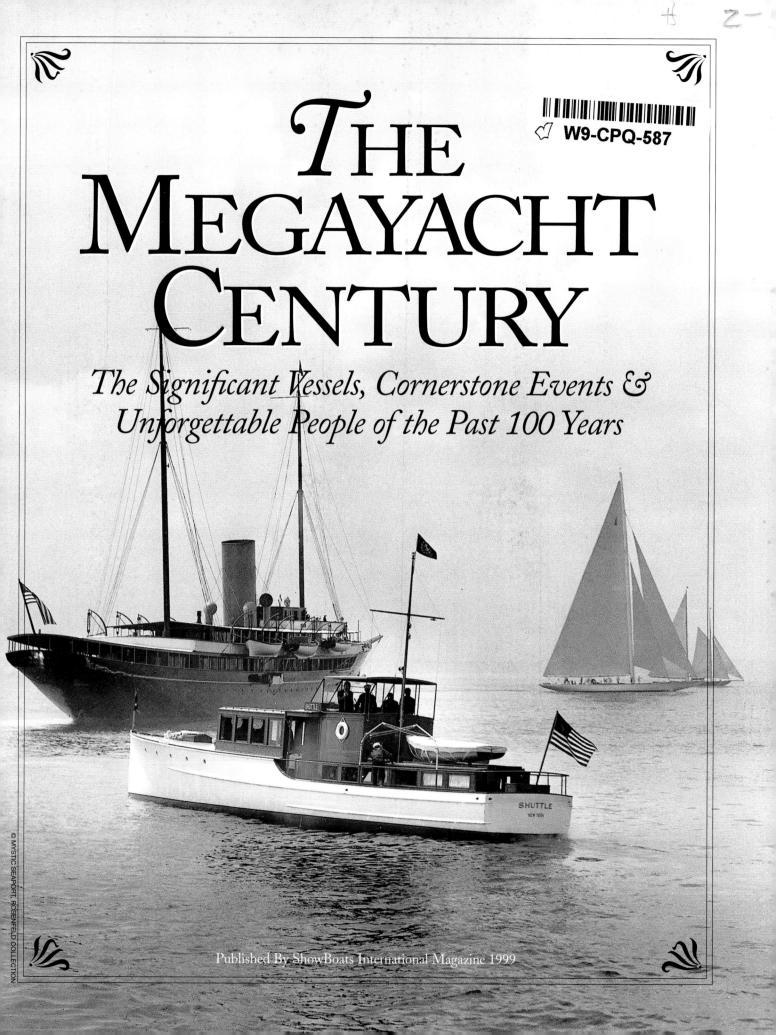

THE MEGAYACHT CENTURY

The Significant Vessels, Cornerstone Events & Unforgettable People of the Past 100 Years

Published By ShowBoats International Magazine 1999

When launched in 1921, *Delphine* was the largest yacht in gross-tonnage measurement (1,255) ever built in the U.S. With her own ice-making plant, she pampered her guests with rudimentary air conditioning.

❧THE❧ MEGAYACHT CENTURY

The Significant Vessels, Cornerstone Events & Unforgettable People of the Past 100 Years

ISBN 0-9674903-0-8

Editor-in-Chief
JAMES R. GILBERT

Executive Editor
MARILYN M. MOWER

Art Director
JANET SANTELICES

Production Supervisor
ANDREW HOFFMAN

Produced by
SHOWBOATS INTERNATIONAL MAGAZINE

LESTER A. ABBERLEY II
Publisher

HACHETTE FILIPACCHI MAGAZINES
1633 Broadway, New York, NY

ON THE COVER:
Giralda at Cowes 1898,
Watercolor 21" x 32-1/2", By Martyn Mackrill

Designed and built by Cox, King and Fairfield in 1894, 306-foot *Giralda* had been built for an American and then sold to the Spanish Navy as a dispatch boat. After his accession to the throne in 1902, however, King Alphonso XIII realized her magnificent lines and had her fitted out as his royal yacht and tender to his Meter Class racing sailboats. The king was a member of the Royal Yacht Squadron and thus *Giralda* was frequently at Cowes. On *Giralda's* starboard is *Victoria* and *Albert II.*

ON THE TITLE PAGE:
Corsair, Rainbow and Shuttle, 1920
© Mystic Seaport, Rosenfeld Collection,
Mystic Conneticut

Prince Albert
of Monaco
aboard the William
Fife-designed *Tuiga.*

❦ FOREWORD ❧

Monaco, September 1999

      The past 100 years of yachting provide an extraordinary perspective from which to gauge many of the people, places and events that have shaped and changed our lives. At the same time, the last century provides, I believe, a perfect proof of the adage that the more things change, the more they remain the same.

      A case in point is my great-grandfather and namesake, H.S.H. Prince Albert I of Monaco. Over the years I have often thought about how he would view the modern age with its lightning-fast technological changes. Certainly he was a man ahead of his own time, a man of singular vision and energy who believed fervently in the power of science and progress to improve man's quality of life. Yet he was also an ardent supporter of the arts, a committed family man, an adventurer and a passionate yachtsman. In short, every inch the prototype of a modern man. His many accomplishments include commissioning the first major transportation tunnels in the world, building the remarkable jetties that turned Port Hercules into a bonafide all-season harbor, and establishing the Museum of Oceanography, the very first oceanographic institution in the world.

      His yachts, L'Hirondelle and Princess Alice not only are among the largest yachts ever built, but they took Prince Albert I on fantastic voyages of discovery. At sea on his yachts he mapped the ocean floor, collected important specimens, discovered new species of life and invented many instruments and techniques that played critical roles in expanding man's knowledge of the sea.

      In the end, I think he would regard the modern age much as I do, with a combination of awe and respect. As I look over the Port of Monaco I see more yachts, and ever-larger yachts. But I also see a resurgence of interest in classical yachting and preserving the important traditions of yesteryear. Most importantly, I also see a growing concern for the protection of our oceans. In short, while it is impossible to ignore the breathtaking changes that have so altered the social, economic and political landscape of our age the best of our ancestors – respect for tradition, a thirst for knowledge and an appreciation for beauty are still alive and well among us as we sail into the next Century.

Albert de Monaco

Princess Alice II
off Monaco in 1906.

THE MEGAYAC
Significant Vessels, Cornerstone Events

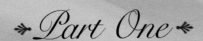

❧ *Part One* ❧

THE YACHTS THAT MADE HISTORY

The construction and use of large yachts is an economic and sociological phenomenon of mankind's recent past. The last 100 years has seen a dramatic shift in the ownership and the homeports of the great yachts. Their enjoyment, however, remains universal.

COURTESY OF KRISTIN LAMMERTING/METEOR

The Rosenfeld and Beken families created the greatest photo archives in the world to record the triumphs – and follies – of yachting. From their files they select their own favorite images.

Constellation

Today's 150-footers don't even make a ripple among the fleet of the 100 largest yachts in service in the past 100 years. In fact, the smallest yacht on our list is 244 feet. A great number of the early large yachts were pressed into military service on all sides during the World Wars and lost forever. Our list spans sail, steam, oil and diesel power.

Alva

MYSTIC SEAPORT MUSEUM/ROSENFELD COLLECTION

Capsule listing of the 100 largest yachts built or in operation in the 20th Century

HT CENTURY
& *Unforgettable People of the Past 100 Years*

WILLY WINKLER

Carinthia VI

SHEILA HILL

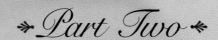

❧ *Part Two* ❧

THE YACHT BUILDERS THAT MADE HISTORY

And I have loved thee, Ocean! And my joy
Of youthful sports was on thy breast to be
Borne like thy bubbles, onward: from a boy
I wanton'd with thy breakers – they to me
Were a delight; and if the freshening sea
Made them a terror – 'twas a pleasing fear,
For I was as it were a child of thee,
And trusted to thy billows far and near,
And laid my hand upon thy mane – as I do here.

~LORD BYRON
Childe Harold's Pilgrimage, Canto IV

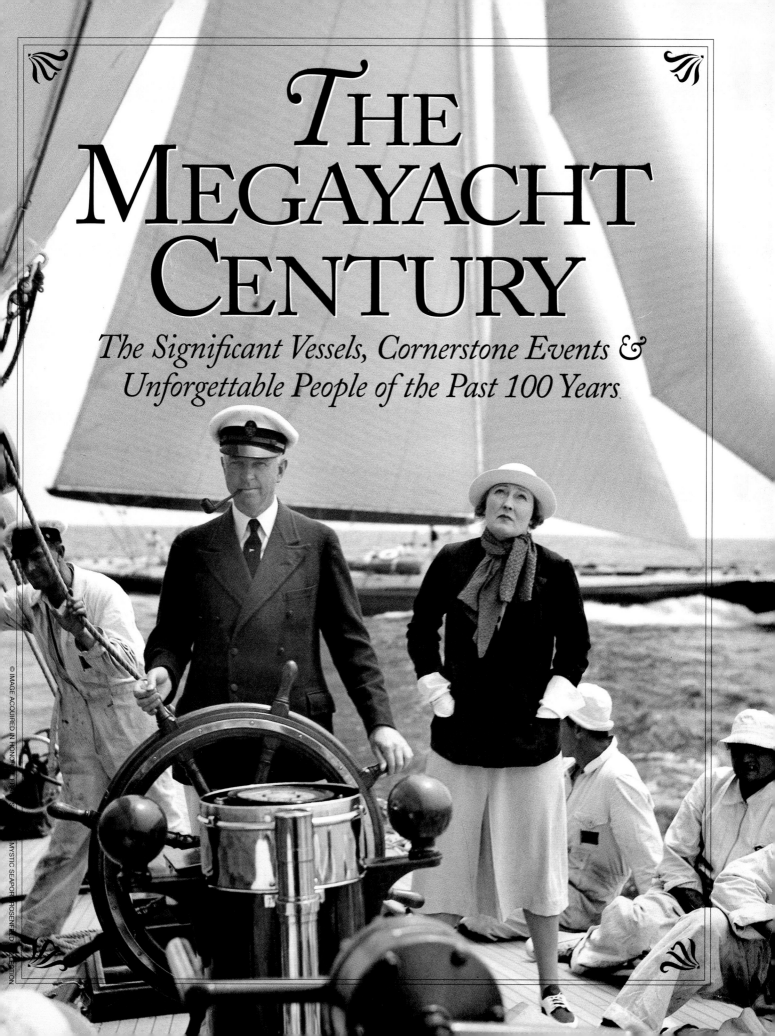

THE MEGAYACHT CENTURY

The Significant Vessels, Cornerstone Events & Unforgettable People of the Past 100 Years

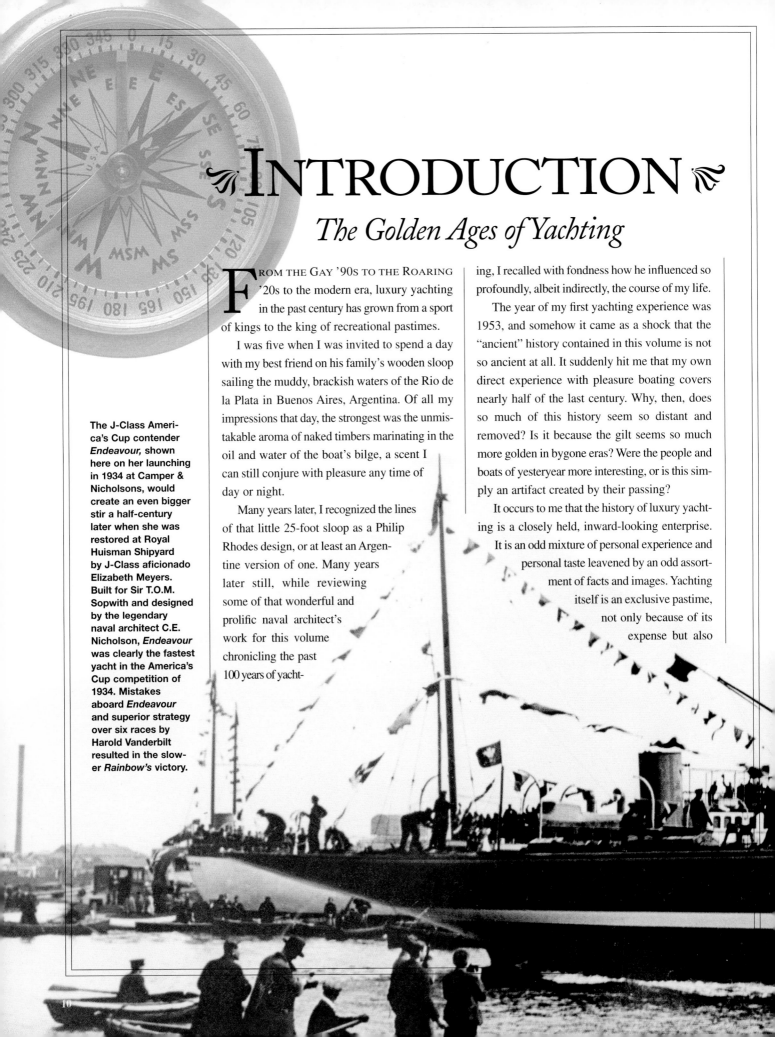

⟫INTRODUCTION⟪

The Golden Ages of Yachting

FROM THE GAY '90S TO THE ROARING '20s to the modern era, luxury yachting in the past century has grown from a sport of kings to the king of recreational pastimes.

I was five when I was invited to spend a day with my best friend on his family's wooden sloop sailing the muddy, brackish waters of the Rio de la Plata in Buenos Aires, Argentina. Of all my impressions that day, the strongest was the unmistakable aroma of naked timbers marinating in the oil and water of the boat's bilge, a scent I can still conjure with pleasure any time of day or night.

Many years later, I recognized the lines of that little 25-foot sloop as a Philip Rhodes design, or at least an Argentine version of one. Many years later still, while reviewing some of that wonderful and prolific naval architect's work for this volume chronicling the past 100 years of yacht-

ing, I recalled with fondness how he influenced so profoundly, albeit indirectly, the course of my life.

The year of my first yachting experience was 1953, and somehow it came as a shock that the "ancient" history contained in this volume is not so ancient at all. It suddenly hit me that my own direct experience with pleasure boating covers nearly half of the last century. Why, then, does so much of this history seem so distant and removed? Is it because the gilt seems so much more golden in bygone eras? Were the people and boats of yesteryear more interesting, or is this simply an artifact created by their passing?

It occurs to me that the history of luxury yachting is a closely held, inward-looking enterprise. It is an odd mixture of personal experience and personal taste leavened by an odd assortment of facts and images. Yachting itself is an exclusive pastime, not only because of its expense but also

The J-Class America's Cup contender *Endeavour,* **shown here on her launching in 1934 at Camper & Nicholsons, would create an even bigger stir a half-century later when she was restored at Royal Huisman Shipyard by J-Class aficionado Elizabeth Meyers. Built for Sir T.O.M. Sopwith and designed by the legendary naval architect C.E. Nicholson,** *Endeavour* **was clearly the fastest yacht in the America's Cup competition of 1934. Mistakes aboard** *Endeavour* **and superior strategy over six races by Harold Vanderbilt resulted in the slower** *Rainbow's* **victory.**

because it is a realm entered only through years of participation. In this sense it is like the history of a family or a neighborhood, short on documentation but long on lore built from shared experience and memories.

Unlike participation in a family, however, people choose to take to the sea in yachts, and the things that draw each person to the water are as different – and as similar – as people themselves. Some are attracted by the hardware of yachting, others merely by the sensations of being at sea. Some seek peace, others adventure. Some want a thrill, others serenity. Some seek company, others solitude. Some want to go fast, others slow. Some want to explore distant lands, others wish to know more deeply the world close to home. And yet throughout there is a bond, an appreciation for the commonality of sights and sounds and smells and motions that are universal to every experience at sea.

The history of yachting is thus at once both immediate and timeless. For those involved in the sport of "messing about in boats" it is as much about personal experience as it is about academics. It is subjective far more than it is quantitative.

While yacht racing has its record books, its premier athletes and enduring personalities, yachting as a pastime is far more about aesthetics than about performance. This is particularly true in the larger yachts which typically are built for comfort and beauty as much as they are for strictly utilitarian purposes, and are used far more for cruising and socializing than for competition.

For this reason, despite its popularity and passionate participation, yachting has not developed the kind of detailed, articulated history of other pastimes such as baseball or even fishing. This is doubly true for luxury yachting, whose documentation relies much more on oral traditions than on neatly compiled records and data.

This is the central and compelling rationale for undertaking this volume. Not only is the historical record woefully weak and fragmented, but of all the different subjects within the larger sphere of yachting, none is more entertaining, physically beautiful and filled with more fascinating characters than luxury yachting.

At the turn of the century, royalty dominated luxury yachting. German Kaiser Wilhelm II, shown here with his family, campaigned a series of racing yachts named *Meteor.* The Kaiser presented the ornate gold "Emperor's Cup" to Wilson Marshall, owner of the schooner *Atlantic* for her record-setting victory in the Great Ocean Race of 1905. At the outbreak of WWI, Marshall auctioned off the cup to benefit the Red Cross, netting a whopping $125,000 for a trophy that later was found to be gold-plated pewter worth only $35!

The advent of mechanized propulsion revolutionized yachting. While it took several decades for diesel engines to become sophisticated enough to become a popular form of yacht power, gasoline engines quickly became an indispensable part of the marine world. In 1899, the U.S. Navy launched its first submarine, *U.S.S. Holland,* powered by a 50hp Otto gas engine. In 1912, Thomas Fleming Day, editor of *The Rudder* magazine, skippered the Matthews-built *Detroit* across the Atlantic Ocean to demonstrate the safety and reliability of gasoline propulsion.

A Sociological View of Yachting

A sociologist might chart the rise in yachting's popularity as a function of increased leisure time, and certainly as reflective of the discretionary disposable income of its participants. Certainly this explains the growth of all forms of yachting since the end of the last World War. The same also can be argued for the other two boom periods of yachting in the last hundred years or so, the Roaring '20s and, especially, the Gay '90s.

The entire field of course, can be explored from the vantage point of almost any segment of human activity or discipline. Man's endless fascination with yachts reflects, for example, the development of science and technology as much as it does the development of social customs and culture. It is a function of economics as much as of physics. It has played important roles in inspiring literature and art and even influenced international politics, not the least of which were the extraordinary rivalries at the turn of the last century between English monarchs and the German Kaiser.

The universality of yachting is demonstrated by the fact that it is enjoyed by young and the old, women and men, strong and weak, wealthy and poor, tall and short, and by smart and stupid people. Yachts represent freedom and independence, an escape from norms and convention. And no matter how sophisticated boats and modern competition have become, all technology and engineering inevitably takes a distant back seat to the awesome, intransigent elemental interaction of water and wind.

The Start of the Modern Era

There is a long and rich tradition of yachting that endures for at least 340 years. Perhaps much longer, but at least that's how long the word "yacht" has been in common usage in Western languages. The word itself comes from the Dutch verb, *jaten,* which simply means to go fast. Of course, wealthy Phoenecians and Romans and heads of state over the years are known to have owned private boats expressly for their personal transportation. But the first record of a boat built entirely for its owner's pleasure appears to be a 52-foot sloop launched in 1661 for King Charles II of England as a present from the royal family of Holland.

Much of that history, like Charles II's little sloop,

focuses on royalty. However, with the explosive development of the industrial revolution in the middle part of the 19th century, particularly in America, yachting begins to attract people who had both the money and the leisure time to enjoy recreation at sea. But it is not until near the end of the century, however, that yachting moves into the mainstream of contemporary life. It is for this reason *The Megayacht Century* deals specifically with the larger yachts of the last hundred years, and not those in the two or more centuries that preceded it. That, and the advent of modern photography, not only provided the first pictorial record of the spectacular comings and goings of yachts and their owners, but served as a driving force in accelerating the popularity of the sport.

Life at the Turn of the Century

Consider for a moment what life was like on the waterfront prior to the turn of the last century. The world, except for the brief conflagration of the Spanish-American War, is enjoying an unprecedented period of peace and prosperity. The industrial revolution is at its peak, fueled by cheap labor and vast supplies of inexpensive raw materials from Third World regions colonized by the world's powers. Technological innovation is rampant. Electricity, telegraph and telephone cables are changing the very landscape and nature of urban life. While mechanized flight is still the fantasy of a few visionar-

ies, steam power has taken over from sail and is itself quickly being replaced by internal combustion engines. On land, horses and trains remain the principal means of transportation. Automobiles are still considered freakish playthings of the rich, noisy aberrations that will never play a useful role.

Nothing, absolutely nothing in the 1890s is more important to the economic, military and social life of a nation than its performance at sea. If people in the 1990s need proof of the adage that the more things change the more they remain the same, they need only go back a century. Time is money, and in the Gay '90s, money is everything. Schooners race weekly to Boston's T Wharf in the North End to ensure the best price for their catch. Steamers race each other across the Atlantic and around the Horn for Blue Ribband bragging rights and, more importantly, for a lion's share of lucrative passenger and freight business. Many yachtsmen of the time have made their money in railroads, but by the turn of the century, business has truly become global, and competitiveness at sea is the key to the future. No impediment of God or nature can stand in man's way, as is evident in 1904, when work begins with renewed fervor on building the Panama Canal.

Business, transportation, foreign policy and military might all revolve around a nation's competency at designing, building and manning the fastest, strongest and largest boats. It's no surprise, then,

Luxury yachts quickly began serving multiple purposes early in the 20th Century. Besides cruising, large yachts were built for enjoying regattas such as the America's Cup, like the 1934 races being observed by a large crowd off *Viking's* stern, top left. An entire class of fast yachts called "commuters" – like this 1929 fleet gathered at the New York Yacht Club's 26th Street docks – were built to ferry industrial and merchant Wall Street barons to the city from their suburban mansions. Above left, Walter Chrysler and friends commuting into Detroit aboard *Frolic III,* his Mathis express cruiser.

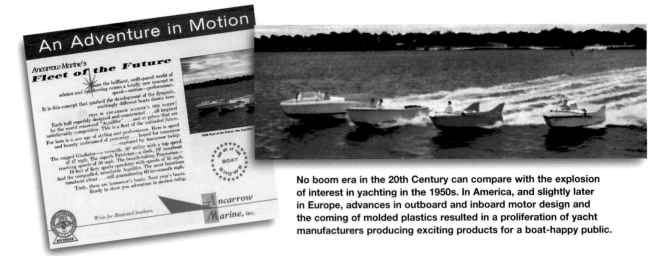

An Adventure in Motion

Ancarrow Marine's
Fleet of the Future

From the brilliant, swift-paced world of science and engineering comes a totally new concept in speed—motion—performance.

It is this concept that sparked the development of the dynamic, excitingly different boats shown here.

THIS IS ANCARROW MARINE'S... 1958 FLEET!

Each hull superbly designed and constructed... all inspired by the world renowned "Aquifier"... and at prices that are unbelievably competitive. This is a fleet of the *unlimited future*. For here is a new age of styling and performance. Here is speed and beauty undreamed of yesterday... hoped for tomorrow... captured by Ancarrow today.

The rugged Gladiator—a versatile, 20' utility with a top speed of 47 mph. The superb Patrician—a sleek, 19' runabout reaching speeds of 50 mph. The breath-taking Praetorian— 19 feet of fiery sports speedster with speeds of 55 mph. And the unequalled, inimitable Aquifier. The most luxurious runabout afloat... still guaranteeing 60 ice-smooth mph.

Truly, these are tomorrow's boats. Next year's boats. Ready to show you adventure in motion today.

Write for illustrated brochure.

Ancarrow Marine, inc.

No boom era in the 20th Century can compare with the explosion of interest in yachting in the 1950s. In America, and slightly later in Europe, advances in outboard and inboard motor design and the coming of molded plastics resulted in a proliferation of yacht manufacturers producing exciting products for a boat-happy public.

Perhaps the most famous space in yachting is the fabled "model room," below, of the New York Yacht Club. It houses more than 1,200 standing and half models, and represents perhaps the best history of the evolution of yacht design. Until 1951, members were required to submit models of any yacht they wished to compete in Club events, a practice originally required for handicapping yachts in an era before they were designed on paper.

that the front page of almost every major newspaper in the world contains the latest ship arrival information, not only which boat has arrived from where, but also how fast it has made its passage. New commercial and recreational vessels of note likewise attract keen attention from the media. Yachting events like the America's Cup, Cowes Week and Kiel Week are front-page news.

From a yachting point of view, the most enduring images of this period are the gatherings of royal yachts in Cowes and the fabled summer cruises of the New York Yacht Club. If this is the Golden Era of yachting, the annual parade of exquisite yachts from New York to Newport and Martha's Vineyard (and sometimes to Boston) serves as its glorious pilgrimage. The Astors entertain parties of 400 with full orchestras on their yachts. Social status is measured in tons and feet. One-upmanship is rampant, and the shipyards of the day are swelled with orders for larger yachts, with penalty

clauses if they are not delivered in time for next summer's cruising season.

Other comparisons are equally interesting. At the turn of the century, riveted steel and wood were the hull materials of choice. A new, state-of-the-art 200-footer could be delivered for less than $250,000 and often took less than a year to build. Operating costs, however, were proportionately much higher than today. A full season's cruising might cost a large percentage of a yacht's purchase price, reflecting the relatively lower cost of construction. Gordon J. Bennett's 311-foot *Lysistrata,* for example, required an annual operating budget – excluding entertaining – of $75,000 in 1907, the equivalent of nearly $2,000,000 today.

While yachting was in the process of becoming more of a middle-class avocation, royal yachts still ruled the high seas at the start of the 20th Century. British, Italian, Russian, German, Spanish and even Siamese royalty dominated the

top of the yacht registers. Many credit the modern-era boom of luxury yachting with the proliferation of royal Arab-owned boats in the late 1970s and 80s. However, Middle Eastern royalty's penchant for yachting actually dates all the way back to the turn of the century, when both the Sultan of Turkey and the Khedive of Egypt owned magnificent cruising yachts.

At any given time, yacht ownership provides an entertaining, even illuminating, cross-section of the world's elite. The decrease in royal-owned yachts during the course of the last century, for example, reflects a steady progression toward more democratic forms of national rule. Likewise, ownership of the world's biggest and most important yachts reflects changing trends in commerce. The rail barons of the 1890s, for example, gave way to the oil barons of the 1920s, who have been replaced in the late 20th Century by Grand Wazirs of the electronic age. Common throughout the last hundred years, however, is the increase of entrepreneurs among ownership, which parallels the increasing importance of Wall Street and other exchanges in the development of private wealth.

Which is the Real Golden Age?

Despite the extraordinary growth in luxury yachting in the past 25 years, many observers believe the modern era has yet to match the glory years at the end of the last century. They point out that in 1896 the rolls of the New York Yacht Club alone contained more 200-plus footers than exist in the entire world today. In 1900 there were 13 yachts over 300 feet plying the sea. Even in the realm of performance, they argue, the yachts of yesteryear – like Charles Flint's 132-foot steam commuter *Arrow* — at 45 knots the fastest boat in the world – compare favorably with today's yachts.

On the other hand, those who argue that the Golden Age of yachting is upon us today point out that the 600 100-foot-plus yachts in existence a century ago represent but a quarter of the large yachts afloat today. And, while the yachts of the 1890s were splendid by the standards of the day, many did not feature such "luxuries" as hot running water and electricity. Howard Gould's 272-foot *Niagra* had a church-size pipe organ in her library. Paul Allen's modern-era *Meduse* goes that one better with full-blown 48-track recording studio, (although it is

FOREST JOHNSON

interesting to note that both yachts made voyages up the Amazon shortly after launching).

Hopefully, the debate over which age provides the richest images will continue forever. Rather than settle this debate, I hope this small volume will help fuel the arguments on all sides.

From my own half-century perspective, I can only say that I still feel the same thrill when I leave land and step aboard a yacht. As a boating journalist for 20 years, I also understand that the more I know about the history of yachting, the more I appreciate the sport and my own time on the water.

Above all other considerations, yachting is about pleasure, and if *The Megayacht Century* helps to increase any reader's enjoyment, then we have done our job. Whether one era of yachting holds preeminence over any other is merely an academic exercise. At the end of every day, let alone any century, I can't imagine a yachtsman or woman believing that anyone else ever had more fun on the water than they did. ✛

~ JIM GILBERT, *Editor-In-Chief*

Turbine-powered *Gentry Eagle,* left, and *Moonraker,* right, flank conventional water jet-powered *Adler* in this 1993 photo notable principally for the combined 30,080 horsepower it showcases. Composite-construction, Norwegian-built *Moonraker,* built for car dealer John Staluppi, briefly hit a record speed of 67 knots before structural damage began occurring to the yacht's hull and its turbine was removed. The image eloquently captures yachting's speed-and-horsepower fascination in the late 1980s and early 1990s.

A strong case.

Just in case.

A Rolex is not only handsome, it is extremely rugged, and the key is its trademark Oyster case sculpted from 18kt gold or stainless steel. The case, combined with the synthetic sapphire crystal and patented Triplock winding crown, creates a virtually impenetrable miniature vault which, for this Submariner, is pressure-proof to 1,000 feet. Its legendary durability has made it the standard of excellence among divers, and is just one reason why this timepiece grows even more impressive the deeper you delve into it.

ROLEX

A CENTURY IN PICTURES

*P*HOTOGRAPHY AND YACHTING ARE A MAGICAL COMBINATION, AND WITHOUT QUESTION THE *art and science of each grew up together in the 20th century. What is remarkable is the fact that two families, one American, one English, are responsible for documenting much of yachting's history. Published in the newspapers and magazines of the day, their pictures told – and still are telling – of the power and dignity of yachts and their inseparable connection with wind and sea. Like the great yachts they photographed, the Rosenfelds and the Bekens are an inseperable part of yachting's golden age.*

The Rosenfelds

In 1903, 13-year-old Morris Rosenfeld borrowed a camera to take pictures of square-rigged ships in New York Harbor. One of his pictures won a magazine contest, and with the winnings he purchased his first camera. In 1908 he opened his own studio in the center of the New York newspaper district. Indeed, he always applied the news photographer's eye to his subjects. To him, a beautiful yacht was such a fine thing it needed no gilding with photographic tricks or filter fakery.

His sons, David, Stanley and William, all participated in the business for a time, but it was Stanley (b. 1913) who truly followed in his footsteps and often drove their little boats, always named *Foto*. Between them they covered every major yachting event, including every America's Cup, since 1905. Stanley's first published photo appeared in 1930. His own style was to showcase the interaction between boats and the environment as well as the human drama of the sport. The Rosenfelds always took care to learn about the boats and their designers and builders. By studying each boat and knowing in what conditions it was designed to excel, the Rosenfelds always managed to capture yachts at their best.

The Bekens

The logo "Beken of Cowes, by Appointment to HRH The Duke of Edinburgh, Marine Photographers established 1888," descreetly adorns the façade of one of the most famous shopfronts in the yachting world. Frank Beken arrived at Cowes on the Isle of Wight in 1888 and was immediately enthralled by the magnificent sight of the beautiful yachts racing in The Solent. Using the new medium of photography he was able to capture that spectacle on glass plate negatives. The bellows portrait cameras of the day were heavy and cumbersome, and Beken invented his own, less delicate camera. However, to steady one on a rolling dinghy generally required two hands. Beken surmounted the problem by inventing a shutter trigger bulb that he held in his mouth and activated by biting.

Frank's son Keith joined the pharmacy and photography business after serving in WWII. He adapted the cameras to take color film and started traveling around the world to broaden the archives. Keith's son Kenneth joined the firm in 1970. Kenneth Beken considers marine photography not work but "a hobby whereby I can collect images of works of art that have lives of their own. Anyone who has ever watched a yacht in heavy seas power her way through the waves that loom and threaten, shaking off white spume as she shoulders ahead, will appreciate the passionate way each of our three generations have thought about our work." ➤

Frank Beken shown here with his famous bite-activated shutter bulb.

THE ROSENFELD PERSPECTIVE

Stanley Rosenfeld

Asked to consider what might have been the most beautiful yachts I ever photographed, I offer a slight variation. I have been active for so long a time and photographed so many yachts and so many situations afloat that I long ago lost the concept of superlatives. I offer instead the most long-lasting memory of magnificent yachts in unforgettable moments caught in images of seeming simplicity, which for me had a number of significant elements that in combination made a strong and lasting impression on me. ~STANLEY ROSENFELD

MAGIC CARPET

MAGIC CARPET GLIDES DOWN LONG ISLAND Sound, barely under steerage way. A slight breeze moves aloft, though no wind riffles the water's surface. Distant wakes have created the few waves that reflect weak sun shrouded by high clouds.

I had more in my mind when I made the photograph. Though the boat is almost still, it was photographed when the hull lifted to a wave and the bow was slightly elevated. This gives a rather solid hull a lightness in the water. It is not bogged down in the calm, but really quite alive. Note the small images of the crew in the cockpit. They are not lolling about: their posture indicates they are awake, alert and attuned to the gentle zephyr overhead that fills their sails. They know that while no wind is on the water, it is aloft and moving.

Forward of the bow is a bell buoy, a key element in the photograph. It is leaning towards the hull of the yacht and proclaiming by its angle that a strong tidal current is setting against the vessel. *Magic Carpet* stems the tide with only a whisper of wind to drive it on. It is this interaction of wind and tide that the crew senses and it brings tautness to their bodies.

Now note the sky. We see an elegant pattern of clouds, with horizontal stripes below and coming in from the upper right-hand corner, a sweep of misty cloud that curves down and carries the eye to the vessel beneath. The sun is muted by the clouds, but its path lights the water beyond the crew so they stand boldly in relief, though they sit quietly on the deck.

The yacht is virtually becalmed, but to the photographer's eye, powerful forces are interacting. This is black and white photography where the photographer is king. I have mentioned nothing of the qualities in the image that come from camera, lens, filter, film, processing and printing, all of which are a part of this image and each of which can dramatically alter the strength and meaning of the photograph. Many strands are gently interwoven to create this image. ✣

$\mathcal{S}$EACLOUD

IN 1939 I WAS ASKED BY MRS. JOSEPH E. Davies (the former Marjorie Post Hutton) to come to Newport, Rhode Island, to photograph her yacht *Sea Cloud,* leaving in a few days to carry her husband the ambassador to his new posting in Russia. The captain of the *Sea Cloud* had arranged for the charter of a venerable, but unfortunately slow, motor launch named *Champion,* as a photo boat. We went out early off Block Island to a pre-arranged rendezvous point, where I waited with no communication between us while *Sea Cloud* went off toward Montauk Point to set sail.

A few hours later, she rose over the horizon, roaring down towards us at 17 knots, while I jockeyed our nine-knot launch into position. I worked with a 5 x7-inch Graphic with an 8-1/4 inch Zeiss lens. It was our custom to fill our film with the subject so it could be enlarged just as it was photographed. I had but a few moments to move both close in for bow shots and then sufficiently far out to fill my viewfinder with a broadside image. It was feverish activity without time for conscious deliberation while we were in shooting range. It was only later I could enjoy the image of the startling length of the hull, the boiling bow wave and the way its whiteness extended the long line of bow and bowsprit, the somewhat ugly glob of the smokestack, the highlight of sun on the sails, their geometric pattern against the sky and their narrow shadows in the water just before the hull.

Beauty for me is found in the elements of the moment. It is the idea as much as the reality that leads eye and mind and pressure on the shutter. Should I have seen that ship sailing not through the path of the sun, but into the end of an era? ✛

THREE
BEKEN GENERATIONS

PROBABLY MY MOST MEMORABLE MOMENTS OF photography at sea were the days before the war began in 1939. One day, we were in a small launch (maximum speed six knots) among five J-Class yachts of 120 feet. *Westward* was tramping down on the start line at 15 knots with seconds to go before the gun. Imagine these six great yachts tacking and cross tacking, and we in the middle of them in our 20-foot launch, our big cameras in our hands and the rubber-ball shutter release in our mouths. We had to steer as well – with eyes in the back of our heads. One had to be a seaman, a yachtsman and a photographer all at the same time.

Probably the second greatest moment at sea was the start of the B/T Round the World Race in 1996. Twelve great yachts headed to round a tall ship moored off Cowes as their first mark. A full westerly gale was pounding them on the nose, their decks awash, water flying high over them . . . and us. Fully five hundred other craft full of spectators out to watch the start were in front of and behind them, big motor craft raising high seas everywhere. It was the roughest, most dangerous and most exhausting photographic event of my life. But from all this we have the most exciting photographs and some wonderful video film.

There is one more occasion which resulted in a picture never to be forgotten. It was during Cowes Week 1996, and a westerly squall was sweeping through The Solent. Small yachts were dismasted and capsized; others more fortunate were racing along at 15-20 knots. Just then, *Silk,* a 41-foot Australian-designed Class I ocean racer streaking past suddenly, slowly began cartwheeling in front of me, throwing one crew member into the water. What were the odds that this would happen in front of you? Not once in a hundred years. And greater still the odds that you would have a camera with you!
~ A. KEITH BEKEN

EACH DAY AFLOAT IS MEMORABLE. EACH OF MY photographs brings back to me the conditions under which the image was taken, whether it be hanging out of a tiny helicopter above the Southern Ocean watching a dozen 12-Meters working up for the America's Cup in 1987, or photographing tall ships off Bermuda. In 1984, I photographed a lovely ship called *Marques* as she headed north, little knowing at dawn the next day she was to be hit by a squall and sunk with the loss of 16 lives.

Without a doubt, the vessels that bring me the greatest pleasure are the classics that have been lovingly restored back to their original splendor. *Endeavour, Shamrock* and *Velsheda* have been photographed by three Beken generations. I was lucky to be in Antigua last spring when they met again some sixty years after their original sparring matches of the Thirties. I'm sure Frank Beken was watching over my shoulder just to make sure that I got the horizon level and the exposure correct!

~ KENNETH BEKEN

B/T Start 1996

In man vs. the elements . . .

Cowes Week 1996

. . . sometimes the elements win.

1984

Marques **would soon sink with all hands.**

1929

As the thoroughbreds of their day, *Velsheda* (above) and *Shamrock III* and *Candida* (below) dominated he J-Class in The Solent.

1999

In 1999, *Endeavour, Velsheda* now in blue topsides, and *Shamrock* raced in Antigua Classic Week. Note the change in their sail inventory.

Keith and Kenneth Beken

1929

View of the owner's cabin on the upper deck.

The unique stateroom on the upper dec

or unique people.

Queen M: as enchanting and majestic as a real queen of the oceans, specially created for the utmost in comfort and elegant enough to sleep twelve guests in style.

Built to the most rigorous international safety standards (M.C.A, G.M.D.S.S and I.C.L.L), Queen M boasts a range of 3,800 nautical miles at 12 knots, a cruising speed of 16.5 and a top speed of 18 knots.

Queen M: the new grand Italian villa from Benetti.

SINCE 1873

Via Michele Coppino, 104 - 55049 Viareggio (Lucca) Italy
tel. +39 0584 - 38.21 - fax +39 0584 - 39.62.32

the world leader

by building more

composite mega-yachts

over 120′ than any other

shipyard in the world.

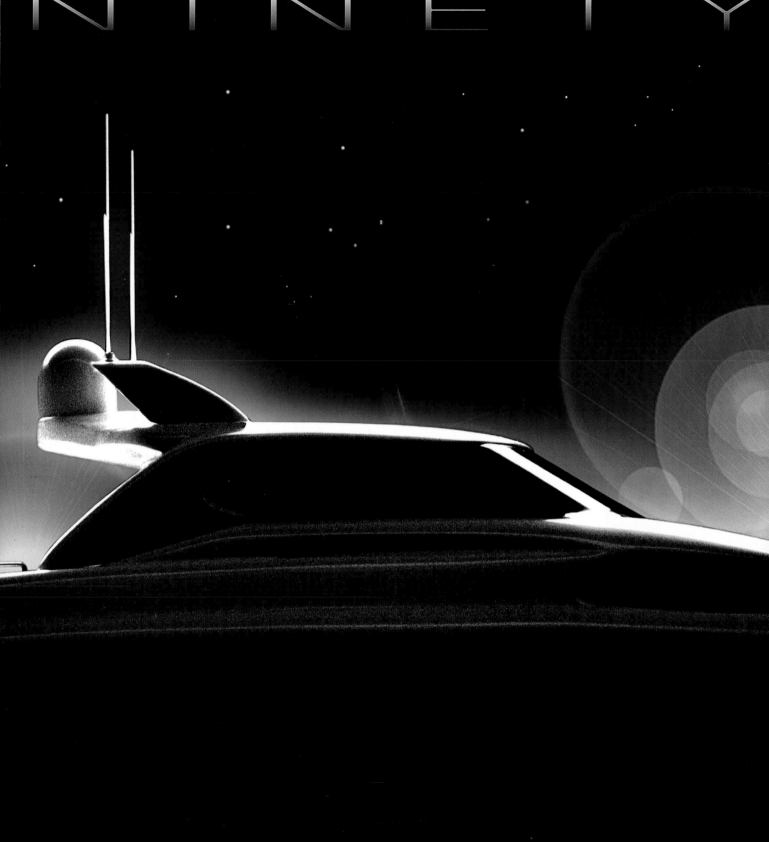

NINETY

Imagine Perfection

LAZZARA
YACHTS

BURGER®

FULFILLING DREAMS SINCE 1863

BURGER BOAT COMPANY

TEL
920-684-1600

1811 Spring Street, Manitowoc, WI 54220

FAX
920-684-6555

www.burgerboat.com

INTRODUCING THE NEW
WESTSHIP 140'.
"2000"

When Herb Postma introduced the first fiberglass motoryacht in 1989,
no one could have predicted the phenomenal reception WESTSHIP yachts have had around the world.

Now, 10 years later, WESTSHIP introduces their new state-of-the-art 140' tri-deck motoryacht.
All of the technologies and advancements in fiberglass yacht building available today and proven WESTSHIP pedigree
are embodied in this magnificent yacht. And, the company's philosophy of
"maximum pleasure thru minimum maintenance"
is strictly adhered to.

The new Westship 140', a yacht built to command everyones attention.

Command Performance.

WESTSHIP
America's Most Technically Advanced Yachts... For The World.

1535 Southeast 17th St., Fort Lauderdale, FL 33316, Phone 954-463-0700, Fax 954-764-2675
e-mail http://www.westshipyachts.com

Perini Navi, Blue-Water Sailing Yachts

March 1999: the 53-metre *S/Y Independence* anchored and sailing off Peter Island - BVI

PERINI NAVI   Via M. Coppino, 114 - 55049 Viareggio - Italia - Tel. +39 0584 4241 Fax +39 0584 424 200
PERINI NAVI USA   One Maritime Drive - Portsmouth, RI 02871- U.S.A. - Tel . 401-683-5600   Fax. 401-683-5611

HEESEN SHIPYARDS,
WHERE CENTURY OLD TRADITIONS

MEET 21ST CENTURY
TECHNOLOGY.

We do.

Our fathers did.

Our grandparents did.

Our great-grandfather did.

Setting standards in yacht construction

since 1875.

IT'S STILL TIME FOR

LÜRSSEN

For over 20 years we have given our clients magic moments of

excitement and freedom.

If you really want the motor yacht you have always dreamed of,

catch our wave and feel the style and quality of the right **board**.

C.B.I. NAVI

The oceans' best address.

Oceanco has taken the lead. A daring expression of excellence to grace the world's oceans.

A fresh approach combining the ultimate in engineering technology and the traditional Dutch skills of the hand and the eye.

The passion, enthusiasm and attitude of all the people at Oceanco elevate our yachts above the rest.

International networks give creative designers and project managers the computer power and tools to produce a far better product.

Whatever the reason, Oceanco is constantly exploring better ways to give the customer what they want.

The Oceans' best address.

Oceanco

For further information contact the Sales office at:
Oceanco
1650 S.E. 17th Street, Suite 200,
Ft Lauderdale, FL 33316 USA
Telephone 1 954 522 4155
Fax 1 954 522 5363
E-mail: Oceanco@aol.com

HOLLAND — MONACO — SOUTH AFRICA — USA

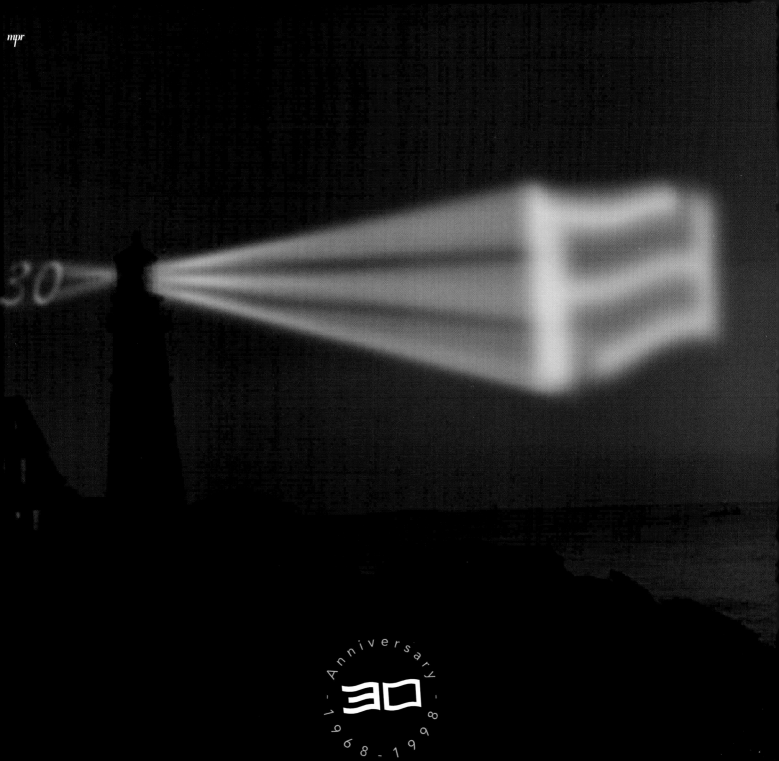

mpr

Cantieri Navali Ferretti

Only a bright past can lead
to an even brighter future.

FERRETTI

WWW.TRIDENTSHIPWORKS.COM

THE CRAFT OF HIGH-TECHNOLOGY SHIPBUILDING.

FROM BOW TO STERN, EVERY TRIDENT YACHT EMBODIES
THE SOPHISTICATED TECHNOLOGY, QUALITY CRAFTSMANSHIP
AND ADVANCED MATERIALS OF THE 21ST CENTURY, TODAY.

MASTER COMPOSITE SHIPBUILDERS℠

A MATERIAL EXPRESSION OF YOUR DREAMS.

EXPRESS YOUR DREAMS IN A MULTI-LAYER COMPOSITE
MEGA-YACHT OF KEVLAR OR CARBON FIBER CONSTRUCTION.
LIGHTER AND STRONGER, POUND-FOR-POUND, THAN STEEL OR
ALUMINUM. SCULPTURALLY FREE FORM AND EXPRESSIVE.

TRIDENT SHIPWORKS, INC.™   5251 WEST TYSON AVENUE, TAMPA, FL 33611   (813) 839-5151   (813) 839-5030 (FAX)

HELIYACHTS

32 m ketch
launched in 1998

Triest
Venice
Pula
Adriatic Sea

YACHTS ·
REFITS ·
REPAIRS ·

DON JUAN, FRERS 95, APRIL 1999.

Aluminum or Composite?
Sail or Power?
Modern or Traditional?
Race or Cruise?
Teak, Birch, Mahogany…

If you have custom needs,
custom desires,
custom dreams…
From 60 to 150 feet:

We build custom yachts.

CNB

■ CNB - 162, quai de Brazza - 33100 Bordeaux - France
Tel. 33 (0) 557 80 85 50 - Fax 33 (0) 557 80 85 51 - E-mail: cnb@cnb.fr - Internet: www.cnb.fr

41

THE CENTURY'S 100 LARGEST YACHTS

Compiled by PAUL O'PECKO

Library Director
MYSTIC SEAPORT MUSEUM, INC.

THE FOLLOWING PAGES present the 100 largest yachts launched or in yacht service during the 20th Century. Where several yachts are of the same length, they are ordered by tonnage. The following list was distilled from approximately 1,000,000 records of registered yachts covering the period 1899 to 1999. There are those who would argue that gross tonnage would have been as good or better a measure than length. However, length becomes the easiest and most reputable benchmark as yachts are refitted through the years. Some of the largest yachts had to be dropped from the list because they were never completed or were never used for their intended purpose due to the onset of wars or revolutions. Still, the smallest yacht on the list is 244 feet. A vessel's name often changed over its lifetime and the name that appears on the list is not necessarily its original name, but the name that appeared in the register when first located. All attempts have been made to list as many of the yacht's names as possible.

The records searched for this report include *Lloyd's Register of British and Foreign Yachts; Lloyd's Register of American Yachts, Manning's Yacht Register; Wood's International Yacht Directory; ShowBoats International magazine; Power & Motoryacht magazine; Erik Hofman's Steam Yachts* and various books and file sources. ➤

462-foot *Mipos*

❦ *The* 100 LARGEST YACHTS ❦

Abdul Aziz (482')

Savarona (408)

1. ABDUL AZIZ** 482'

Rig: Power **Gross Tons:** 8457 **Designer/ Builder:** *Maierform GmbH/Helsingor Vaerft (Denmark)* **Owner:** *Saudi Arabia/King Fahd (1991)* **Year Launched:** *1984* **Propulsion:** *Diesel* **Source:** *SBI1991/Wood's 1994*

Renamed *Prince Abdul Aziz* in 1996. Abdul Aziz was a forward-thinking warrior statesman who codified the tribes into the kingdom of Saudi Arabia in 1932. The yacht is always shadowed by an escort ship equipped with missiles.

2. MAHROUSSA** 478'

Rig: Schooner **Gross Tons:** 3762 **Designer/ Builder:** *O. Lang/Samuda Bros.* **Owner:** *Egyptian Viceroy/H.H. The Khedive of Egypt (1907)* **Year Launched:** *1865* **Propulsion:** *Turbines/sail* **Source:** *Hofman/Brit. Lloyd's 1907;1965/Royal Yachts 1997*

Originally a paddle steamer, the paddles were removed and screws added when the yacht was lengthened to 420 feet in 1905. Stretched again, she belonged to King Farouk who sailed into exile aboard her in 1952. Replated and renamed *Al Hourria,* she was the Egyptian Navy's training ship and is occasionally used as the Egyptian presidential yacht.

3. MIPOS** 462'

Rig: Power **Designer/Builder:** *Lürssen Werft/HDW Nobiskrug* **Year Launched:** *1999* **Propulsion:** *Diesel* **Source:** *Frankfurter Allgemeine Zeitung*

This yacht was too large for Lürssen's Bremen facilities and so was built in Kiel in HDW's yard under Lürssen direction. MIPOS is the yacht's project name, which stands for Mission Impossible.

4. VICTORIA & ALBERT III 430'

Rig: Schooner **Gross Tons:** 5005 **Designer/ Builder:** *William White/Pembroke Dockyard* **Owner:** *British royal yacht (1899-1955)* **Year Launched:** *1899* **Propulsion:** *Steam/sail* **Source:** *Hofman/ Brit. Lloyd's 1907*

When launched, *Victoria & Albert* was fitted out so heavily that she had an extreme list to starboard and was stranded at dockside. With her consort long dead, Queen Victoria supposedly wanted this yacht named *Balmoral* after her favorite residence. The Queen never went aboard the yacht. Scrapped in 1955.

5. STANDARDT 420'

Rig: Schooner **Gross Tons:** 4334 **Designer/ Builder:** *Burmeister & Wain (Des. & Build), Denmark* **Owner:** *H.I.M. The Emperor of Russia (1895-1917)* **Year Launched:** *1895* **Propulsion:** *Steam* **Source:** *Hofman/ Brit. Lloyd's 1907*

Standardt was almost identical in size to the 1899-built *Victoria & Albert* but had a huge promenade deck and three masts to beat other royals at flag-flying. The last Russian royal yacht, she had the same name as Peter the Great's 1703 yacht built in England. Later a Russian Navy mine-laying vessel, *Marti* (1917-1963), she disappears from records in the mid '60s.

6. BRITANNIA 412'

Rig: Power **Gross Tons:** 5769 **Designer/ Builder:** *Sir Hugh Casson/John Brown & Co.* **Owner:** *British royal yacht* **Year Launched:** *1954* **Propulsion:** *Power* **Source:** *SBI July '91/Brit. Lloyd's 1965*

A very young Elizabeth II took over the construction of this vessel after her father's death and christened her two months before her coronation. She traveled over a million miles as ambassador on her original engines before decommissioning. She carried a crew of 21 officers and 256 yachtsmen.

7. SAVARONA** 408'

Rig: Schooner **Gross Tons:** 4646 **Designer/ Builder:** *Gibbs & Cox/Blohm & Voss* **Owner:** *Cadwalader, Mrs. E.R. (1931-1938) Turkey (1938-1994)/ STT Marine Trading (1994)* **Year Launched:** *1931* **Propulsion:** *Steam/sail — Diesel (1994)* **Source:** *Hofman Wood's 1994/PMY/SBI 1991*

Formerly *Savarona III; Gunes Dill; Savarona.* She was built for an American heiress who then gave her to Kemal Ataturk to be Turkey's state yacht. She was bought from the Turkish Navy in 1990 and refitted under the direction of Don Starkey as a charter yacht.

8. ALEXANDER** 400'

Rig: Power **Designer/Builder:** *Luebecker Flender-Werke (Des. & Bld.) (Ger).* **Owner:** *Latsis, John (1991)* **Year Launched:** *1976/1986* **Propulsion:** *Power* **Source:** *PMY Aug '91, '97/SBI1991*

Formerly *Regina Maris;* formerly listed at 343'. She is the largest of the Latsis fleet and

*** Yachts currently in service*

Mipos (462')

Britannia (412')

❦ *The* 100 LARGEST YACHTS ❦

Sea Cloud (359')

Lady Moura (344')

regularly loaned out to friends, the younger British royals among them. Among her endearing qualities, she has a kindergarten aboard.

9. SAVOIA II 390'

Rig: Power **Gross Tons:** 4989 **Designer/ Builder:** Royal Italian Arsenal (Des. & Bld.) (Spezia) **Owner:** Italian royal yacht **Year Launched:** 1921 **Propulsion:** Steam turbines **Source:** Brit. Lloyd's 1927; 1950

Formerly *Citta di Palermo.* Converted to a royal yacht for Victor Emmanuel III in 1925, although the real power lay with Mussolini. She was classified as a Royal Warship and carried guns. She was sunk by Allied aircraft in 1943.

10. HOHENZOLLERN 383'

Rig: Schooner **Gross Tons:** 3756 **Designer/ Builder:** German Admiralty/Vulcan-Stettin **Owner:** German imperial yacht **Year Launched:** 1893 **Propulsion:** Steam/sail **Source:** Hofman/ Brit. Lloyd's 1894; 1907

The Hohenzollern family ruled Brandenburg, then Prussia, and finally Germany from the 15th century through 1918 when Kaiser Wilhelm II abdicated his throne at the end of WWI. A new yacht of the same name was in design before WWI and at over 500 feet would have dwarfed any other yacht in existence.

11. AL SALAMAH** 380'

Rig: Power **Designer/Builder:** Maierform GmbH/Hellenic Shipyards (Greece) **Owner:** Saudi Royal Yacht **Year Launched:** 1973 **Propulsion:** Diesel **Source:** SBI July 1991/

PMY Aug. '91

Formerly *Atlantis,* formerly *Prince Abdul Aziz,* she belongs to Prince Bin Sultan Bin Abdul Aziz, minister of defense. She used to belong to John Latsis, who gave her to King Fahd.

NOTE: *When two yachts are of the same length, they are sorted first by tonnage, then by alphabetical order.*

12. ATLANTIS II** 380'

Rig: Power **Designer/Builder:** Maierform GmbH/Hellenic Shipyards (Greece) **Owner:** Niarchos, Stavros (1996) **Year Launched:** 1981 **Propulsion:** Diesel **Source:** SBI July '91/PMY Aug. '91, Aug. '97

Rarely used by the late Niarchos in his final years, she once was an elegant Cote d'Azur destination for the jet set. She is permanently berthed at the Yacht Club de Monaco.

13. SEA CLOUD** 359'

Rig: Bark **Gross Tons:** 2323 **Designer/ Builder:** Cox & Stevens/Krupp Germania Werft **Owner:** Hutton, Mrs. E.F. (1932); Davies, Joseph E. (1939) **Year Launched:** 1931 **Propulsion:** Oil/sail **Source:** Lloyd's 1939; Brit. Lloyd's 1965

Formerly *Hussar,* later, *Angelita, Patria* and now *Sea Cloud.* Mrs. Hutton kept the yacht when the Huttons divorced, but he kept the name, thus the change to *Sea Cloud.* When Marjorie bought Clarence Birdseye's patents for freezing food, she had a freezer installed on *Sea Cloud.* When her second husband was ambassador to Russia, the yacht became their

Baltic residence. Now in charter.

14. MARGARITA 352'

Rig: Schooner **Gross Tons:** 1830 **Designer/ Builder:** G.L. Watson/Scott & Co. (Scot.) **Owner:** Drexel, Anthony J. **Year Launched:** 1900 **Propulsion:** Steam/sail **Source:** Manning's 1900; Hofman; Brit. Lloyd's 1930

Margarita had a crew of 90 and cost £100,000. Her coal-fired 5,000 horsepower was equal to that of the White Star liner *Britannic.* Sold to the Marquis of Anglesley in 1911, she was renamed *Semiramis.* As *Alacrity,* in WW I she was fitted with an arsenal of two breech-loading guns, two Colt rapid-fire guns, and 30 rifles. A charter yacht between wars, she was sunk on active duty during WWII.

15. VANADIS 345'

Rig: Schooner **Gross Tons:** 1115 **Designer/ Builder:** Tams, Lemoine & Crane/A & J. Inglis (Scot.) **Owner:** Billings, C.K.G. (1909) **Year Launched:** 1908 **Propulsion:** Steam/sail **Source:** Lloyd's 1915; Hofman; Brit. Lloyd's 1909;1930

Later *Poryv; Finlandia;* and *lanara.* She was another yacht conscripted and sent to the China Sea to defend the British Empire. After WW I she was purchased by Lt. Commander Montague Grahame-White who kept a large fleet for charter in the Pacific.

16. LADY MOURA** 344'

Rig: Power **Gross Tons:** 6539 **Designer/ Builder:** Luigi Sturchio/Blohm & Voss (Germany) **Owner:** Al-Rashid, Nasser. (1997) **Year Launched:** 1990 **Propulsion:** Diesel **Source:**

Hohenzollern (383')

Atlantis II (380')

❧ *The* 100 LARGEST YACHTS ❧

Corsair IV (344')

Limitless (315')

Probably the most expensive yacht ever delivered, due in large measure to her elegant and elaborate Luigi Sturchio interior and the portable "beaches" that fold out of her hull port and starboard. Her name is a contraction of Rashid and the owner's former wife, Mouna, for whom the yacht was originally built.

17. CORSAIR IV 344'

Rig: Power *Designer/Builder:* Henry J. Gielow/Bath Iron Works *Owner:* Morgan, J. "Jack" P. *Year Launched:* 1930 *Propulsion:* Electric Turbine *Source:* Lloyd's 1930

After giving his father's *Corsair III* to the U.S. Coast and Geodetic Survey in '29, Jack, also commodore of the NYYC, ordered a new and 40' longer one, but also with a black hull.

18. AL SAID** 340'

Rig: Power *Designer/Builder:* Picchiotti (Des. & Bld.) *Owner:* Sultan Qaboos of Oman (1991) *Year Launched:* 1982 *Propulsion:* Diesel *Source:* SBI July'91/PMYAug.'91

In the yard's heyday, the Sultan reportedly paid Picchiotti $39 million for this massive yet still attractive yacht. She features enclosed bridgedeck wing stations like a cruise ship.

19. POLIARNIA ZVEZDA 336'

Rig: Power *Gross Tons:* 3270 *Designer/Builder:* Baltic Shipbldg. (Des. & Bld.) (St. Petersburg) *Owner:* H.I.M. The Emperor of Russia (1888-1917) *Year Launched:* 1888 *Propulsion:* Steam *Source:* Brit. Lloyd's 1890; 1907; 1911; 1915

Built by Alexander III, who became czar after his father's assassination in 1881. The names means Pole Star and she is similar in design to the British royal yachts. In 1913 she was Lloyd's fifth largest yacht.

20. ORION 333'

Rig: Schooner *Gross Tons:* 3097 *Designer/Builder:* Fried. Krupp/ Germania Werft (Kiel) *Owner:* Forstmann, Julius (1930) *Year Launched:* 1929 *Propulsion:* Diesel/sail *Source:* Lloyd's 1930

21. ATMAH 333'

Rig: Schooner *Gross Tons:* 1665 *Designer/Builder:* G.L. Watson/Fairfield Shipbldg. *Owner:* Rothschild, Baron Edmond and J.A. (1898-1939) *Year Launched:* 1898 *Propulsion:* Steam/sail *Source:* Hofman

22. MOINEAU 327'

Rig: Power *Gross Tons:* 2400 *Designer/Builder:* Canadian Vickers (Des. & Bld.) *Owner:* Rexach, Mrs. Lucienne Benitez (1961) *Year Launched:* 1942 *Propulsion:* Steam *Source:* Brit. Lloyd's 1961

Formerly *R.C.N.S. Annam; U.S.S. Natchez;* converted to a yacht in 1952.

23. MANSOUR** 326'

Rig: Power *Gross Tons:* 3743 *Designer/Builder:* Blythswood S.B. Co. (Des. & Bld.) (Glasgow) *Owner:* Saudi Royal Yacht (1965) *Year Launched:* 1936 *Propulsion:* Steam *Source:* Brit. Lloyd's 1961

Formerly *Al Amir Saud; Fort Townshend;* classed as a yacht in 1954.

24. CHRISTINA** 325'

Rig: Power *Gross Tons:* 1526 *Designer/Builder:* Canadian Vickers, Ltd. (Des. & Bld.) *Owner:* Onassis, A.S. (1965); Papanicolaou, John (1998) *Year Launched:* 1943 *Propulsion:* Steam *Source:* Brit. Lloyd's 1965/PMY Aug.'91/SBI July '99

Formerly *Stormont* (converted to a yacht in1954); later *Argo,* now *Christina O* and completely refit for luxury charter service for up to 36 guests.

25. ROVER 320'

Rig: Schooner *Gross Tons:* 1881 *Designer/Builder:* Alexander Stephen & Sons (Des. & Bld.) *Owner:* Lord Inchape (1930-1932) *Year Launched:* 1930 *Propulsion:* Oil/sail *Source:* Hofman

Later *Southern Cross.*

26. MAYFLOWER 318'

Rig: Schooner *Gross Tons:* 1779 *Designer/Builder:* G. L. Watson/ J.& G. Thompson *Owner:* U.S. presidential yacht (1902-1929) *Year Launched:* 1897 *Propulsion:* Steam/sail *Source:* Hofman

Used by Presidents Taft, Wilson, Harding and Coolidge. She was originally built for Ogden Goelet but converted for Coast Guard use in 1898, later becoming the presidential yacht.

27. LIMITLESS** 315'

Rig: Power *Designer/Builder:* Lurssen (Des. & Bld.) *Owner:* Wexner, Les *Year Launched:* 1997 *Propulsion:* Diesel/electric *Source:* PMY (Aug. 1997) SBI (July 1998)

Christina (325')

Mayflower (318')

❧ *The* 100 LARGEST YACHTS ❧

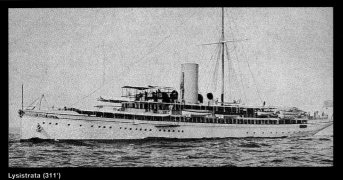

Lysistrata (311')

Corsair III (304')

The owner deliberately requested a *Carinthia VI* look-alike from his design team, headed by Jon Bannenberg and Tim Heywood. The yacht is designed for 25-knot cruising and carries its own covered swimming pool.

28. LYSISTRATA 311'

Rig: Steam **Gross Tons:** 1942 **Designer/ Builder:** G.L. Watson/W.Denny & Bros. **Owner:** Bennett, J. Gordon (1904) **Year Launched:** 1900 **Propulsion:** Steam **Source:** Lloyd's 1904-05

Newspaperman Bennett inherited the *New York Herald* from his father and built a succession of racing schooners. This magnificent yacht was built to one-up Vanderbilt's *Valiant*, A.J. Drexel's *Margarita* and Morgan's third *Corsair*. She carried her crew aft (a departure) and had a speed clause (17.5kts.) in her contract and the demand that she be built under a roof. She cost £105,000 to build.

29. TRICK ONE** 311'

Rig: Power **Designer/Builder:** The A Group/ Oceanco **Year Launched:** 1999 **Propulsion:** Diesel **Source:** SBI Jan. 98; Sep. 99

The largest yacht launched in Holland is scheduled to go in the water before the turn of the century. She is destined for the Middle East.

30. IOLANDA 310'

Rig: Schooner **Gross Tons:** 1647 **Designer/ Builder:** Cox & King/Ramage & Ferguson (Scot.) **Owner:** Plant, Morton F. (1910) **Year Launched:** 1908 **Propulsion:** Steam/sail **Source:** Lloyd's 1910/Brit. Lloyd's 1950

Later *White Bear.* On her initial trip to her home port of New London, Conn., she flew a 220-foot "homeward-bound" pennant from the main topmast. Among her accommodations was a "surgery and hospital," including an x-ray machine. Her only American-made fitting was a steel galley stove.

31. NAHMA 306'

Rig: Schooner **Gross Tons:** 1740 **Designer/ Builder:** G.L. Watson/J & G. Thompson (Scot.) **Owner:** Goelet, Robert (1897-1922) **Year Launched:** 1896 **Propulsion:** Steam/sail **Source:** Manning's 1899/ Brit. Lloyd's 1907/Hofman

"Nahma" supposedly means King Bird. *Nahma* and *Mayflower* were sister ships. She spent WWI in the U.S. Navy.

32. VARUNA 306'

Rig: Schooner **Gross Tons:** 1574 **Designer/ Builder:** G.L. Watson/A.&J. Inglis (Scot.) **Owner:** Higgins, Eugene (1897-1909) **Year Launched:** 1896 **Propulsion:** Steam/sail **Source:** Manning's 1899/ Brit. Lloyd's 1907/Hofman

Varuna is Sanskrit for "the encompasser of the Universe." In the Hindu Rig-Veda he is creator and lord of the waters, the night and the West. This *Varuna* was double-bottomed and built for safety with eight transverse bulkheads and eight boats, including two 30' steam launches.

33. LIBERTY 304'

Rig: Schooner **Gross Tons:** 1607 **Designer/ Builder:** G.L. Watson/Ramage & Ferguson (Leith,Scot) **Owner:** Pulitzer, Joseph (1910)

Year Launched: 1908 **Propulsion:** Steam/sail **Source:** Lloyd's 1910; Brit. Lloyd's 1930

In 1930, *Yachting Monthly* called *Liberty* "perhaps one of the finest examples of a Watson steam-yacht." Quite a compliment, considering the number of vessels that came off G.L. Watson's board. Later *Glencairn.*

34. CORSAIR III 304'

Rig: Schooner **Gross Tons:** 1136 **Designer/ Builder:** J. Beavor-Webb/T.S. Marvell & Co. **Owner:** Morgan, J. Pierpont (1899-1930) **Year Launched:** 1898 **Propulsion:** Steam/sail (twin screw) **Source:** Manning's 1899; Hofman

Morgan's third yacht of this name often entertained European royalty during Cowes Week. Naval service from 1917 to 1919 and 1942 to 1944. U.S. Coast and Geodetic Survey service from 1930 to 1942.

35. APHRODITE 302'

Rig: Bark **Gross Tons:** 1147 **Designer/ Builder:** Charles Ridgely Hanscom/Bath Iron Works **Owner:** Payne, Col. Oliver H. (1899) **Year Launched:** 1898 **Propulsion:** Steam/sail **Source:** Manning's 1899; Lloyd's 1913

Carried over 17,000 square feet of canvas, yet was predominantly a steam-powered yacht.

36. EVERGREEN** 302'

Rig: Power **Designer/Builder:** Diana Yacht/Hayashikane (Japan) **Owner:** Yung-Fa Chang **Year Launched:** 1998 **Propulsion:** Diesel **Source:** PMY Aug. 1997/SBI Jan. '98

Built for the Taiwanese owner of the huge

Trick One (311')

Liberty (304')

❧ *The* 100 LARGEST YACHTS ❧

Erin I 287

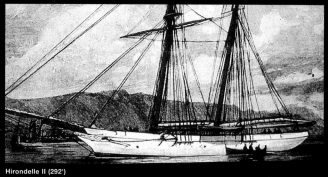

Hirondelle II (292')

shipping company of the same name, she is designed for large-scale entertaining. Reportedly for sale at $70 million.

37. NAHLIN 300'

Rig: Schooner **Gross Tons:** 1391 **Designer/ Builder:** G.L. Watson/John Brown **Owner:** Lady Yule (1930-1937) **Year Launched:** 1930 **Propulsion:** Oil/sail **Source:** Hofman

Equipped in the "most up-to-date manner," she carried a Sperry gyroscope compass and automatic steering gear. Interior design by Sir Charles Allom. *Nahlin* supposedly means "fleet foot." Later *Luceafarul; Liberatatea.*

38. LORENA 300'

Rig: Schooner **Gross Tons:** 1303 **Designer/ Builder:** Cox & King/Ramage & Ferguson (Leith) **Owner:** Barber, A.L. (1904-05) **Year Launched:** 1903 **Propulsion:** Steam/sail **Source:** Lloyd's 1904-05; Brit. Lloyd's 1939

Later *Atalanta; Kan Lu;* lengthened 1923 and repowered.

39. ALBION 300'

Rig: Schooner **Gross Tons:** 1116 **Designer/ Builder:** William White/Swan, Hunter & Wigham Richardson **Owner:** Newnes, George (1905-1908) **Year Launched:** 1905 **Propulsion:** Steam/sail **Source:** Hofman

In 1930 she was purchased by Sir Thomas Lipton and renamed *Erin II.* She served as a tender for his last America's Cup attempt with *Shamrock V.* Her designer also designed *Victoria & Albert III* and her most distinguishing fea-

ture was her single bell-shape funnel. Broken up in 1936.

40. ALDER 294'

Rig: Power (Diesel) **Gross Tons:** 2076 **Designer/ Builder:** Henry J. Gielow/Pusey & Jones **Owner:** Thompson, William Boyce (1930) **Year Launched:** 1928 **Propulsion:** Diesel **Source:** Lloyd's 1930

Formerly *Savarona.*

41. ALEXANDRA 293'

Rig: Power **Gross Tons:** 2157 **Designer/ Builder:** A. & J. Inglis (Des. & Bld.) **Owner:** British Royal Yacht **Year Launched:** 1907 **Propulsion:** Steam **Source:** Brit. Lloyd's 1911

A replacement for *Osborne,* she was a miniature version of *Victoria & Albert* and used for cross-Channel service. After WWI she was sold to a Norwegian passenger steamer line. She was sunk in 1940.

42. HIRONDELLE II 292'

Rig: Schooner **Gross Tons:** 1321 **Designer/ Builder:** Forg & Chant Mediterenee (Des. & Bld.) (La Seyne) **Owner:** Prince Albert I of Monaco **Year Launched:** 1911 **Propulsion:** Steam/sail **Source:** Brit. Lloyd's 1926; Royal Yachts

The second of Prince Albert I of Monaco's yachts, the name means "swallow," a bird he is said to have admired for its adventurous resolution. Like *Princess Alice,* she was designed for oceanographic research. She disappears from registers after 1926.

43. GIRALDA 289'

Rig: Schooner **Gross Tons:** 1265 **Designer/ Builder:** Fairfield Shipbldg. (Des. & Bld.) (Glasgow) **Owner:** King of Spain (1911) **Year Launched:** 1894 **Propulsion:** Steam/sail **Source:** Brit. Lloyd's 1911

See cover. She was built for American Col.MacCalmont and was owned by the Portuguese government for a short time before becoming the royal yacht for King Alfonso XIII. She disappears during the Spanish Civil War.

44. CASSANDRA 287'

Rig: Schooner **Gross Tons:** 1286 **Designer/ Builder:** A.S. Chesebrough/Scott's Shipbldg. (Greenock, Scot) **Owner:** Rainey, Roy A. (1909) **Year Launched:** 1908 **Propulsion:** Steam/sail **Source:** Lloyd's 1909; Brit. Lloyd's 1939

Later *Casiana; Banahaw.*

45. ERIN I 287'

Rig: Schooner **Gross Tons:** 1057 **Designer/ Builder:** Scott Shipbldg. (Des. & Bld.) **Owner:** Lipton, Sir Thomas (1898-1914) **Year Launched:** 1896 **Propulsion:** Steam/sail **Source:** Hofman

Formerly *Aegusa. Erin* acted as convoy for *Shamrocks I, II,* and *III* during their transatlantic passages and tender during the America's Cup. She had a magnificent interior described as a riot of Victorian ornateness. She could cruise at 15.5 knots, which made her a valuable commodity in 1914. Lipton put her at the disposal of the Red Cross to ferry doctors to mobile hospitals in France. She was torpedoed in the Mediterranean with the loss of six lives.

Alexandra (293')

Nahlin (300')

The 100 LARGEST YACHTS

Sapphire (285')

Kingdom 5kr (282')

46. SAPPHIRE 285'
Rig: Schooner **Gross Tons:** 1207 **Designer/ Builder:** G.L. Watson/John Brown **Owner:** Duke of Bedford (1912-1919) **Year Launched:** 1912 **Propulsion:** Steam/sail **Source:** Hofman

47. ARCTIC** 285'
Rig: Power **Designer/Builder:** C. Kusch (Conversion)/Schichau Unterwasser **Owner:** Kerry Packer **Year Launched:** 1969/con. 1995 **Propulsion:** Diesel **Source:** PMY Aug. 91; Aug. '99/SBI File

An appropriate name for a converted ice-class tug that circles the globe.

48. MAHA CHAKRI 284'
Rig: Schooner **Gross Tons:** 2229 **Designer/ Builder:** Ramage & Ferguson (Des. & Bld.) **Owner:** King of Siam (1900) **Year Launched:** 1892 **Propulsion:** Steam/sail **Source:** Brit. Lloyd's (1900)

Her odd hermaphrodite rig seemed an afterthought, and she had a ram bow and enclosed stern, unusual for the day. As her predecessor carried a gun in the bow, it was assumed she did as well.

49. OSBORNE 284'
Rig: Schooner **Gross Tons:** 1850 **Designer/ Builder:** E.J. Reed/Pembroke Dockyard **Owner:** British Royal Yacht **Year Launched:** 1870 **Propulsion:** Steam paddle/sail **Source:** Hofman/ Brit. Lloyd's 1894; 1907

Named after one of the royal residences. She cruised regularly in the Med with the Prince and Princess of Wales. The Prince was in love with yachting and also used her as his tender at Cowes Week. Scrapped in 1908.

50. KINGDOM 5KR** 282'
Rig: Power **Gross Tons:** 1768 Jon Bannenberg/M&B Bennetti (Italy) **Owner:** Prince al-Waleed (1997); Donald Trump (1991); Adnan Kashoggi **Year Launched:** 1980 **Propulsion:** diesel **Source:** PMY Aug. '91/Wood's '94/SBI '91; file

Formerly *Trump Princess; Nabila*. Besides her size, her fame includes scenes in a James Bond film and the fact that she bankrupted Benetti during construction.

51. WARRIOR 282'
Rig: Schooner **Designer/Builder:** G.L. Watson/ Ailsa Shipbldg. (Scot.) **Owner:** Vanderbilt, Fred. W. (1904) **Year Launched:** 1904 **Propulsion:** Steam/sail **Source:** Lloyd's 1904-05

Later *Wayfarer*. Upon her completion, Vanderbilt joined the captain and crew in Troon before heading to France to finish furnishing the interior. *Warrior* then went to Kiel and off on a cruise to Norway. Her elaborate bathrooms were fitted with "hot-water geysers."

52. CAROLINE 279'
Rig: Power **Gross Tons:** 1839 **Designer/ Builder:** Henry J. Gielow/Bath Iron Works **Owner:** Johnson, Eldridge R. (1939) **Year Launched:** 1931 **Propulsion:** Oil **Source:** Lloyd's 1939

53. ALCEDO 275'
Rig: Schooner **Gross Tons:** 983 **Designer/ Builder:** G.L. Watson/D&W Henderson (Glasgow) **Owner:** Rothschild, Baron N. de (1895-1905) Drexel, George W.C. (1906-'17) **Year Launched:** 1895 **Propulsion:** Steam/sail **Source:** Lloyd's 1910/ Hofman

Formerly *Veglia*. Torpedoed during naval service in WW I.

54. NIMET ALLAH 273'
Rig: Schooner **Gross Tons:** 1704 **Designer/ Builder:** R. Erbach/Deutsche Werke (Kiel) **Owner:** Achilles Yacht Co. (1935) **Year Launched:** 1934 **Propulsion:** Oil/sail **Source:** Brit. Lloyd's 1939

55. CUTTY SARK 273'
Rig: Schooner **Gross Tons:** 883 **Designer/ Builder:** Yarrow (Des. & Bld.) **Owner:** Keswick, H. (1920-1926) **Year Launched:** 1920 **Propulsion:** Steam/sail **Source:** Hofman

An unorthodox-looking yacht, *Cutty Sark* was being built as a destroyer but was completed instead as a private yacht in 1920. Her lines remained those of a WWI destroyer.

56. NIAGARA 272'
Rig: Bark **Gross Tons:** 1444 **Designer/ Builder:** W.G. Shackford/Harlan & Hollingsworth **Owner:** Gould, Howard (1899) **Year Launched:** 1898 **Propulsion:** Steam/sail (twin screw) **Source:** Manning's 1899

Thomas Fleming Day claimed her rig was a modified topsail schooner akin to that of the Confederate raider *Alabama*. A top sailboat competitor, Gould used her as a tender for his racing sloop *Niagra*.

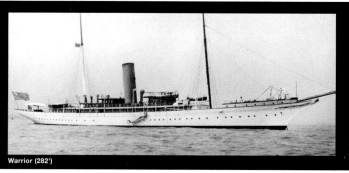

Warrior (282')

Maha Chakri (284')

❦ *The* 100 LARGEST YACHTS ❦

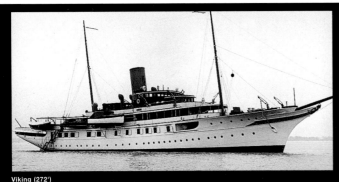

Viking (272')

Golden Odyssey (266')

57. VIKING 272'

Rig: *Schooner* **Gross Tons:** *1300* **Designer/Builder:** *T.D. Wells/Newport News Shipbldg.* **Owner:** *Baker, George F. Jr. (1930)* **Year Launched:** *1929* **Propulsion:** *Electric turbines/sail* **Source:** *Lloyd's 1930, 1939*

Later *Noparo. Viking* was capable of cruising 7,000 miles at 12 knots without shore service. Along with a figurehead of a Viking carved by a Norwegian sculptor, *Viking* carried a Chris-Craft sedan, a Banfield cruiser, and a Jardine Seaskiff on her davits.

58. JEANNETTE 270'

Rig: *Schooner* **Gross Tons:** *931* **Designer/Builder:** *G.L. Watson/John Brown* **Owner:** *Livesay, Harry (1911-1936)* **Year Launched:** *1911* **Propulsion:** *Steam/sail* **Source:** *Hofman*

59. DORIS 270'

Rig: *Schooner* **Gross Tons:** *910* **Designer/Builder:** *G.L.Watson/John Brown* **Owner:** *Joel, Solomon B. (1910-1931)* **Year Launched:** *1910* **Propulsion:** *Steam/sail* **Source:** *Hofman; Brit. Lloyd's 1939*

Later *Eileen; Girundia II.*

60. IELA 269'

Rig: *Schooner* **Gross Tons:** *498* **Designer/Builder:** *Cox & King/Ramage & Ferguson (Leith, Scot.)* **Owner:** *King of Italy* **Year Launched:** *1902* **Propulsion:** *Steam* **Source:** *Brit. Lloyd's 1904; 1930*

Formerly *Rannoch,* she also belonged to Italy's last king, Victor Emmanuel III.

61. AL YAMAMAH** 269'

Rig: *Power* **Designer/Builder:** *Helsingor Vaerft (Bld. & Des.) (Denmark)* **Owner:** *Saudi royal yacht (1991)* **Year Launched:** *1981* **Propulsion:** *Diesel* **Source:** *PMY Aug.1991/SBI July '91, file*

Formerly *Quadissiyat Saddam* under Iraqi ownership, she now belongs to the Crown Prince of Saudi Arabia.

62. ARCTURUS 268'

Rig: *Power* **Gross Tons:** *2475* **Designer/Builder:** *Pacific American Fisheries (Des. & Bld.)* **Owner:** *Beebe, William (1926)* **Year Launched:** *1919* **Propulsion:** *Steam* **Source:** *Brit. Lloyd's 1926*

Formerly *Clio.*

63. HI-ESMARO 267'

Rig: *Power* **Gross Tons:** *1333* **Designer/Builder:** *Henry J. Gielow/Bath Iron Works* **Owner:** *Manville, H.E. (1939)* **Year Launched:** *1929* **Propulsion:** *Oil* **Source:** *Lloyd's 1931; 1939*

64. CYPRUS 267'

Rig: *Schooner* **Gross Tons:** *1286* **Designer/Builder:** *Cox & Stevens/Seattle Con. & Drydock* **Owner:** *Jackling, D.C. (1915)* **Year Launched:** *1914* **Propulsion:** *Steam/sail* **Source:** *Lloyd's 1915*

Initially built in 1913, *Cyprus* was lengthened by 31 feet the following year. The owner loved the way the vessel handled on its initial voyage, but felt there was not enough room to accommodate those accompanying him.

65. ALEXANDRIA 267'

Rig: *Power (paddle)* **Gross Tons:** *716* **Designer/Builder:** *Baltic Shipbldg. (Des. & Bld.) (St. Petersburg)* **Owner:** *Emperor of Russia 1903* **Propulsion:** *Steam* **Source:** *Brit. Lloyd's 1911*

66. GOLDEN ODYSSEY** 266'

Rig: *Power* **Gross Tons:** *1855* **Designer/Builder:** *Platou (Norway)/Blohm & Voss (Germany)* **Owner:** *Prince Khalid bin Sultan* **Year Launched:** *1990* **Propulsion:** *Diesel* **Source:** *PMY Aug. '97/Wood's 1994/SBI Jan. 93*

His Highness had her lengthened 16' in 1995. The dining salon has a breath-taking wall-size aquarium with an aft glass wall that exposes the swimming pool.

67. ALVA 264'

Rig: *Power (Oil)* **Gross Tons:** *2265* **Designer/Builder:** *Cox & Stevens/Krupp Germania Werft (Kiel)* **Owner:** *Vanderbilt, W.K. (1931)* **Year Launched:** *1931* **Propulsion:** *Oil* **Source:** *Lloyd's 1931; 1939*

Vanderbilt, an extensive traveler and writer, took *Alva* on a 30,000-mile world cruise soon after her launching in 1931.

68. NOURMAHAL 264'

Rig: *Schooner* **Gross Tons:** *1969* **Designer/Builder:** *Cox & Stevens/Krupp* **Owner:** *Astor, Vincent (1930)* **Year Launched:** *1928* **Propulsion:** *Diesel/sail* **Source:** *Lloyd's 1930*

This was the largest of Vincent Astor's yachts named *Nourmahal.* The name meant "light of the harem."

Hi-Esmaro (267')

Nourmahahal (264')

❧ *The* 100 LARGEST YACHTS ❧

Norge (263')

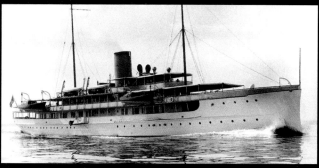

Delphine (258')

69. NORGE** 263'

Rig: Power **Gross Tons:** 1628 **Designer/Builder:** C.E. Nicholson/Camper & Nicholson **Owner:** King Haakon of Norway (1950) **Year Launched:** 1937 **Propulsion:** Diesel **Source:** SBI July '91/Brit. Lloyd's 1950

Formerly *Philante,* she was built for T.O.M. Sopwith as the support ship for his America's Cup contenders named *Endeavour.* The name was a contraction of Phyllis and Tom, Phil and T, with an "e" added to improve pronunciation. During WW II she was in the British Navy, and afterwards the people of Norway raised £250,000 to buy her as a present for their king.

70. IOLAIRE 263'

Rig: Schooner **Gross Tons:** 862 **Designer/Builder:** W. Beardmore & Co. (Des. & Bld.) **Owner:** Currie, Sir Donald (1902) **Year Launched:** 1902 **Propulsion:** Steam/sail **Source:** Brit. Lloyd's 1902; 1939

71. CONSTELLATION** 262'

Rig: Power **Designer/Builder:** The A Group/Oceanco **Owner:** Emir of Qatar **Year Launched:** 1999 **Propulsion:** Diesel **Source:** SBI '99

The first of a pair of sister ships being built for the Qatar Royal Family. The steel hulls are built in South Africa, and the yachts are finished in Holland.

72. ERTRUGRUL 260'

Rig: Schooner (3 masts) **Gross Tons:** 935 **Designer/Builder:** J.R. Perrett/W.G. Armstrong-Whitworth & Co. (Newcastle-on-Tyne) **Owner:** Mohammed V (1904); president of Turkey (1950) **Year Launched:** 1904 **Propulsion:** Steam/sail **Source:** Brit. Lloyd's 1904; 1950

Also, spelled *Erthogroul,* she was built for the last Ottoman emperors and then came to Kemal Ataturk when he took over the country. She was replaced by *Savarona* in 1936.

73. HONOR 260'

Rig: Schooner **Gross Tons:** 915 **Designer/Builder:** G.L. Watson/Ramage & Ferguson **Owner:** Baron De Forest (1905-1911) **Year Launched:** 1905 **Propulsion:** Steam/sail **Source:** Hofman

Later *Eros.*

74. AZTEC 260'

Rig: Schooner **Gross Tons:** 848 **Designer/Builder:** Gardner & Cox/Crescent Shipyard **Owner:** Burrage, A.C. (1904) **Year Launched:** 1902 **Propulsion:** Steam/sail twin screw **Source:** Lloyd's 1904-05/Brit. Lloyd's 1950

Later *Beaver.* Fitted with double bottom for safety. Space between the bottoms used to store water. Top speed was 18.5 knots, a good rate for a steam yacht.

75. KATOOMBA 260'

Rig: Schooner **Gross Tons:** 626 **Designer/Builder:** G.L. Watson/Ailsa Shipbldg. **Owner:** Heriot, Madame (1904); Drexel, Anthony J. Sr. (1930) **Year Launched:** 1903 **Propulsion:** Steam/sail **Source:** Brit. Lloyd's 1904; 1950

Later *Salvator; Sayonara; Heliopolis.*

76. DANNEBROG** 259'

Rig: Power **Gross Tons:** 1054 **Designer/Builder:** Naval Dockyard (Denmark) (Des. & Bld.) **Owner:** Danish Royal Yacht **Year Launched:** 1931 **Propulsion:** Diesel **Source:** PMY Aug. 1991/Brit. Lloyd's 1935; 1965

The second yacht of this name, she was built for King Christian X and has been continuously owned by the Danish Crown ever since. Except for the broken sheer line, she looks like a classic Victorian steam yacht. She is actively cruised by the royal family.

77. DELPHINE** 258'

Rig: Schooner **Gross Tons:** 1255 **Designer/Builder:** Henry J. Gielow/Grt. Lakes Eng. Works (Detroit) **Owner:** Dodge, Horace E. (1923) **Year Launched:** 1921 **Propulsion:** Oil fuel/sail **Source:** Lloyd's 1923; PMY Aug. '97

Delphine was built with a ram or naval-type bow instead of a traditional overhanging clipper bow because the designer needed to fit as much accommodation as possible into the vessel, yet make it small enough to pass through the canal system to get from the Great Lakes, to the sea. She is now undergoing a refit.

78. MASSARRAH** 258'

Rig: Power **Designer/Builder:** National Bulk Carriers (Des. & Bld.) (Japan) **Owner:** Sheik Ahmed Yamani (1997) **Year Launched:** 1960 **Propulsion:** Diesel **Source:** PMY Aug.1991; Aug. '97/SBI July '91, files

Formerly *Ultima II* and previously owned by Dr. Al Rashid, who replaced her with *Lady Moura.*

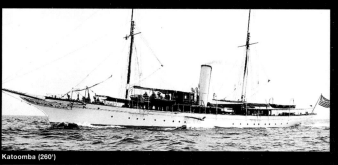

Katoomba (260')

Constellation (262')

❧ *The* 100 LARGEST YACHTS ❧

Lone Ranger (Simson) 255'

American (254')

79. UNITED STATES 256'

Rig: Schooner **Gross Tons:** *2054* **Designer/ Builder:** *Manitowoc Shipbldg. (Des. & Bld.)* **Owner:** *Green, E.H.R. (1917-1919)* **Year Launched:** *1909* **Propulsion:** *Steam* **Source:** *Hofman*

Built as Great Lakes passenger vessel and converted to a yacht because Col. Green did not have time to have one built for the upcoming yachting season. All of the yachts available for purchase were too small. His ship was one of the largest and costliest in the world at that time.

80. NORTH STAR 256'

Rig: Schooner **Gross Tons:** *819* **Designer/ Builder:** *W.C. Storey/Nav. Con. & Arm Co. (Barrow, England)* **Owner:** *Vanderbilt, C.* **Year Launched:** *1893* **Propulsion:** *Steam/sail* **Source:** *Lloyd's 1904-05/YTG May 07*

Formerly *Cherokee; Sybarite; Venetia.* When built, she could carry 225 tons of coal, allowing her to travel 5,000 miles at 12 knots. *Yachting* magazine said that her drawing room and library rivaled any found on Fifth Avenue.

81. LONE RANGER** 255'

Rig: Power **Designer/Builder:** *C. Kusch (conversion)/Cantiere Navale (Italy)* **Owner:** *Setton, Jack* **Year Launched:** *1972/ converted 1994* **Propulsion:** *Diesel* **Source:** *PMY Aug. '91; Aug. '97/ SBI July '95*

Formerly *Simson S; Simson; Lone Wolf.* Owner Jack Setton traded in his Feadship for a yacht that could carry more toys, including a 40-foot offshore cruiser and a 60-knot Cougar

speed boat and some aircraft, as well as a pool.

82. AMERICAN 254'

Rig: Ship **Gross Tons:** *851 A.Watt (Builder)* **Watt, Archibald (1904-05)** **Year Launched:** *1898* **Propulsion:** *Steam/sail* **Source:** *Lloyd's 1904-05*

83. NOMA 252'

Rig: Schooner **Gross Tons:** *763* **Designer/ Builder:** *TAMS, Lemoine & Crand/Burlee Dry Dock* **Owner:** *William B. Leeds* **Year Launched:** *1902* **Propulsion:** *Steam/sail* **Source:** *Lloyd's 1904-05*

Later *Vega.*

84. WESTWARD 251'

Rig: Schooner (4 masts) **Gross Tons:** *2001* **Designer/Builder:** *A/S Rodby Havns Jernskibs (Rodby Havn)* **Owner:** *Robinson, M.A. (1930)* **Year Launched:** *1920* **Propulsion:** *Sail/oil* **Source:** *Brit. Lloyd's 1930*

Formerly *Danefolk,* one of the largest racing schooners of all time.

85. LADY SARYA** 250'

Rig: Power **Gross Tons:** *1436* **Designer/ Builder:** *Rinaldo Gastaldi/Cantiere Navale Apuania (Italy)* **Owner:** *Sheik Yamani (1991)* **Year Launched:** *1972* **Propulsion:** *Diesel* **Source:** *SBI 'July '91/PMY Aug. 1991/Wood's 1994*

Her name is sometimes misspelled *Sarah,* but this yacht is rarely missing from Sardinia. Her owner also owns *Massarah.*

86. ROUSSALKA 250'

Rig: Schooner **Gross Tons:** *1433* **Designer/ Builder:** *W. Denny (Des. & Bld.)* **Owner:** *Guinness,*

Walter (1931-1933) **Year Launched:** *1905* **Propulsion:** *Oil* **Source:** *Hofman*

Built as a cross-Channel steamer, she was converted to a yacht in 1931.

87. TRIAD 250'

Rig: Schooner **Gross Tons:** *1182* **Designer/ Builder:** *Caledonian Shipbldg. (Des. & Bld.)* **Owner:** *Schenley, G.A. (1909-1912)* **Year Launched:** *1909* **Propulsion:** *Steam/sail* **Source:** *Hofman/Brit. Lloyd's 1913*

88. NOURMAHAL 250'

Rig: Bark **Gross Tons:** *745* **Designer/ Builder:** *Gustav Hillman/Harlan & Hollingsworth* **Owner:** *Astor, John Jacob (1899)* **Year Launched:** *1884* **Propulsion:** *Steam/sail* **Source:** *Manning's 1899*

Nourmahal was used for gunboat service during the Spanish American War. Her original owner went down with the *Titanic* in 1912. His son later built a larger boat of the same name.

89. NAZ-PERWER 249'

Rig: Schooner **Gross Tons:** *708* **Designer/ Builder:** *Ramage & Ferguson (Des. & Bld.) (Leith)* **Owner:** *Youssouf Kamal (1932); King Farouk I of Egypt (1950)* **Year Launched:** *1930* **Propulsion:** *Oil/sail* **Source:** *Brit. Lloyd's 1930;1950; 1965*

Later *Intisar; Fakhr El Bihar.* One of King Farouk's earlier yachts.

90. VANADIS 248'

Rig: Power (diesel) **Gross Tons:** *1451* **Designer/ Builder:** *Cox & Stevens/Germania Werft* **Owner:** *Billings, C.K.G. (1924); Williams, Harrison (1930)*

North Star (256')

Westward (251')

❧ *The* 100 LARGEST YACHTS ❧

Leander (246')

Montkaj (246')

Year Launched: *1924* **Propulsion:** *Diesel* **Source:** *Brit. Lloyd's 1924/ Lloyd's 1930*

Later *Warrior*.

91. CYPRUS 248'
Rig: *Power (Diesel)* **Gross Tons:** *1033* **Designer/Builder:** *Cox & Stevens/Germania Werft (Kiel)* **Owner:** *Jackling, D.C. (1930)* **Year Launched:** *1929* **Propulsion:** *Diesel* **Source:** *Lloyd's 1930*

92. TALITHA G** 247'
Rig: *Power* **Gross Tons:** *1080* **Designer/Builder:** *Cox & Stevens/Krupp Germania Werft (Germany)* **Owner:** *Getty, J. Paul II (1991); Russell A. Alger (1931)* **Year Launched:** *1930* **Propulsion:** *Diesel* **Source:** *PMY Aug. 1991/Wood's 1994; Brit. Lloyd's 1931*

Formerly *Reveler; Chalena; USS Beaumont; Carola; Elpetal; Jezebel*. Later, Wood's lists her at 280 feet overall. All other sources list 247'. Refitted under the direction of Jon Bannenberg in 1994 in true 1930s fashion.

93. JOSEPHINE 247'
Rig: *Schooner* **Designer/Builder:** *Neafie & Levy (Des. & Bld.)* **Owner:** *Widener, Geo. & Jos. & P.A.B. (1899)* **Year Launched:** *1899* **Propulsion:** *Steam/sail* **Source:** *Manning's 1899*

Cost approximately $400,000 to build in 1899. Was finished in time to view the 1899 America's Cup races.

94. LEANDER** 246'
Rig: *Power* **Designer/Builder:** *Peenewerft Shipyard (Des, & Bld.) (Germany)* **Owner:** *Gosling, Sir*

Donald (1997) **Year Launched:** *1992* **Propulsion:** *Diesel* **Source:** *PMY Aug. 91/ SBI Sept. 93*

The follow up to his *Brave Goose, Leander* is a very pricey charter yacht and also used for the owner's entertaining. The interior is traditional English country-estate in style.

95. MONTKAJ** 246
Rig: *Power* **Designer/Builder:** *Terence Disdale/Amels (Holland)* **Owner:** *Saudi Royal Family* **Year Launched:** *1995* **Propulsion:** *Diesel* **Source:** *PMY Aug. 1995/SBI Nov.'95, file*

Certainly one of the prettiest modern yachts over 200 feet, *Monkaj* keeps a low profile.

96. PRINCESSE ALICE II 245'
Rig: *Schooner* **Gross Tons:** *1368* **Designer/Builder:** *Laird Bros. (Des. & Bld.) (Birkenhead)* **Owner:** *Prince of Monaco (1900)* **Year Launched:** *1898* **Propulsion:** *Sail/steam* **Source:** *Brit. Lloyd's (1900)*

Used by Prince Albert I of Monaco for his endeavors in early marine exploration and contributed substantially to the development of oceanography as a formal scientific enterprise.

97. VALHALLA 245'
Rig: *Ship* **Gross Tons:** *1218* **Designer/Builder:** *W.C. Storey/Ramage & Ferguson* **Owner:** *J.F. Laycock; Earl of Crawford(1902)* **Year Launched:** *1892* **Propulsion:** *Sail/steam* **Source:** *Hofman*

One of the best examples of the fully rigged steam auxiliary type. Under her second owner, an ornithologist, she made many voyages to remote lands to discover new species (he also

reported a sea serpent off the coast of Brazil). She raced in the 1905 Emperor's Cup, which was won by *Atlantic*.

98. ISABEL 245'
Rig: *Schooner* **Gross Tons:** *710* **Designer/Builder:** *Cox & Stevens/Bath Iron Works* **Owner:** *Willys, John N. (1917)* **Year Launched:** *1917* **Propulsion:** *Steam* **Source:** *Hofman*

Built for the man who developed Willys cars and Curtiss airplanes, she was faster by 8 knots than her contemporaries and was snapped up by the Navy for $611,553. Fitted with four three-inch guns and four torpedo tubes, she was commissioned as a destroyer rather than armed yacht, the only yacht ever so honored. She was returned to yacht status as Navy's Pacific flagship.

99. NARCISSUS 245'
Rig: *Schooner* **Gross Tons:** *661* **Designer/Builder:** *Fairfield Shipbldg. (Des. & Bld.) (Glasgow)* **Owner:** *Mundy, A.E.M. (1905)* **Year Launched:** *1905* **Propulsion:** *Steam (turbines)/sail* **Source:** *Brit. Lloyd's 1905;1911; 1930*

First twin-screw yacht with Charles Parsons turbines which were a breakthrough in power.

100. ARAS 244'
Rig: *Power (oil)* **Gross Tons:** *1332* **Designer/Builder:** *Bath Iron Works* **Owner:** *Chisholm, Hugh J.* **Year Launched:** *1931* **Propulsion:** *Oil* **Source:** *Lloyd's 1939/ Brit. Lloyd's 1950*

Built for the originator of the transportation publishing business, she was later *Williamsburg*.

Princess Alice II (245')

Vanadis (Warrior) 248'

The CENTURY'S 100 LARGEST YACHTS

By Their Most Well-Known Names

1. ABDUL AZIZ**	482'	35. EVERGREEN**	302'	69. NARCISSUS	245'
2. AL SAID**	340	36. GIRALDA	289'	70. NAZ-PERWER	249'
3. AL SALAMAH**	380'	37. GOLDEN ODYSSEY**	266'	71. NIAGARA	272'
4. AL YAMAMAH**	269'	38. HI-ESMARO	267'	72. NIMET ALLAH	273'
5. ALBION	300'	39. HIRONDELLE II	292'	73. NOMA	252'
6. ALCEDO	275'	40. HOHENZOLLERN	383'	74. NORGE**	263'
7. ALDER	294'	41. HONOR	260'	75. NORTH STAR	256'
8. ALEXANDER**	400'	42. IELA	269'	76. NOURMAHAL	264'
9. ALEXANDRA	293'	43. IOLAIRE	263'	77. NOURMAHAL	250'
10. ALEXANDRIA	267'	44. IOLANDA	310'	78. ORION	333'
11. ALVA	264'	45. ISABEL	245'	79. OSBORNE	284'
12. AMERICAN	254'	46. JEANNETTE	270'	80. POLIARNIA ZVEZDA	336'
13. APHRODITE	302'	47. JOSEPHINE	247'	81. PRINCESSE ALICE II	245'
14. ARAS	244'	48. KATOOMBA	260'	82. ROUSSALKA	250'
15. ARCTIC**	285'	49. KINGDOM 5KR**	282'	83. ROVER	320'
16. ARCTURUS	268'	50. LADY MOURA**	344'	84. SAPPHIRE	285'
17. ATLANTIS II**	380'	51. LADY SARYA**	250'	85. SAVARONA**	408'
18. ATMAH	333'	52. LEANDER**	246'	86. SAVOIA II	390'
19. AZTEC	260'	53. LIBERTY	304'	87. SEA CLOUD**	359'
20. BRITANNIA	412'	54. LIMITLESS**	315'	88. STANDARDT	420'
21. CAROLINE	279'	55. LONE RANGER**	255'	89. TALITHA G**	247'
22. CASSANDRA	287'	56. LORENA	300'	90. TRIAD	250'
23. CHRISTINA O**	325'	57. LYSISTRATA	311'	91. TRICK ONE**	311'
24. CONSTELLATION	262'	58. MAHA CHAKRI	284'	92. UNITED STATES	256'
25. CORSAIR III	304'	59. MAHROUSSA**	478'	93. VALHALLA	245'
26. CORSAIR IV	344'	60. MANSOUR	326'	94. VANADIS	345'
27. CUTTY SARK	273'	61. MARGARITA	352'	95. VANADIS	248'
28. CYPRUS	267'	62. MASSARRAH**	258'	96. VARUNA	306'
29. CYPRUS	248'	63. MAYFLOWER	318'	97. VICTORIA AND ALBERT III	430'
30. DANNEBROG**	259'	64. MIPOS**	462'	98. VIKING	272'
31. DELPHINE**	258'	65. MOINEAU	327'	99. WARRIOR	282'
32. DORIS	270'	66. MONTKAJ**	246'	100. WESTWARD	251'
33. ERIN I	287'	67. NAHLIN	300'		
34. ERTRUGRUL	260'	68. NAHMA	306'		

*** Indicates Existing Yachts*

8 ZEALOUS

The Bentley Arnage. 413 pound-feet of relentless torque. 18 handcrafted feet of shameless luxury. It's time to answer your id's impassioned plea. 1-877-300-8803 toll-free or www.bentleymotors.co.uk

How the Challenger 604 i

mproving Marine Life.

There's where you live – and where you *live*.
The Challenger* 604 connects the two quickly,
comfortably, effortlessly. Fly Los Angeles to Antigua,
Fort Lauderdale to Palma, Nice to Nantucket.
Chances are, no matter where you moor your yacht,
you're no more than a nonstop flight away with
the 604's 4,000-nautical-mile range. And you're sure
to enjoy the voyage because, port to starboard,
there's more room on board a Challenger 604 than
on any other corporate jet.

For information on this remarkable vessel and how it
can help enhance your marine life, call (800) 268-0030
in North America. Internationally, call (514) 855-7698.

BOMBARDIER
AEROSPACE

Ask Us For The World

July 1, 1997:   China Takes Rule of Hong Kong From the U.K.

Good for Us.

Business is booming in Hong Kong and Cheoy Lee Shipyards is taking advantage of it.

By 2001, China's shipbuilding industry is expected to produce more than 10% of the world's commercial shipping tonnage, and Cheoy Lee will contribute significantly.

Shipbuilder to the world since the family run business began in 1870, Cheoy Lee has consistently produced some of the finest luxury yachts and commercial vessels.

Today, due in part to the succession of Hong Kong from the British to the Chinese, Cheoy Lee is entering an unprecedented era of growth. A new state-of-the-art manufacturing facility will help meet world-wide demand and keep Cheoy Lee at the forefront of yacht and ship construction.

Cheoy Lee's extensive line of motoryachts are expertly crafted specifically for the American market and priced competitively. The yachts range in size from the 50' Sportsfish to 150' Megayachts. Reap the rewards of Cheoy Lee's 130 years of shipbuilding.

SHIP BUILDERS TO THE WORLD

Cheoy Lee

FOR MORE THAN A CENTURY.

Cheoy Lee Shipyards, Ltd.
89 + 91 Hing Wah St. West
Lai Chi Kok, Kowloon, Hong Kong
(852) 2-307-6333 • fax (852) 2-307-5577
cheoylee@hkstar.com

Cheoy Lee Shipyards North America
1497 S.E. 17th Street
Fort Lauderdale, FL 33316
(954) 527-0999 • fax (954) 527-2887
info@cheoyleena.com

Compass Point Yachts, Inc.
809 Fairview Place N., Ste. 150 • Seattle, WA 98109
(206) 625-1580•Fax (206) 682-1473
compasspt@aol.com
San Diego Office: (619) 523-5490 • Fax (619) 523-5493
scoveyachts@earthlink.net

YACHTASIA
B40 Club de Mar
E 07015 Palma de Mallorca, Spain
+34-971-699-040
Fax +34-971-691-802
info@yachtasia.com

Put more **value** on board.

When navigating the world's investment waters, you
want a private bank on your side whose experience and
ingenuity can spell the difference between mediocre
and superior performance. That's why it makes sense
to travel with Bank Julius Baer. Committed to protecting
and adding value to client wealth since 1890, we are in
the mainstream of the world's premier asset managers.
For detailed information, just call on Bank Julius Baer.
For that something extra.

Julius Bär
THE FINE ART OF PRIVATE BANKING

The
Millennium
Collection

Brioni

Photograph: Bill Muncke

100%
entertainment for
visionaries™

Proven at sea and supported right around the world
by Linn Approved Marine Affiliates

LINN

total entertainment©
for superyachts

UK Tel: +44 **(141) 307 7777**   UK Fax: +44 **(141) 644 4262**
USA Tel: +1 **(904) 645 5242**   USA Fax: +1 **(904) 645 7275**
e-mail: **info@linnmarine.com** internet: **www.linn.co.uk** or **www.linninc.com**

If every sea voyage was this calm, you'd never need our antenna.

Whether it's flat calm or gale force conditions, you can depend on Sea Tel® for reliable, uninterrupted satellite television at sea. New generation, patented, 3-axis stabilised antennas and communications systems provide unparalleled performance with radome-enclosed dishes from 45.7 cm to 1.2 metres across. DTH TV-at-Sea brings hundreds of channels of entertainment onto your yacht from service providers worldwide. WeSat Weather-at-Sea systems provide global weather information from geostationary satellites.

So whether you're cruising the Carribean or the Med, nothing beats a Sea Tel. Because every system is backed by two decades of industry leadership, a worldwide network of service technicians, a legendary 2-year warranty and 24-hour, 7 day a week support.

No matter what the conditions, no matter what your needs, look to the leader. Look to Sea Tel.

For the dealer nearest you or for info, call
Sea Tel Europe **44 (0) 1703 671155**
Sea Tel, Inc. **925.798.7979** or visit **www.seatel.com**

Look to the leader. Look to Sea Tel.

©1999 Sea Tel, Inc.

Global Power Systems is The Gold Standard in Onboard Shore Power Converters Worldwide.

We invited yacht owners, designers and builders worldwide to compare all of the shore power converters on the market. They returned to Global Power Systems for superior design, construction and value, backed by the strongest performance guarantee in the industry. Discerning owners prefer Global Power Systems.

GP3000
S E R I E S

30 - 50kva
Size: 24"w X 30"d X 52"h
Weight: 1100 lbs.

72 - 120kva
Size: 45"w X 30"d X 39"h
Weight: 1800 lbs.

YACHT OWNERS PREFER GLOBAL FOR

1. Styling that complements their yachts' designs
2. Non-interruptible, reliable power transfer
3. Patented noise-free, distortion-free output
4. Proven state-of-the-art technology
5. Compliance with the standards, including CE
6. Demonstrated high motor-starting capability
7. Unsurpassed output efficiency
8. Compact, lightweight, and extremely rugged self-contained unit
9. The only true marinized shore power converter, built to withstand the harsh marine environment

---

You'll appreciate the Global Power Team's professionalism and experience. We stand ready to assist you in selecting the power sizing to meet your requirements in yachts 50- to 300-feet. We will provide electrical wiring recommendations, installation advice, on-site engineering help and complete documentation. We can assist with single- or three-phase power, 8kva to 360kva. Contact us today about the Global product for your yacht and the dealer nearest you.

GP2000
S E R I E S

8 - 18kva
Size: 30"w X 12"d X 22"h
Weight: 270 lbs.

24 - 40kva
Size: 14"w X 30"d X 39"h
Weight: 500 lbs.

GLOBAL POWER'S WORLDWIDE HEADQUARTERS
Phone 206-301-0515 • Fax 206-301-0660
1500 Westlake Ave. North, Suite 4, Marina Mart Building
Seattle, Washington USA 98109

Global Power Systems is a Thermo Voltek company, a subsidiary of Thermo Electron.

SIGNIFICANT VESS

CORNERSTONE

EV

UNFORGETTABLE

PEPLE

❖ *of the Past 100 Years* ❖

EL S

ENTS

E DITORS' NOTE: THE WRITTEN, PHOTOGRAPHIC AND ANEC-dotal records relating to boats, yachts and all things marine occurring roughly over the past one hundred years have never been gathered in one place. Choosing from among thousands of events and many thousands of boats and yachts for those of most lasting significance will, no doubt, spark debate. On the following pages, we believe, the events and especially the yachts represent the first, the fastest, the biggest, or the best of their type or class. In some cases they represent folly or futility. In others, staggering achievement. What they all share is their direct and incontrovertible impact on the development of luxury yachting during the 20th Century. ➢

ONLY THE BEGINNING

ACAJOU

FOR RICHNESS of finish there is just nothing like mahogany. And that's partially why 137-foot *Acajou* – French for mahogany – is so special. In 1984 not-yet-famous Jon Bannenberg was hired by French builder Chantiers Navals de L'Esterel to put a yacht spin on its line of patrol-boat hulls drawn by Andre Mauric. The first thing JB did was convince L'Esterel not to paint the mahogany hull – she is the largest bright-finished boat ever. Despite the fact marine plywood disallowed compound curves, *Acajou* was sleek and exciting – especially at 34 knots. Among her avant garde features were a forward observation lounge and a TV that rose from the center of a table in the master suite.

✥ *Taking it from the Top* ✥

A B D U L   A Z I Z

It's FITTING THAT THE RICHEST MAN in the world owns the largest yacht in the world. Her dimensions are mind-boggling: 482 feet on a 60-foot beam. King Fahd was introduced to yachting in the early '70s by John Latsis, who actually bought the King his first yacht as a gift. *Prince Abdul Aziz,* the king's current yacht, was launched in 1984 at Helsingor, a Danish commercial yard, with assistance from Vospers. The yacht, however, is anything but commercial looking. Her long bow is kept open for landing the royal helicopter – a smart plan that both enhances the yacht's looks and the King's security. She is powered commercially with a pair of 12-cylinder Pielstick diesels. She is beautifully appointed and contains, among other salons, a large movie theater. *Abdul Aziz* is moored in a special facility in Jiddah and rarely leaves the Red Sea.

AJAX NEWS & FEATURE SERVICE

BROWARD'S FIRST STEP

IN 1953 FRANK DENISON BEGAN building minesweepers in Fort Lauderdale, Florida, launching a 144-footer every 45 days and repairing all manner of craft. Impressed by the yard's refit and repowering of one of his designs, the renowned naval architect John Wells contacted Denison about building a wood 96-footer ordered by Elmer Bobst, chairman of Warner Lambert Pharmaceuticals. Broward's first yacht, *Alisa V,* was a yacht in every sense of the word and one of the largest launched in the 1950s. Broward built the

ALISA V

boat in just 11 months. She was powered by two 600-hp diesels and ran continuously at 14.5 knots. In 1957 she set a record running from Miami to New York in just 57 hours.

1900
- New York YC creates first one-design class: The Seventies
- **Joshua Slocum** publishes *Sailing Alone Around the World*
- First Olympic yachting events held during Paris Games
- **Enrico Forlanini** runs first hydrofoil catamaran

1901
- *Columbia* defeats *Shamrock II* in America's Cup
- The Henry B. Burger Shipyard builds its first motor cruiser utilizing the Kahlenberg Company's new gasoline engine. The 85-footer was named *Vernon Jr.*

Joshua Slocum

Atlantic

1903
- *Atlantic,* a 185-foot schooner designed by **William Gardner,** is launched.
- Universal Rule developed for J-Class
- Herreshoff's *Reliance,* at 144 feet the largest racing cutter ever, is launched to defend the America's Cup. She set 16,000 sq. ft. of sail on a 196-foot mast.
- First edition of *Lloyd's Register of American Yachts*
- First Harmsworth Trophy for motorboat speed won by *Napier* at 19.53 mph

- First radio time signal for navigation
- In a precursor to RADAR, Christian Hulsmeyer, Germany, patents reflected radio waves for object detection
- Work begins on the Panama Canal
- First Gold Cup Regatta for powerboats

1904

CORBIS

ILLIAM KISSAM VANDERBILT II NAMED this 264-foot Krupp-built diesel yacht for his mother. Relatively unscathed by the Great Depression, in the summer of 1931 he began a nine-month, round-the-world cruise aboard what amounted to a gentleman's ship. Like his grandfather Cornelius, he had a fondness for big yachts and described *Alva* as, "the most powerfully constructed yacht in existence." Mr. and Mrs. Vanderbilt crossed the Atlantic from the West Indies, cruised through the Med and the Red Sea, went on to the East Indies and Australia, then came home by way of the South Seas, the Galapagos, and the Panama Canal. The cruise fulfilled Rosamond and W.K. Vanderbilts's wanderlust, and also

ALVA

filled their Long Island estate with specimens of marine life and aboriginal curiosities.

❊ *A Fantastic Fife* ❊

ALTAIR

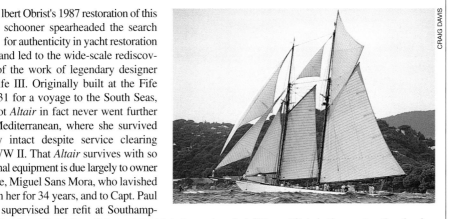

lbert Obrist's 1987 restoration of this schooner spearheaded the search for authenticity in yacht restoration and led to the wide-scale rediscovery of the work of legendary designer William Fife III. Originally built at the Fife yard in 1931 for a voyage to the South Seas, the 107-foot *Altair* in fact never went further than the Mediterranean, where she survived remarkably intact despite service clearing mines in WW II. That *Altair* survives with so much original equipment is due largely to owner number five, Miguel Sans Mora, who lavished attention on her for 34 years, and to Capt. Paul Goss who supervised her refit at Southampton Yacht Services. Retaining all her original interior and period fittings *Altair* is the most authentic classic sailing yacht afloat. In the last 10 years *Altair* has been more actively sailed than ever and has become a regular winner on the Mediterranean classic circuit.

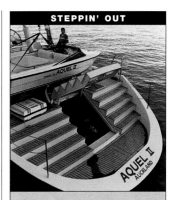

AQUEL II

ESIGNED IN THE MID-1980s FOR a client making the transition from motor yachts to sailing, the brief for Dubois Naval Architects demanded sleek, modern looks and great functionality. Advances included concealed winches (developed in conjunction with Seaway Products), hidden sheets and ventilators, and a stylish wing to hold the SatCom dome. It is 123-foot *Aquel II's* stepped transom, however, that everyone remembers. Ed Dubois' racing boat background was evident here with this marvelously functional adaptation of the sugar-scoop stern. Built in New Zealand, *Aquel II* helped pioneer that country's megayacht industry.

Kaiser Wilhelm Trophy

1905
• Kaiser Wilhelm Trophy won by *Atlantic* skippered by **Charlie Barr.** Her monohull record would stand for 90 years
• **Guglielmo Marconi** invents directional radio antenna
• **Cameron B. Waterman** patents first successful outboard motor
• First London to Cowes motorboat race
• 120' *Vitesse* powered by two 3-cylinder Seabury engines is the first gas-powered commuter. She goes 30 knots.

1906
• British Yacht Racing Assn. first "Metre Rule" (23, 15, 12, 8, & 6)
• International Yacht Racing Union, the governing body of sail, introduces class system

1907
• First radionavigation warnings issued by U.S. Navy Hydrographic Office
• *Yachting* magazine begins publication
• Abeking & Rasmussen launches first project, a 5m *Arbeitsboot*
• At the urging of *Rudder Magazine* editor **T.F. Day,** the Cruising Club of America hosts First Bermuda Race
• First Transpac sailing race to Hawaii from Los Angeles

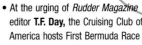

✷ *Record Holder* ✷

ATLANTIC

*A*TLANTIC SAILED FROM SANDY HOOK, New Jersey, to England in May of 1905 in a race with ten other yachts for the Kaiser's Cup. Driven to the potential of her lean hull form and 18,500 square feet of sail by Captain Charlie Barr, on the seventh day of racing she logged a staggering 341 nautical miles. When she passed the warship marking the finish, she had crossed the ocean in 12 days, 4 hours, 1 minute, 19 seconds. This record would stand for more than 90 years. One of the world's great schooner yachts, 185-foot *Atlantic* was designed by William Garden and built of steel for Wilson Marshall of New York. Her second owner was Cornelius Vanderbilt. She lasted into the late 1970s. Too big and costly to properly maintain, she sank at her last mooring in tidewater Virginia. In 1997, the NYYC hosted The Atlantic Challenge, a race for large cruising yachts in *Atlantic's* memory.

© MYSTIC SEAPORT/ROSENFELD COLLECTION

BIGGEST BURGER

BURGER BOAT COMPANY

ARARA

*B*UILT TO A design by Jack Hargrave, Burger Boat Company launched 125-foot *Arara* in August 1977. Not only was it the largest fully-found aluminum motor yacht launched to that time in the U.S., but she was and remains the largest Burger yacht. Built for the Illinois Tool Company for corporate entertaining up and down the Mississippi River as well as along the Eastern Seaboard, the yacht was ahead of her time with state-of-the-art fire resistant materials and a sewage treatment system. Uniquely, she featured individual cabins with private heads for each of her seven crew.

ORIENTAL WAY

YANTI RAFFLES SHIPYARD

ASEAN LADY

*W*HEN BRIAN CHANG took delivery of 158-foot *Asean Lady* in 1983 from Nisshe Shipyard in Japan, she was one of the largest GRP yachts ever built, and certainly the largest modern-era yacht built for an Asian yachtsman. But more than her size and choice of construction material, *Asean Lady* is significant for establishing far-ranging patterns of use that Asian yachtsmen emulate to this day. Chang, a passionate diver and fisherman, has put 11,500 hours on her engines, in the process setting the standards for Pacific luxury cruising that influenced such significant Asian yachtsmen as Vee King Shaw (*Seashaw*) and Goh Cheng Liang (*White Rabbit*).

Dixie II

1908

- **Clinton Crane's** speedboat *Dixie II* does 36.6 mph (31.6 knots)
- **H. Anschutz-Kaempfe** makes first gyroscopic compass

1909

- **Joshua Slocum** and *Spray* disappear at sea
- **Kaiser Wilhelm II** takes delivery of 154.75-foot *Meteor IV*, the first *Meteor* built in Germany and crewed by Germans
- Ole Evinrude invents lightweight outboard (to shorten trip across lake to buy ice cream for his fiancée)
- *M/V Cartago* sends first wireless report of a storm at sea

Evinrude outboard

1910

- **Prince Albert I** of Monaco founds Institute for Oceanography
- **Mathis Yacht Building Company** opened in Camden, New Jersey, by **John Mathis** and **Johan Trumpy** with $20,000 capital stock. Their first houseboat yacht was 69'8" *Cocopomelo*
- **Jacques-Yves Cousteau** born at St. Andre-de-Cubzac, France.

MUSÉE OCÉANOGRAPHIQUE

Prince Albert I

❧ *Waltzing Matilda* ❧

AUSTRALIA II

WHEN THE LOW BLACK SCHOONER *Amer-ica* trounced the British fleet in a race around the Isle of Wight in 1851, a grand sporting saga known as the America's Cup began. For the next 132 years, the New York Yacht Club defeated a succession of challengers for the prize. That monopoly was finally broken in 1983 by Alan Bond's syndicate and *Australia II*. Designed by Ben Lexcen, whose real name was Bob Miller, the 12-Meter yacht sported a breakthrough keel with canted wings. Although the keel was carefully shielded from view during the trials, it was widely rumored that it had appendages and aerial photography confirmed the fact. The NYYC tried and failed to defeat Australia in the courtroom and on the water when Dennis Conner and *Liberty* went down to defeat in seven races. Later analysis suggests that *Australia II's* sail program coordinated by North Sail's Kiwi genius Tom Schnackenberg might have been just as important, but it is the keel and the new thinking it spawned that changed sailboat design forever.

THE ULTIMATE COMMITTEE BOAT

BLACK KNIGHT

A QUADRENNIAL FIXTURE at the America's Cup starting line off the coast of Newport, Rhode Island, *Black Knight's* stately black hull, bright super-structure and rows of uniform-clad officials came to symbolize the New York Yacht Club's dominance of the Cup. Built in 1955 as *Cassiar* by Goudy & Stevens for General Mellon, this lovely 85-foot wooden motor yacht remains a nostalgic reminder of the way things used to be.

TUBE OF MAHOGANY

BABY BOOTLEGGER

In THE 1920s, GEORGE CROUCH DREW A NUMBER of successful mahogany speedboats and raceboats. But when he designed *Baby Bootlegger*, he permitted pure aesthetics to direct the outcome. An extraordinary mahogany tube with a rolled sheerline, a fast bottom, and the heads of 60,000 brass screws gleaming under perfect skins of varnish, this boat defined an era when bootleggers were prominent and speedboats were often called "Baby." This most extraordinary runabout of the Jazz Age is still around, perfectly restored by Mark Mason, including her 1920s Hispano-Suiza V8 engine.

1911

- **William Gardner** and **Francis Weisguth** design the *Star*, a 22-foot, hard-chined sloop with a fin and bulb keel for Olympic competition
- **Gar Wood** begins powerboat racing
- **Elmer Ambrose Sperry** patents the gyrocompass
- Forbes ship logs introduced to operate through hull bottom, not dragged astern
- **Captain Charlie Barr,** three-time winner of the America's Cup dies at age 47 while skipper of the schooner *Westward*
- First radio direction finder installed on *S.S. Mauretania*

Charlie Barr

1912

- *Maple Leaf IV,* **The Duke of Westminster's** 40' hydroplane, at 50 knots, is the fastest boat in the world
- **Glenn Curtiss** builds his first flying boat
- **Charles Nicholson** designs innovative *Istria* (15-Meter) with dinghy that fit into a sunken cockpit and a two-part "fish-pole" mast. In the U.S. it was called a Marconi rig, in the U.K. the term was Bermuda rig
- *Meteor IV* triumphs at Kiel Week, invented by The Kaiser to establish a German yachting tradition to rival Cowes Week.
- **John Jacob Astor** and 1,500 others lost with the *Titanic*
- **Rudolf Diesel** dies

Charles Nicholson

FIBERGLASS FOREVER

BOUNTY

AFTER WW II THE wooden Bounty Class designed by Philip Rhodes and built by Coleman as a family sloop was stretched to 40 feet and modified for fiberglass construction. The easily handled Bounty was the most talked about boat at the 1957 New York Boat Show and paved the way for the fiberglass revolution. Bounty's East Coast dealer was Vince Lazzara, then of Chicago, who helped popularize them by racing his own boat in the Chicago-Mackinaw race. Lazzara would later apply Bounty's formula of pairing big interiors on an easily driven hull to his Gulfstar Line and later to his own 60-foot staysail schooner.

⚜ *End of an Era* ⚜

BRITANNIA

SEEMINGLY THE last in a long line of British royal yachts, *Britannia* replaced the third *Victoria and Albert.* Initially planned for King George VI she was completed in 1954 for Queen Elizabeth II and the Duke of Edinburgh. Controversy over the building cost of the yacht led to her being designed to quickly convert into a hospital ship. While this facility was never used, *Britannia's* career combined both state and private royal occasions. Queen Elizabeth once explained her affection for the yacht by noting that *Britannia* was the only royal home that she and Duke had any hand in creating. She served their family on many occasions including, most famously, during the Prince and Princess of Wales' honeymoon. *Britannia's* final official role was at the 1997 handover of Hong Kong to China. After 43 years use as a vessel of state, pleasure and business, the 412-foot *Britannia* remains as stately as ever, although she is tied to the dock as a tourist attraction in Edinburgh, Scotland.

AJAX NEWS & FEATURES SERVICE

WAVE TAMER

CAMARGO IV

FEADSHIP TOOK ANOTHER LEAP FORWARD WHEN *CAMARGO IV* WAS launched in 1961 for Julius Fleischmann of Cincinnati, Ohio. This 116-foot steel yacht with aluminum superstructure was the largest yacht that de Vries Scheepsbouw had launched to date. Of particular note, however, were her breakthrough hydraulically operated stabilizer fins. These fins reduced roll from 15 to 1.5 degrees. Even Prince Bernhard came to see the accomplishment. Other notable features included autopilot, automatic fire fighting system, watermaker and four TV sets with Ampex stereo sound.

FEADSHIP

1913

- De Voogt International Yacht & Ship Design opens for business
- Kaiser Wilhelm commissions *Meteor V*
  - First diesel megayacht, 163' *Pioneer* designed by **Charles Nicholson**
  - **Alexander Winton** introduces the gasoline internal combustion engine to large power yachts. Marinized diesel engines would not be practical until the mid-1920s

Meteor V

1914

- **N.G. Herreshoff** designs the first 12-Meter yacht
- WWI cancels America's Cup racing
- Panama Canal opens for international shipping
- **Ambrose Sperry** invents the first autopilot
- Fr. Lurssen Werft burns to the ground, setting the stage for the current shipyard in Vegesack, Germany

Panama Canal opens

CORBIS

1915

- Amels Shipyard opens in Makkum, Holland. By century's end, it will have launched 400 vessels
- U.S. Coast Guard established

AS SWORDS INTO PLOWSHARES

CARINTHIA VI

HE COINCIDENTAL TIMing of 1973's worldwide oil crisis and the delivery of his new 233-foot motor yacht powered by three 20-cylinder 2,700-hp MTUs did little to dampen the spirits of *Carinthia's* owner. Following the sinking of *Carinthia V* on her maiden voyage, he was just happy to have a yacht. Radically styled for her day by Jon Bannenberg (see page 7), she featured shutters over her windows for privacy. *Carinthia VI* benefited from Lürssen's expertise with high-speed military boats. Built to Lloyd's certification, she topped out at 24 knots.

CHRIS'S BIG CRAFT

CHRIS CRAFT ROAMER

HRIS CRAFT IS PERHAPS THE ONLY COMPANY IN America to have manufactured large production boats in wood, metal and fiberglass. For nearly two decades the legendary builder's largest, most luxurious yachts were known as Roamers, a name retained from the Holland, Michigan, tugboat yard acquired by Chris Craft in 1955. Over the years, steel and aluminum models

were offered, and because Chris Craft was a familiar name, owners otherwise reluctant to invest in a metal boat took the plunge. Used 60-foot models became so popular that attorney F. Lee Bailey founded a company just to restore them.

PIVOTAL FEADSHIP

CAPRI

HE *CAPRI 55* was the largest yacht and therefore queen of the 1953 New York Boat Show. Some 100,000 visitors came aboard to admire her smooth steel hull — most U.S. yards were still building in wood — her laid teak decks, and her varnished teak house. Her exquisite mahogany interior joinerwork enveloped deluxe quarters for eight. She was a spec product of the First Export Association of Dutch Shipbuilders (Feadship) built especially for the U.S. market. Although Feadship had been marketing yachts to Americans since 1951, and had shown a nice 40-footer at the '52 New York show, the size, beauty and power of *Capri* made a lasting impression. The advancements developed by the Feadship partners for U.S. buyers would shape both Feadship and the luxury yacht market that followed.

❦ *Nautical Art Deco* ❧

CHANTICLEER

NE OF THE GREAT POSTWAR MOTOR yachts, *Chanticleer* was sculpted into being in 1946-47 by DeFoe Shipbuilding of Bay City, Michigan. These 118-foot semi-custom yachts called Cruisemasters by Tom Defoe were styled with the curvaceous influence of 1930s and '40s industrial design. Of the six

that he built, *Chanticleer* became the most famous. Acquired in 1953 by OMC Chairman Ralph Evinrude, and his wife, singer Francis Langford, *Chanticleer* took her owners cruising from April to October nearly every year from a base on Florida's Gold Coast to northern adventures high in the Great Lakes. Sometimes she ranged farther – often to Cozumel and Isla de Mujeres. In 1957, she cruised to the U.S. West Coast and in 1965 made a transatlantic passage and a grand tour of the Med from Gibraltar to the Black Sea. This was ambitious, trendsetting cruising for the time, just what Ralph Evinrude had in mind when he bought her and perhaps what Tom DeFoe had in mind when he gave these capable cruisers their name.

1917

- *Isabel,* the only megayacht delivered in the U.S. during the war, is launched from Bath Iron Works. She was a 245' steam-powered auxiliary schooner designed by Cox & Stevens.

1918

- **Alexander Graham Bell** tests a high-speed hydrofoil boat
- **Johnson and Gmack** begin building fishing boats in Sturgeon Bay, Wisconsin. The yard that would become Palmer Johnson launches its first yacht 10 years later.

1919

- Radio Corporation of America (RCA) founded
- Hakvoort shipyard founded
- Atlas Imperial Engine Co., of California introduces rail fuel injection

1920

- **King George V** refits the G.L. Watson-designed "big-class" *Britannia* (1893) and beats the American schooner *Westward,* among others, at Cowes. In 1923, *Britannia* won 23 of 26 starts.
- Antwerp Olympics prove superiority of Bermuda rig over gaff rig
- *Miss America II* built by **Gar Wood** sets record of 80.567 mph
- Huisman Shipyard celebrates its 100th anniversary

The Big Class Britannia

- Fishing schooner *Bluenose* launched in Canada. She would become the most famous Gloucester schooner.

❧ *Incomparable Entertainer* ❧

CHRISTINA

No other artifact defines the era of the jet setters quite so completely as the Aristotle Onassis' yacht

"**A**FTER YOU GET TO A CERTAIN point, money not only ceases to be a problem, it ceases to be important. What matters is to be happy and content," said Aristotle Onassis. Thus, in 1954, the undisputed leader of the Jet Set created the most fabulous yacht the world had ever seen. She was born a military frigate, the *Stormont,* in 1943. At the cost of over $4 million, Onassis transformed her into a 325-foot floating palace. The task was skillfully executed at the Howaldt-Kiel shipyard under the direction of naval architect Caesar Pinnau.

Technically, she was a high-performance cruiser capable of hitting 22 knots. In fact, she was a self-contained floating city capable of generating enough power to light up Monaco, one of Onassis' favorite ports. Among her innovations were an onboard hospital complete with an operating room. All portholes and doors were electrically monitored for security, and she had an automatic fire suppression system. For fun, there were toys galore — a small car, a seaplane, four launches, a high speed hydrofoil, two speedboats, and a six-ton sailboat.

Christina was opulence personified. Her focal point was the open stern lounge with its centerpiece ancient mosaic inlaid dance floor

framed in polished bronze. With the push of a button, the dance floor converted into a full-sized swimming pool with fountains. Forward, through Japanese lacquer doors, guests congregated in the immense game room. Here was the Steinway where La Callas practiced and Sinatra swung. Two Yuan-dynasty bronze lions guarded the gemstone-encrusted fireplace. The

yacht's famous glass-topped circular bar had footrests and handholds of ornately carved whales' teeth and ivory. Much has been made of the fact the bar stools were covered with whale foreskin. Onassis' enjoyed politely informing his female guests they were "sitting on the world's largest genital!"

On the main deck, the glorious circular main dining hall featured murals by Mareel Vertes, and an original Vermeer. The grand reception hall accommodated a full orches-

tra and 200 guests.

Onassis' private domain was a full upper deck apartment. Among its appointments were a Louis XIV desk, a pair of gold sabers from King Faud, Turkish dueling pistols, antique armor, El Greco's "The Ascension," and a priceless amethyst, jade and ruby Buddha. Onassis' cream and sea-green bedroom was decorated with Venetian antiques and Greek, Russian and Byzantine icons. The bathing salon was an exact copy of the bath of King Minos with a sunken bathtub of blue, white and gold mosaics and gold dolphin-shaped faucets. Guests were accommodated in nine air conditioned and soundproofed three-room suites named after Greek islands.

Onassis' entertaining was legendary. Star-studded parties often featured Moulin Rouge dancers from Paris, Athenian bouzouki players and flamenco dancers from Seville. Renowned guests included Douglas Fairbarks Jr., Cary Grant, John and Jackie Kennedy, Greta Garbo, Marlene Dietrich, Elizabeth Taylor, Richard Burton, Princess Margaret, Gregory Peck, King Farouk, Cole Porter, John Wayne and Charles de Gaulle. Maria Callas, Prince Rainier and Princess Grace, and Sir Winston and Lady Churchill were often in residence. A crew of 65 catered to their needs.

In 1978, *Christina* was given to the Greek government by Onassis' heirs for use as a presidential yacht. By the late '80s, however, she was little used and neglected. In 1998, a new owner purchased her, giving her a total refit. *Christina O,* as she is now called, will begin the next century as a luxury charter yacht capable of carrying up to 36 guests.

— John Randall Lassiter, III, Olympiships

1921

- Int'l Hyrographic Bureau, Monaco, established to standardize nautical charts
- First radio-direction-finding beacon installed
- "Big Class" racing restarted in Europe and US after WWI
- *Nyria* (23-Meter) first large yacht with English-named Bermuda rig
- **John Alden** designs his first *Malabar* Schooner

1922

- First effective echo sounder
- **Marconi** posits potential for radio-reflection detection
- Admiralty List of Wireless Signals initiated
- Chapman's *Piloting* first published

Nyria

1923

- Bermuda Race revived; **John Alden's** *Malabar IV* wins
- **Gar Wood** launches 50-knot *Cigarette,* half her 70' length was filled with 5 Liberty engines and fuel.
- First direct-reversing diesel appears

❋ *Smoke Signals* ❋

COCHISE

*C*OCHISE IS NOTABLE, NOT only for her speed, but for her obviously influential appearance. She looked like a patrol boat, a natural considering her design ancestry. Built in 1971 by Cantieri Baglietto of Verazze, Italy, for Austrian-born John van Neuman, who was at the time the major Volkswagen-Porsche importer for the Southwest U.S., *Cochise* was painted battleship gray with the pennant number JvN5 painted in black on her superstructure. Constructed of mahogany and marine plywood, this 65-footer was powered by twin CRM 18D/S-2 diesels, each developing 1,350-

hp for a top speed of 42 knots. Interesting additions were the bow-mounted twin cannons and smoke-screen laying equipment with which van Neuman used to terrorize the chic Jet Set at anchor off St.Tropez.

AT THE FOUR-FRONT

CLUB MEDITERRANÉE

AJAX NEWS AND FEATURE SERVICE

*F*OR A SINGLE-HANDED race across the Atlantic, a giant four-masted vessel of 242 feet is hardly a likely candidate. Yet, with *Club Mediterranée*, Frenchman Alain Colas took on the 1976 Observer Singlehanded Transatlantic Race. In the process, he demonsrated that very large yachts need not require very large crews – a concept central to the development of modern megasailers. French industrialist Bernard Tapie later saved the yacht from the drudgery of an ill-maintained charter operation in the Pacific. He renamed her *Phocea* and transformed her into a cruiser with four hydraulically controlled rigs trimmed at the touch of a toggle switch. She was completely refitted at Lürssen in 1998-99 for Mouna E. Ayoub.

REALLY SMOKIN'

CIGARETTE

*T*HE MAN BEHIND THE BOAT, DON Aronow, made Cigarette a synonym for fast open boats and, over the years, added others — Formula, Donzi and Magnum among them — to the boating lexicon. Aronow gained prominence in 1962, when, as a novice, he took fourth place in the Miami-Nassau powerboat race. He died in 1987, murdered in his car on "Thunderboat Row," the Miami street he had made famous.

1924

- First vane-type self-steering introduced on sailing yachts

1925

- International Rule adopted, leads to creation of J-Class
- First Fastnet Race won by *Jolie Brise*, a 50' **Alexandre Paris** cutter built in 1912 at Le Havre
- First Transpac race to Tahiti
- Codecasa Shipyard celebrates its 100th anniversary

AJAX NEWS AND FEATURE SERVICE

Jolie Brise

1926

- Concordia shipyard founded by the Howland family and C. Ray Hunt
- **Thomas Fleming Day**, influential editor of *Rudder* magazine dies.

1927

- "Genoa" jib makes debut on 6-Meter *Lilian*
- Dragon class designed by **Johann Anker**
- Camper & Nicholsons delivers 699-ton schooner *Vira*, soon renamed *Creole*
- Ratsey & Lapthorn debut the symmetrical spinnaker.

❧ *Suburb to City at 40 Knots* ❧

THE COMMUTERS

Uniquely American in their ingenuity and excess, commuters once were the rage

MANHASSET FLYER

APHRODITE

OHN HAY WHITNEY COMMISSIONED HIS third *Aphrodite* from the Purdy Boat Company in 1936-37 specifically to beat his brother-in-law Charles Payson's commuter *Saga* on their sprints into Manhattan from adjoining Long Island estates. The 74 by 14-foot 6-inch uniquely beautiful *Aphrodite* was powered by two 800-horsepower V-12 Packard engines. **Fast, elegant, and a survivor,** *Aphrodite* was restored in the 1980s and is now a family boat in Florida. She's also an inspiration. *Liberty*, launched in 1996 by Hodgdon Yachts of Boothbay Harbor, Maine, to lines by Bruce King, is a dead ringer for her, although *Liberty* is all hightech composite construction.

WNERS OF LARGE yachts today may commute to work by fax, phone and modem from office suites on vessels anchored in exotic locations. In the early days of this century, going to work on a yacht meant stepping aboard from the dock of a waterfront estate and settling into a wicker chair for a light breakfast served by the steward while the yacht steamed toward Manhattan or Detroit. By the 1920s, the trip into town from Glen Cove or Grosse Point likely had become a race with a fellow commuter, wicker chair abandoned for a firm grip on the rail.

Marine commuting and the class of yachts it spawned is a uniquely American phenomenon beginning in the 1880s and lasting through 50 years of social, financial and nautical extravagance. Fleets of commuter yachts traveling between city and suburb – as many as 300 altogether– reached their zenith in the Roaring '20s then, with a few exceptions such as Laurance Rockefeller's 66-foot *Dauntless*, disappeared by 1950.

In 1890, J. Pierpont Morgan rode the Hudson River to Wall Street at 15 knots aboard his second *Corsair,* a 242-foot steam yacht as large and luxurious as any domicile. A decade later, textile entrepreneur Matthew C.D. Borden jaunted

Chris Craft began offering commuters in 1928. Allez carried 30 people at 30 knots.

in from Atlantic Highlands aboard his *Little Sovereign* at speeds over 30 miles per hour. This third of Borden's commuter yachts was a 112-foot by 11-foot canoe with two Herreshoff triple-expansion steam engines. The era of one-upsmanship was firmly at hand.

Advances in speedboat design and the development of powerful aircraft engines made the fast commuter yachts possible. The yachts were split into two camps. The more sedate ones were built by Lawley, Luders, Nevins, Great Lakes Boat Building, and Consolidated. They were recognizable by their long, slim, white-painted semi-planing hulls. Varnished house structures sheltered all the conveniences of a hotel suite. A windshield set into the deck sheltered a forward cockpit, and the covered aft decks served as smoking lounges. Two big gas engines in well-insulated engine rooms typically turned out 25- to 35-

---

1928

- *Niña* wins Transat (first for small boats) and Fastnet races
- First U.S. team competes in Olympic sailing
- British designer, **Uffa Fox's** invents the V-section and planing hulls. His dinghy *Avenger* wins 52 of 57 races.
- Hinckley opens for business

Avenger

1929

- Sparkman & Stephens open for business in Manhattan
- **G.L.Watson** delivers 209' *Virginia* for Major Courtauld. She looked like a steam yacht but held two Gardner diesels and could cross the Atlantic twice before refueling.
- Mrs. Oliver Grinnell bolts a barber chair to her skiff to create the first fighting chair

Sir Thomas Lipton

1930

- **Sir Thomas Lipton** dies after losing his fifth attempt to win the America's Cup. **Harold S. Vanderbilt's** Starling Burgess-designed *Enterprise* beat *Shamrock V* in four straight races. *Enterprise* was the first jib-headed J-Class and debuted the duralumin mast.
- First Southern Ocean Racing Conference (S.O.R.C.) series sailed
- Polystyrene, Polyvinyl-chloride, and Freon invented
- **Barton** invents the bathysphere
- Blohm + Voss completes its first motor yacht, 408' *Savarona*

Howard Gould's 110-foot Niagara IV was built in 1903.

mph speeds without a lot of noise.

In the other camp, led by Gar Wood, John Hacke and George Crouch were those who enjoyed an adrenaline rush along with their coffee and *Wall Street Journal.* Wood's 50-footers powered by twin Liberty V-12s provided 50-mph sprints into the city. Others with 40- to 50-mph capabilities came along during the '20s and '30s – notably Ralph Pulitzer's 45-mph *Phantom,* the 50-mph step-bottomed *Whim III* built by Consolidated for Harrison Williams, and Adolph Zukor's 45-mph *Lotty K* with two 550-hp Packards. Among the superstars were Caleb Bragg's 50-mph-plus *Rascal* and a fancy speed-boat built around two Packard V-12s by the Purdy brothers of Long Island, Gordon Hammersley's *Cigarette.*

The Depression took a toll on yacht commuting, but didn't stop it, and those who could afford it commissioned some of the world's great yachts between the crash of '29 and the war clouds of '39. Standouts of this period include Charles Shipman Payson's 69-foot Wheeler *Saga* and Jock Whitney's 74-foot Purdy-built *Aphrodite.*

What faltering economies and great wars couldn't stop, interstate highways did. Commuters were extravagant and they were fun. They will not pass this way again.

Peter Rouss' 225-foot Winchester offered a 30-knot commute.

JAZZ AGE POWER

CIGARETTE

 AR WOOD GAINED FAME FOR SETTING a world water speed record of 80 mph in 1921. His marinized versions of the WWI Liberty V-12 aircraft engines delivered roughly 450 horsepower. Wood's prototype commuter had four Liberties, although one or two were enough for most sportsmen. New York tabacco millionaire and sometime speedboat racer Gordon Hamersley ordered five engines for the 70-foot commuter he bought from Wood in 1923. Hamersley's boat, purpose-built for getting the Baron of Wall Street from his Long Island home to his Manhattan office, would be his fastest *Cigarette* and the ultimate commuter in an era of ultimates. Her intriguing name, suggesting long and slim, was perfect for a boat with only an 11-foot, 6-inch beam. She was one of several famous *Cigarettes,* one of them a Brooklyn rum boat that more than 40 years later inspired Don Aronow to give the same name to his deep-Vee speedster.

1931

- **Olin Stephens'** *Dorade* wins transatlantic and Fastnet races, establishing Stephens' skill and the validity of lighter boats
- Stevens Institute of Technology opens Small-Boat Towing Tank
- Krupp launches 360' *Hussar II* designed by Gibbs and Cox for **E.F.Hutton** and **Marjorie Post.** When they divorce in '37 she keeps the boat and renames it *Sea Cloud.*
- The Chris-Craft Corporation unveils a new concept in family boating at the New York Boat Show – the Cabin Cruiser

1932

- Comet class created

Ed Monk at work

1933

- **Ed Monk** pens Plan No. 1, a 50-foot motorboat for himself. Named *Nan,* it would be his office and home for many years
- The first international dinghy competitions held in Oyster Bay
- *Sequoia II* commissioned as the U.S. Presidential Yacht

1934

Mr. & Mrs. Sopwith

- Sir **T.O.M. Sopwith's** J-Class *Endeavour I* is faster but loses to *Rainbow* in America's Cup
- First experimental pulse-signal used to detect aircraft in the U.S.
- First Miami-Nassau sailboat race

EBONY FLYER

CREOLE

THIS LEGENDARY black 190-foot three-master was brain child of C. E. Nicholson, who imagined her as an ideal long-distance cruising yacht, equally capable under power or sail. Upon her launching she was described as "the most aggressive-looking schooner ever built." Her owner must have agreed, because he ordered 15 feet lopped off her masts. Since her launching in 1927, *Creole*'s history includes both wartime service in the Royal Navy and a stint as a training ship. In the post-war years, *Creole* has been alternatively indulged and neglected. Both Stavros Niarchos and Maurizio Gucci spent lavishly on her ensuring that she remains one of the most distinguished classics afloat.

❧ *Morgan Opus* ❧

CORSAIR IV

THE FOURTH OF THE Morgan family's *Corsairs* was designed by Henry Gielow and built by Bath Iron Works in 1930. She was the largest of the *Corsairs* and the most impressive motor yacht to come from the drawing boards of the Gielow office and the builder's yard. At 344 feet with a 42-foot beam and 18-foot draft, this ship in yacht's clothing, powered by twin General Electric steam turbines was built for J.P. "Jack" Morgan, the great J.P.'s son and heir. With her black hull, clipper bow, raked masts and funnel—and let us not forget her sheer size—*Corsair* was an impressive presence at the yachting events of the 1930s, flying the burgee of the NYYC. She also did some cruising—to the West Indies, the Panama Canal, and the Galapagos in 1934, as well as many Florida-New England passages.

During World War II, she was sold to the British Navy for $1, an appropriate gesture for this family that had solicited and safeguarded British investments in America for generations. Sadly, she ended her days as a California cruise ship and was wrecked at Acapulco.

ALDEN'S CLASS

CURLEW

LAUNCHED IN 1926 FOR CHARLES ANDREWS of the New York Yacht Club, *Curlew* is one of the finest examples of the great John G. Alden-designed fast passage-making schooners. Alden loved the schooner rig and showed it to advantage on *Curlew*. Bigger than the *Malabar* series, this 82-footer was built in Wiscasset, Maine, at Fred Pendleton's shipyard and campaigned successfully for years in the club's ocean racing class. Later, *Curlew* served as a training vessel at King's Point, and like many yachts of her day, performed patrol duty during World War II.

1935
• Nylon patented

1936

• *Ticonderoga (Tioga)* launched. Designed as a family cruiser, this 72' Herreshoff ketch held more than 30 elapsed-time racing records.
• Berlin Olympics televised
• After the death of **King George V,** *Britannia* is broken up and scuttled according to his will.
• Ventor Boatyard in Atlantic City launches a 3-point hydroplane based on **Adolph Apel's** patent

Ranger

1937

• J-Class yachts *(Ranger, Endeavour II)* sail their last America's Cup. **Starling Burgess** and **Olin Stephens** outdid themselves on *Ranger's* design. She won four straight. The decision was made to sail in smaller, Meter boats.
• *Ranger* debuts rod rigging and first Rayon sail cloth for Genoa jib
• First seagoing RADAR tested, U.S.S. Leary
• British "Gee," first high-frequency hyperbolic nav system proposed
• First composite plastic of flax fiber and phenolic resin developed in the U.K.

MRS. DODGE'S DIVERSION

DELPHINE

 HEN HORACE DODGE, SR. DIED IN 1920, MRS. DODGE inherited a 257-foot steam yacht designed by Henry Gielow that was still under construction by the Great Lakes Engineering Works. Anna Dodge loved the yacht, a three-deck, plumb-stem beauty certified by the steamboat inspectors for Great Lakes and coastwise passenger service. As a yacht she had a crew of 54 to serve fewer than 20 in the owner's party. Mrs. Dodge loved *Delphine* so much that even though the insurers considered her a total loss after a fire and sinking in the Hudson River, she had *Delphine* raised and rebuilt. *Delphine* served the Dodge family into the 1950s, spent 40 more years in a variety of cruise-ship and school-ship schemes, and is currently being restored as the grand yacht she was in the 1920s.

A BETTER IDEA

EVON

 1973, FORD FOUND AN eager customer for the first turbines produced by its Power Products division. Ford touted the low horse-power-to-weight ratio, cleaner burn, and a vibration-free ride. From the stock 450hp, Broward Marine got Ford to boost the output to 550 hp., on a pair for an 87-footer named *Evon*, making her the first civilian yacht with twin turbines. According to Frank Denison, the whining turbines were later replaced with small diesels.

NOTHIN' BUT NET

ECO

 ROBABLY THE MOST progressive motor yacht of the 1990s, *Eco*, now *Katana*, was designed by Martin Francis and built at Blohm & Voss for the late Mexican billionaire Emilio Azcarraga. Her molded glass windows alone cost a king's ransom. This 74-meter yacht can reach 38 knots, thanks to two diesels and a 10,000-hp turbine engine all linked to waterjets. She also maintains a speed of 18 knots throughout a transatlantic crossing. She was refitted in 1999 at Lürssen under Francis' direction for her new owner, software genius Larry Ellison. Changes include an aft deck basketball court, a smashing Oriental décor and a more attractive paint job. From superlative performance to distinctive aesthetics, this 1991 issue remains at the leading edge of a new generation of ultra-fast megayachts.

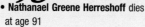

DORADE

T JUST 22 YEARS OF AGE, OLIN STEPHENS reinvented the racing yacht when in 1930 when he designed *Dorade*, a 52-foot yawl commissioned by his father. It was Olin's first major yacht. *Dorade* featured a slim 10 feet of beam and had a yawl rig, in stark contrast to the schooner yachts and "Big Class" sloops that had dominated ocean racing in the 1920s. *Dorade* won the 1931 Transatlantic Race in decisive fashion, finishing a full day ahead of the rest of the fleet. She followed that remarkable achievement by winning England's famous Fastnet Race. With these performances, the firm of Sparkman & Stephens began to dominate deepwater sailboat racing, although it is *Dorade's* innovative deck-mounted ventilators that most sailors remember. Olin Stephens is now an active 92 years old, and his autobiography has just been published by Mystic Seaport. *Dorade* is 60 years old and sailing, wonderfully restored, in Italy.

1938

- **Nathanael Greene Herreshoff** dies at age 91
- **Count Theo Rossi Di Montalera** is the first European to win the Gold Cup and the last to win in a conventional monohull. Hydroplanes have dominated power boat racing ever since.
- Yacht construction shifts from wood with the launch of the first all-steel yacht in the U.S., the 81' **Phillip Rhodes**-designed ketch, *Tamaris*, by Burger Boat Company
- Gray introduces marinized GM 6-71 engine

Herreshoff

1939

- British demonstrate multicavity magnetron for RADAR
- Polyethylene begins to be manufactured in U.K.
- **C. Ray Hunt** designs the *Concordia Yawl*
- International Game Fish Association formed

1940

- Terylene (better known in U.S. as Dacron) invented in U.K
- Detroit Diesel begins engine production for tanks and landing craft
- Zodiac manufactures prototype inflatable boat

Zodiac's inflatable boat

FAIRFORM FLYER 40

In THE 1920s, when Frank Pembroke Huckins created his first boat, he named the design "Fairform," after the family's milling business, and "Flyer," because the planing hulls were light and non-pounding. He developed his Quadraconic Formulae design solution for planing hulls before WWII, and its formula still guides the company. The 1946 Sportsman 40 is the quintessential Huckins, and its proportions scaled up to encompass the Corinthian, Atlantic and Linwood lines, remained virtually unchanged until 1966 when the first wide Quadraconic was introduced. In 1997 Huckins reintroduced the now retro-hip Sportsman 44.

F-100

CRAIG DAVIS

G IOVANNI AGNELLI HAS ALWAYS ENJOYED his time on the sea. He usually prefers to be sailing and has done so with exceptional yachts like *Extra Beat* and, more recently, *Stealth*. But spending most of his time in the Mediterranean necessitated building a tender with range and protection in the event of a mistral or sirocco. In 1980, one of his tenders was built by CRN Ancona. Never one to follow the crowd, Agnelli told designer Gerhard Gilgenast that function rather than a yachty look was key. At 109 feet, the 26-foot beam, 140-ton *F100* is a bit of a tanker. But with her single 1,000 hp MAG6M331 engine, *F100* was a precursor to today's expedition-style yachts. She was also the first yacht built with a functional swim platform, and remains the smallest to carry a helicopter, which lands on the coachroof.

✦ *Lightweight Heavyweight* ✦

EVVIVA

BILL MUNCKE

T HE 161-FOOT TRI-deck *Evviva* is one of the largest and most efficient fiberglass boats ever built. Her 420,000 pounds can move at an astounding 30 knots powered by twin MTU 16V396 diesels. Naval architect William Garden and stylist Donald Starkey brought the newest lightweight materials, from Nomex honeycomb to Kevlar and carbon fiber, to the project. Builder Admiral Marine works contributed craftsmanship and ingenuity, part of which was molding all components with unpainted gel-coat surfaces. Perfect molds were created for everything — 180 altogether — including monster molds for both hull and main deck. This technical achievement was orchestrated by *Evviva*'s owner, Bayliner founder Orin Edson, who, as Garden commented, "pushed us all into the 21st Century."

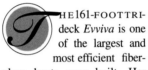

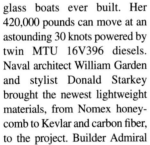

1941
- Rad Lab at MIT assigned development of LORAN (Long Range Navigation) and RADAR (Radio Direction and Ranging)

1942
- Gee system operational for Royal Air Force
- First Inertial Navigation System is used in German V-2 rockets
- Experimental LORAN chain is set up on the East Coast of the U.S.
- Schooner *America* crushed under snow-covered shed in Annapolis, Maryland.

1943
- **Vito Dumas** completes circumnavigation in *Lihg II*
- First Standard LORAN A system (N. Atlantic Train) fully operational
- SS (Skywave Synchronized) LORAN tested
- **Jacques Cousteau** invents Aqualung

1944
- Skywave Synchronized LORAN operates in Europe/Africa for Allied night bombing
- Decca system (called "QM") used for navigation in Normandy invasion

LORAN LINEAR INTERPOLATOR

❧ *Expeditious Eagle* ❧

GENTRY EAGLE

Tom Gentry, offshore powerboat racer, engineer, and sportsman, built this monster deep-V in 1988 to set records and push some engineering envelopes. With two 16-cylinder turbocharged MTU diesels delivering 7,000 horsepower to KaMeWa waterjets, and a 4,500-hp Lycoming gas turbine driving an Arneson surface propeller, the 110-foot *Gentry Eagle* set new records for Miami to New York and Miami to Nassau. In the summer of 1988 the superboat was turned back from a transatlantic record after pounding through 1,300 miles of rough water. During 1990-91 she was converted to a more civilized service as the Gentry family yacht and has since cruised from Alaska to Mexico to the Mediterranean.

FORTUNA

King Juan Carlos' *Fortuna* remains as unusual a royal yacht today as when she was first built in 1977. A far cry from stately displacement yachts normally chosen by monarchs, 86-foot *Fortuna* was commissioned for the speed-loving Spanish King. Incorporating cutting edge materials and technology, including then nascent waterjet propulsion, Don Shead succeeded in designing a gas turbine vessel able to reach a top speed of 52 knots, a record that remained unbeaten among yachts for almost a decade. Her choice of builder was unusual, too. American builder Palmer Johnson won the job based on its record of building race-winning sailboats.

APPLE OF HIS EYE

GOLDEN DELICIOUS

When Northwest apple grower Bill Gammie ordered a custom 98 footer from Westport Shipyard in 1987, little did he know he would revolutionize yachting. Taking as its starting point Westport's stock expandable hull mold (designed by Jack Sarin), the client and Sarin created a beautiful and useful new superstructure with no exterior wood and a full-beam salon. The short, enclosable aft deck and well-protected cockpit were purely Northwest in their origins. The casual interior with its huge family room/galley forward paved the way for an important trend. When Florida marketer extraordinaire Herb Postma saw the boat, he formed an entire company, Westship, around the concept, eventually growing the boats to 112 feet.

1945

- First Sydney-Hobart Race
- First commercial RADAR offered for sale
- First Low-Frequency (LF) LORAN tested
- Navaglobe LF nav system tested
- DuPont buys rights to Terylene and renames the fiber Dacron. It leads to the most important advances in sailmaking of the century.
- Cantieri di Pisa opens its doors
- **Ray Hunt** publishes his first power boat design

1946

- Eleven years after it was commercially available, Nylon sailcloth is introduced
- Cyclan (Cycle Matching LORAN) is developed
- Hinckley Boat Co. launches its first *Sou'wester*

Thor Hyerdahl

1947

- **Laurent Giles** introduces the masthead jib on 38 foot *Myth of Malham*, built for John Illingworth. A radical boat with short overhangs, she wins Fastnet twice
- Explorer/adventurer **Thor Hyerdahl** and *Kon Tiki* complete Atlantic passage
- **Earle Wakefield** opens Admiral Marine in Seattle
- **Luigi Nervi** develops ferro-cement boatbuilding
- Radux nav system is proposed
- Britisher **Ann Davidson** becomes the first woman to sail across the Atlantic alone
- Fraser Yachts opens its doors as a brokerage office in San Diego
- Famed naval architect **W. Starling Burgess** dies

DAHM'S DEMAND

INSPIRATION

NSPIRATION WAS designed by Ron Holland and launched in 1985 by Jongert for Herbert Dahm. *Inspiration* was the prototype of the well-known Jongert modern series. Dahm's brief demanded "a cruising boat with full extensive cruising interior and appliances, capable of sailing around the world and competing at almost the same speed as the full-blooded ICAYA maxi yachts." This tall order definitely helped push the development of the racer-cruiser concept. *Inspiration* was raced successfully in the cruising class at many ICAYA regattas.

❧ *Super Sloop* ❧

HYPERION

EW YACHTS, PAST OR PRE-sent, have generated as much pre- and post-launch interest as 151-foot German Frers-designed *Hyperion*, launched in 1998 at Royal Huisman Shipyard. Part of the hype is due to her awesome size. At the time of her launch, she was the largest sloop in the world (soon to be eclipsed by John Williams' *Georgia*) equipped with not only the tallest mast ever built, but also the largest single-piece carbon fiber structure ever built. Her tailored interior contains just three state-rooms in the owner's accomodation. But much of the interest in *Hyperion* is also due to her computer genius owner, Dr. Jim Clark. Clark, who helped popularize the Internet with his Netscape browser, applied the same never-take-no-for-an-answer philosophy in building his yacht as in amassing his considerable fortune. All parts and operations manuals on board are in HTML format, naturally.

ONE COOL CRUISE

ITASCA

AUGUST 26TH 1994, *ITASCA* completed the 55th traverse of the Northwest Passage. The record book further notes it was the first single-season eastward traverse by a private yacht. Owner William Simon had once anticipated making the trip aboard his sailboat, but when the 175-foot salvage tug came on the market, he realized her greater size would enable a more thorough expedition. From experience gained on a Canadian icebreaker, *Itasca's* hull and systems were retrofitted for her rendezvous with the ice. Her interior was also redesigned in Seattle by Judy Bell-Davis for the extremes of polar cruising. Five months later Itasca and Simon cruised the Antarctic.

1948

- **Frank Denison** opens Broward Marine on Ft. Lauderdale's New River doing repairs and military contracts
- Elco introduces its 30' sport model for family sport fishing
- **Guy Lombardo** sets a new measured mile record of 114.8 in *Tempo VI*

1949

- FEADSHIP is formed. The acronym stands for: First Export Association of Dutch Shipbuilders
- International 5.5-Meter created
- *Corsair IV* lost off Mexico
- First Orlon spinnaker introduced
- The last commuter yacht, **Laurence Rockefeller's** 65'10 *Dauntless,* designed by S&S, rolled down the ways at Jakobson shipyard on Oyster Bay
- John Rybovich and sons open boatyard

Frank Denison

Broward Marine's early yacht construction

STANDARD BEARER

JAMAICA BAY

NDER THE COMMAND OF CAPtain John Appleby, the magnificent *Jamaica Bay* came to define the classic style and superb service that was to be expected in a luxury charter. Designed by DIANA Yacht Design with an interior by Felix Buytendijk, this remarkable 42-meter Amels motor yacht is arguably the most successful charter yacht ever built and is considered to be the most beautiful boat designed by the late Joost Beekman.

✷ *In Atlantic's Wake* ✷

JESSICA

TODAY'S HOT TREND in retro sailing craft owes its beginnings to *Jessica*, a contemporary yacht with a most traditional appearance. When launched in 1984, the entirely new design by Arthur Holgate embodied features and fittings that most observers of the post-Jacuzzi yachting scene thought were lost forever. Second owner Alan Bond bought her and renamed her *XXXX* to promote his beer brand, turning her into a party girl in the process. When Bond's empire collapsed in 1992, she was snapped up by George Lindemann who renamed her *Adix* and hired skipper Paul Goss (see *Altair*) to turn her into the best new/old yacht possible. At Pendennis Shipyard, naval architect Gerard Dijkstra provided a new stern, a more powerful rig, a faster keel, and lengthened her to 183 feet on deck (212' overall) in the process. Her magnificent interior is pure turn-of-the-century elegance. As *Adix*, her Dacron sails have been dyed to look like Egyptian cotton, she is a regular on the international racing circuit.

PRETTY BREEZE, INDEED

JOLIE BRISE

ALTHOUGH YACHTS had been racing annually from Brooklyn to Bermuda since 1906, Britain entered long-distance offshore racing somewhat reluctantly. The 1925 Fastnet race, the first ocean race in Europe, began off Ryde in The Solent, turned at Fastnet Rock off the Irish Coast, and finished at Plymouth after a grueling 600 miles. Three quarters of a century later, it is the cornerstone of the British racing scene. Ironically, the boat that won the first was neither British nor a racing yacht. She was a French-built pilot cutter and sometime fishing boat designed by Alexander Paris. E.G. Martin had her refit as a yacht in 1923. The 56-foot *Jolie Brise* won the Fastnet three times ('25, '29, '30) until the advent of lighter racing yachts eclipsed the utility boats.

Corsair IV, designed by Henry Gielow, was lost off Mexico in 1949.

1950

- RADAR becomes standard equipment on all merchant ships
- **C. Ray Hunt** designs his first motor yacht, a 42-foot, 55-mph express cruiser for Bradley Noyes, *Ticonderoga*

1951

- International 5.5 Meter becomes an Olympic class
- 100th anniversary of that little race between *America* and the Royal Yacht Squadron
- Hood Sails, in consultation with **C. Ray Hunt**, debuts the horizontal cut for spinnakers

❧ *The 3 Remaining Js* ❧

ENDEAVOUR, SHAMROCK V & VELSHEDA

The Ultimate Ocean Thoroughbreds

HE J-CLASS WAS THE CULMINA-tion of the Big Class — an always loose grouping of big racing yachts that formed the pinnacle of the sport of yacht racing from the mid 1800s to the beginning of World War II. Between 1930 and 1937, 10 J-Class yachts were built, four in Britain and six in the U.S., principally as competitors

PHOTOS © MYSTIC SEAPORT/ROSENFELD COLLECTION

Endeavour

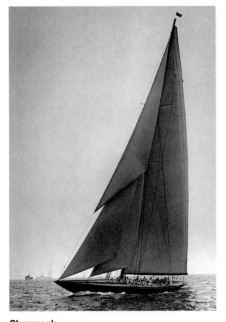

Shamrock

for the America's Cup in 1930, 1934 and 1937.

Of the original 10, the three remaining Js all were designed by C. E. Nicholson and built by Camper and Nicholsons. The 1980s saw the first bloom of J-Class restoration fever when Sir Thomas Sopwith's derelict 1934 Cup challenger *Endeavour* was acquired by American yachtswoman Elizabeth Meyer. The hands-on Meyer, working with Royal Huisman Shipyard, not only rescued 131-foot steel-hulled *Endeavour*, but put her back in racing trim with an

interior completely sympathetic with the original. Meyers also oversaw the reconversion of *Shamrock V* back to her original racing rig, although she was not as grandly refit. A new owner, however, began a complete restoration in 1999, supervised by Meyers.

The 1933 non-cup *Velsheda*, which had been used previously as a houseboat, was returned to sailing form in a highly authentic, though low budget project in the 1980s. Her glory days are back, however, courtesy of a 1997 refit that

1952

- **John Rybovich** creates the tuna tower for 34' *Miss Chevy IV*
- The *S.S. United States* set a new record for transatlantic crossing: 3 days, 10 hours, 40 minutes
- **Ted Hood** and his father purchase four pillowcase looms in Salem, Massachusetts, to begin weaving their own Dacron sail cloth

CORBIS

Blue Riband winner *USS United States*

1953

- *H.M.R.Y. Britannia* (412') launched on the Clyde and christened by *Queen Elizabeth II*
- Monofilament fishing line becomes commercially available
- **Jan Jongert** opens a shipyard in Opperdoes, Holland, for building punts and small motor boats
- Largest swordfish ever taken on tackle: 1,182 lbs. caught off Chile

GUY GURNEY

Shamrock, **Velsheda** and **Endeavour** race together at Antigua after a hiatus of 62 years.

added a steering cockpit, a second deckhouse and carbon fiber spars. Below decks, she has an elaborate period-style interior. In 1999 the two former cup challengers ended their lonely duels when *Velsheda* joined them in Antigua for the first real J-Class racing since 1937.

Oddly, the Js were never conceived as yachts to last through the ages. As the ICAYA maxi yachts of their day, they represented the state-of-the-art in racing craft, designed to be replaced after a season or two. Their interiors were designed only to house the owner or master when necessary. Opulence was reserved for their motoryacht tenders. The staggering beauty and elegant low hulls, 160-foot-high masts and their remarkable power under sail have led to the most improbable end of all . . . their rescue and reverence some 60 years hence.

BEKEN MARITIME SERVICES LTD.

Velsheda in original paint

1954

- First polyester working sails are developed
- The Ocean Cruising Club is formed — for

Jon Bannenberg

membership you must accomplish an offshore passage of no less than 1,000 miles in a boat no longer than 70 feet.
- Italy's Baglietto shipyard celebrates its 100th anniversary
- **Jon Bannenberg** opens a design studio in London. His first yacht is *Tiawana*.

1955

- **Eric** and **Susan Hiscock** circumnavigate in *Wanderer III*
- Burger launches America's first welded aluminum boat, 36' *Virginia*
- **John G. Alden** retires after designing 900 boats
- **Chris Craft** buys Roamer Boat Corp. and begins offering steel Chris Craft yacht models.

1956

- First fiberglass production sailboats are launched
- **Harold W. Johnson** opens Alaska Diesel Electric to provide reliable power to the Bering Sea fishing fleets
- **Frank Denison** launches Broward Marine's first custom yacht, 96' *Alisa V*, designed by John Wells
- **Renato "Sonny" Levi** pens his first fast cruiser, *Speranica Mia*

1957

- **Sir Myles Wyatt** donates The Admiral's Cup trophy for a new international ocean racing team competition. The series incorporates the Fastnet race, the Channel race and three inshore races.
- First LORAN C chain is established on East Coast of the U.S.
- First "Sputnik" launched by USSR inspired satellite navigation research
- The first all-welded aluminum sailboat, 58-foot *S&S Dyna*, launched by Burger Boat Company.
- **Lowell North** begins building Dacron sails for his Star boat in his garage. When they prove faster than anyone else's, he quits his engineering job to open North Sails.

KAKKI M

IN THE MID-1940s, naval architect William Garden began to establish a sweeping aesthetic for both express cruisers and motor yachts, the former often with clipper bows, moderate beam, broken sheerlines and dramatic angles. His seagoing motor yachts were given a trend-setting small-motorship look. *Kakki M* carries on the motorship tradition impressively at 104-feet by 22-feet. She carries on some other traditions in her construction material — almost entirely wood, shaped by Seattle's famous Vic Franck shipyard. Two D-353 Caterpillar diesels give *Kakki M* an easy cruising speed of 12 knots. Garden lists her as one of his two most important boats. Her cruising adventures have included Alaska, the Great Lakes, both coasts of the U.S. and Canada, and the islands of the South Pacific.

✳ *Plastic Fantastic* ✳

K Z-1

ALTHOUGH THE 1988 AMERICA'S Cup was waged more in the courtroom than on the race course, New Zealand's entry sponsored by Michael Fay reshaped the America's Cup by forcing the design of the current IACC class, which is the most significant post-war change to the event. More importantly, *KZ-1* embodies New Zealand's penchant for, and abilities with, light displacement composite yachts. By making them reliable and acceptable, *KZ-1* also pioneered very large carbon fiber masts, leading directly to their use aboard large cruising yachts. From that stage, Kiwi spar manufacturers went on to revolutionize

NEIL RABINOWITZ

furling booms. The Bruce Farr-designed "Winged Wonder" measured 90 feet on the water — Fay insisted on challenging under the original terms of the Deed of Gift — and required a crew of 30. Deceptively light, it was an exceptional monohull, but no match for Dennis Conner's 60-foot catamaran.

THE GENIUS OF G. L. WATSON

KALIZMA

BUILT IN 1906 BY RAMAGE AND FERguson, *Minona* was Watson's quintessential Edwardian steam yacht all clipper bow and fantail stern. A tall funnel carried away the soot from the coal fires for her triple-expansion engine. This 165-foot survivor of service in two world wars and many refurbishments has a most glamorous history. Renamed *Kalizma* and owned for seven years by Richard Burton, she is remembered as the place where he gave Liz Taylor the famed 69-carat diamond. Peter de Savary used her as his tender for his 1983 America's Cup challenge. Discreetly available for charter, she spends her time in Southeast Asia.

AJAX NEWS AND FEATURE SERVICE

1958

- America's Cup sailed in 12-Meters for the first time: *Columbia* designed by **Olin Stephens** beats *Sceptre* designed by **David Boyd**
- U.S. Coast Guard takes responsibility for coastal nav stations
- First satellite Doppler navigation system proposed
- **Norm Nordlund** and **Walt Silva** open a yard in Tacoma, Washington, building 26' plywood boats

Ted Hood

1959

- St. Lawrence Seaway opened
- Hatteras begins building boats with *Knit Wit*, a 41' fiberglass convertible designed by **Jack Hargrave** for **Willis Slane**
- **George Nicholson** opens Camper and Nicholsons Brokerage. His first custom yacht project: 1963 *Rampager*
- **Ted Hood** designs and builds his first centerboard ocean racer *Robin*. She wins 10 of 14 races her first year
- **Henry Rasmussen** dies, leaving control of A&R Shipyard to his grandson **Hermann Schaedla**
- Sea Ray is founded in Detroit, Michigan

LADY MOURA

HILE "ONLY" 17TH ON THE LIST OF THE century's largest yachts, in terms of sheer tonnage (6,539 gross tons) *Lady Moura* is the 2nd largest yacht in history. At a reported construction cost of $200 million, 344-foot *Lady Moura* is also the most expensive yacht ever built. Her amenities include a large swimming pool and gym on her fifth deck, a 45-foot tender, a jet helicopter and 68-90 crew. Built by Saudi oil-and-gas billionaire Dr. Nasser Al-Rashid for his former wife, Mouna, *Lady Moura* set modern day standards for sheer vol- ume and, thanks to Italian designer Luigi Sturchio, for levels of interior styling.

DEB LEX

L'AQUASITION

NQUESTIONABLY one of the most photographed and copied yachts of the 1990s, waterjet-propelled 145-foot *L'Aquasition* helped define the genre of modern semi-displacement cruising motor yachts. *L'Aquasition* is also remembered as the most important exterior styling project by designer Gerhard Gilgenast. As Heesen Shipyard's 1990 follow up to the record-breaking 1988 speedster *Octopussy*, *L'Aquasition* was quite an encore and proved her builder capable of delivering exceptional finish with technological sophistication. The yacht, delivered to Fruit of the Loom CEO Bill Farley, also helped consolidate the growing reputation of interior designer Paola Smith.

✷ *From the Heartland* ✷

LA BARONESSA

HARMON STUDIOS

T THE BEGINNING OF THE CENTURY, with the exception of Lake Union Dry Dock in Seattle, Washington, America's yacht-building centers were on the Eastern Seaboard. Motor yachts of substance were usually built at such yards as Bath Iron Works and Newport News Dry Dock. The landscape changed after the Great Depression and the advent of income taxes when Americans simply stopped building great yachts. World War II, fought by the U.S. in two oceans with its attendant need for troop and merchant ships, clinched the evaporation of large-scale yacht building on the East Coast. When large yacht building returned to the U.S. in the late 1980s, it was in different regions – the Gulf Coast, Florida, the Pacific Northwest and Wisconsin. Post-war, builders from a state known more for its cheese have held the title of America's Largest Aluminum Yacht Builder. (See Builders That Made History) The current title holder is Palmer Johnson for its 1998 launch *La Baronessa*. Built for a repeat customer from Asia, 195-foot *La Baronessa* was a group effort, with S&S supplying naval architecture and Nuvolari & Lenard supplying design. Winner of a *ShowBoats* Award for Most Innovative Motor Yacht, *La Baronessa* is a beautiful floating city with 10,000-mile range. In addition to being the largest yacht launched in the U.S. since 1930, *La Baronessa* is currently the world's largest aluminum yacht (tied for second are *Izanami* and *The Other Woman*). A contract has been signed, however, for an aluminum ketch to be built at Perini Navi that will measure 208 feet when delivered in 2002.

1960

- First OSTAR is won by **Francis Chichester,** who is later knighted
- First satellite launched by U.S. for navigation experimentation
- TIG a.k.a. heli-arc welding invented, making precision aluminum welding possible
- **Richard Betram's** *Moppie* debuts the Hunt deep-V hull in the Miami-Nassau race
- After three generations, the Smith family sells Chris Craft to NAFI. Annual sales were $40 million

Jack Hargrave and Hatteras founder Willis Slane

1961

- Yachtsman/Yachtswoman of the year award intitiated. First winners are **Buddy Melges** and **Timothea Schneider**
- **Pat Haggerty** buys Palmer Johnson Shipyard

Moppie

A COPIED CAT

LEGACY

WHEN BROTHERS DICK and Brad Lazzara, sons of pioneering GRP builder and designer Vince Lazzara, set out in the early 1990s to create a new boat building company, they decided not simply to develop a new line of motor yachts, but to reinvent the way yachts are built. Studying the modern automobile assembly process, they created a modular approach to all aspects of yacht construction. The first product of Lazzara Yachts, a 76-foot 1993 flybridge motor yacht named *Legacy* built for Richard and Paula Herschelman, is likely one of the most copied small yachts in history. Designed to fill the active-boater niche between a motor yacht and convertible sportfisherman, her often-emulated features included a flybridge hardtop, and personal watercraft storage pods.

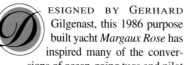

✤ *The Hull That Launched a Hundred Ships* ✤

MARGAUX ROSE

DESIGNED BY GERHARD Gilgenast, this 1986 purpose built yacht *Margaux Rose* has inspired many of the conversions of ocean-going tugs and pilot vessels in the ensuing years. Purposefulness of line and the rugged quality of her Schweers shipyard construction and single-screw efficiency highlighted an alternative view of the essential characteristics of a yacht, which many subsequent owners have been happy to adopt. Forgoing finesse, 152-foot *Margaux Rose (now Louisiana)* offered new possibilities, not least of which was

the celebrated hot air balloon launched from her elevated foredeck. In the process, this yacht heralded the advent of the expeditionary, or discovery, yacht.

THE ULTIMATE FASHION STATEMENT

LIMITLESS

LIMITLESS SERVES AS THE ULTIMATE private retreat for the owner of a clothing empire who appreciates the latest and greatest of everything. Another of Lurssen's top secret projects, this 315-footer launched in 1997 achieves a top speed of 25 knots on a clever diesel/electric power plant and is equipped with infrared cameras, radar and forward reading sonar for running at night and an incredible security system. She also sports the first Intering anti-roll system on a yacht. At her owner's request, she is a styling derivative of *Carinthia VI*, built 20 years earlier.

JIM RAYCROFT

1962

- Australians first challenge for America's Cup in *Gretel* designed by **Alan Payne**
- 100th anniversary of founding of the American Bureau of Shipping
- **Laurent Giles'** 111' motor sailer *Blue Leopard* breaks displacement speed barrier ($s = \sqrt{1.5\ LWL}$) under power and sail to establish light displacement standards sailing yachts.

Blue Leopard

1963

- CRN opens for business in Ancona, Italy
- **John Trumpy** dies

Eric Tabarly

AJAX NEWS & FEATURE SERVICE

1964

- French naval officer **Eric Tabarly** wins the second OSTAR in a 44' catamaran
- Huisman Shipyard begins building sailing yachts in aluminum. In 1968 S&S would put Huisman on the map with the commission for *Running Tide*.
- **Bob Bavier** skippers **Olin Stephens'** *Constellation* to victory in the America's Cup

WINGED HULL

MERCURY

ELIVERED IN 1960 BY Vosper & Co. of Portsmouth, England, 102-foot *Mercury* was based on the design of Brave Class Royal Naval patrol boats. Designed by Cmdr. Peter du Cane, *Mercury* was built for Greek shipping tycoon Stavros Niarchos. Powered by three Bristol Siddeley Proteus gas turbines developing 4,250hp each, *Mercury* was the first gas turbine yacht to exceed 50 knots and could under ideal conditions top out at 60 knots. She was built of double diagonal planked mahogany on aluminum frames. A large forward semi-circular main deck salon with ample windows made up for the limited below-decks accommodations.

MALCOLM WOOD

❧ *Race Me, Cruise Me* ❦

MARI CHA III

NEIL RABINOWITZ

HE TECHNOLOGY AND DESIGN BEHIND 141-foot *Mari Cha III* borrows heavily from the grand prix domain and is probably one of the most complete examples of technology transfer from racing to cruising. Designed by Frenchman Philippe Briand, the yacht was required to span both applications. Aggressive lines combined with rigorous weight-saving features characterize the carbon fiber New Zealand-built ketch. These attributes fulfilled the owner's demands for a vessel capable of breaking ocean passage records. The Edwardian-style John Munford interior, featuring Nomex cores and mahogany veneers, answered the demand for cruising elegance. In racing mode, parts of the interior are removed and the hydraulic winches are converted to a mechanical system. The success of the project was demonstrated in early 1999 when *Mari Cha III* set a new transatlantic record for monohulls of eight days, 23 hours, 59 minutes.

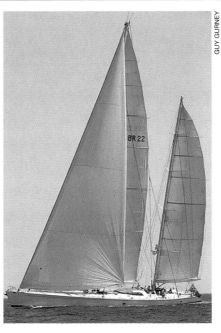

GUY GURNEY

MARINA

AUNCHED IN 1987, *Marina* was actually the third yacht to wear the Perini Navi brand but the first to have fully automatic sail handling. Every sheet and halyard on this 82-footer led under deck to its own captive reel winch equipped with a tension measurement device that could be set to match sailing conditions. Instead of gusts overpowering the boat, the reels would automatically ease the sheets. Even the anchor could be raised and lowered from the helm station. True to her Italian roots, she is the most luxurious single-hander ever launched, with a rich teak interior, marble counter tops, and leather upholstery.

1965

- **Jack** and **Ivor Jones** open Delta Marine in Seattle building race boats. They soon switch to fishing boats, crabbers and later to yachts.
- **Robert Manry** sails transatlantic in 13'8" *Tinkerbell*
- San Lorenzo Shipyard opens, building small yachts in wood.

1966

- Nautor's Swan begins building boats, its first designer was S&S
- **Bill Trip** designs the Columbia 50

AJAX NEWS AND FEATURE SERVICE

Hobie Cat

1967

- **Francis Chichester,** age 65, sets new solo records with his one-stop circumnavigation following the route of the clipper ships.
- *Intrepid* sailed by **Bus Mosbacher** wins America's Cup
- **Hobie Alter** begins production of the Hobie 14 Catamaran. They cost $1,000.
- The maxi yacht *Ondine* is launched by Abeking & Rasmussen.
- WestBay Boat Builders opens.

MOLLIHAWK

THE NICHOLSONS bought *Mollihawk* while England battled through World War II because they needed a place to live while the family patriarch, Commander Vernon Nicholson, was away in the Royal Navy. One of the places he was away to was the West Indies, and he fell in love. After the war the family refitted the old schooner, a 70-footer designed by Linton Hope and built in 1903, they sailed her to Nelson's Dockyard, Antigua. There they set up camp aboard the vessel and ashore in the 1745 Paymaster's House. Soon enough, winter vacationers at the island's Mill Reef club began asking whether *Mollihawk* might take them for a sail down island. Sensing an opportunity, in 1949 *Mollihawk* became the first vessel of today's huge West Indies charter fleet and the cornerstone of Nicholson Yacht Charters, a family enterprise that transformed Nelson's Dockyard and the rest of the Caribbean tourism infrastructure. As for *Mollihawk,* reports Julie Nicholson, "She's still giving people pleasure — on the bottom near St. Thomas where she's a great attraction for divers."

6. Ray Hunt invented the deep-V powerboat hull in 1957, but typically didn't do much about it until 1959 when Miami yacht broker and sailboat racer Dick Bertram asked him for a 30-footer with a bottom capable of taming the Gulf Stream and winning the Miami-Nassau Race. The result was *Moppie.* Powered by two 275-hp Interceptor V8s and driven by Sam Griffith, Bertram's *Moppie* won the rough race at an average speed of more than 20 knots. Except for Jim Wynne's's 23-footer, also designed by Hunt, the rest of the fleet didn't finish until the next day. *Moppie* was the pro-

MOPPIE

totype for the legendary Bertram 31, the foundation of the Bertram's glory days.

❧ *The Pride of Germany* ❧

METEOR V

COURTESY OF KRISTIN LAMMERTING/METEOR

WHILE MANY CONSIDERED the 1909 *Meteor IV* to be one of the most beautiful racing yachts ever, Kaiser Wilhelm II replaced her in 1914 with another Max Oerst design also built at Germania Werft. The last in a string of Big Class yachts commissioned by Wilhelm, 156-foot *Meteor V* was his last bid to build a yacht that could consistently beat *Britannia,* owned by his uncle, the Prince of Wales. In addition to beautiful furnishings and handmade carpets, she carried an upright piano in the salon and had a full owner's suite with office. In the bow and stern were bunks for 30 crew.

AJAX NEWS & FEATURE SERVICE

Robin Knox-Johnson

1968

AJAX

Chay Blyth

• **Robin Knox-Johnson** in *Suhaili* is the only sailor to finish (312 days) the first non-stop circumnavigation race, sponsored by the *Sunday* (London) *Times.* In 1970 **Chay Blyth** would shave 20 days off that time sailing east to west.

• **Alessandro** and **Norberto Ferreti** open a shipyard in Marignano, Italy.

• Naval architect **Laurent Giles** dies.

1970

Black Molly I

• **Baron Marcel Bich** attempts first America's Cup challenge for France. He steers fourth race in formal attire and white gloves

• **Herbert Dahm** begins his remarkable association with Jongert by taking delivery of the innovative *Black Molly I.*

• Chris-Craft begins offering integrated electronic command consoles for all boats over 41 feet.

❧ *Size Redefined* ❧

NABILA

DNAN KHASHOGGI'S *NABILA* remains an epoch-defining yacht. Her sheer size dwarfed all contemporary yachts except Stavrus Niarchos' *Atlantis*. Her Jon Bannenberg styling and Luigi Sturchio interior combined with the Benetti yard's craftsmanship to define the look for a generation of large yachts. Not withstanding these achievements, Khashoggi's assiduous insistence on the terms of the contract led to Benetti's bankruptcy. In turn, the 'Arms to Iran' scandal resulted in Khashoggi's downfall, and the yacht passed into the ownership of Donald Trump. Trump was seduced by the yacht's breathtaking interior and, on the strength of a brochure, parted with $28 million, a fraction of her original $70 million cost. While *Trump Princess* may have contributed to the spread of super yachting from the Gulf States into

AJAX NEWS & FEATURES SERVICE

the U.S., it was The Donald's own financial problems that returned the 86-metre yacht to the Mediterranean. Refitted at Amels in 1992 and now known as *Kingdom 5KR*, she is owned by consummate Saudi businessman Prince Al-Whalid bin Talal.

TRUMPY'S TRIUMPH

NEPENTHE

HEN IMMIGRANT SHIPWRIGHT Johan Trumpy arrived in New York in 1902 from Norway, America was in the midst of a major ship-building boom. After years of helping design warships at New York Shipbuilding, Trumpy was convinced there was a need for building coastal motor yachts for viewing regattas and for cruising between the U.S. Northeast and Florida. Johan – or John as he was now called – began working at John H. Mathis Company in Camden, New Jersey, and by 1910,

at the age of 31, had convinced the owners of the soundness of his ideas. Early that year the Mathis Yacht Building Company was born with Trumpy as a minor stakeholder, a position he would parlay to full ownership by 1939. From 1910 and for the next 63 years no name would become more synonymous with American luxury yacht building than Trumpy.

Of the 448 boats built by Trumpy (the company moved to Annapolis in 1943 and became John Trumpy and Sons), 90-foot *Nepenthe* was one of the more luxurious.

Built in 1917 for James Deering, the builder and owner of the lovely Vizcaya estate on Biscayne Bay in Miami, *Nepenthe* epitomizes the shallow-draft houseboat style of cruiser that was to become so successful over the next half-century and beyond. Delivered with tender at a cost of $37,650, she was used as officer's quarters at the Key West Naval Base during World War I before being returned to Deering for winter cruising in south Florida, the Bahamas and Florida Keys, and summer use in and around New York.

1971

- Lurssen launches its first modern yacht, 233-foot *Carinthia VI*, the first German mega yacht of the postwar era, for its richest retailer Helmut Horten.
- Huisman Shipyard outgrows its Ronduit yard and moves to Vollenhove.
- The Hobie 16 is introduced. By 1999, it would be the most produced boat in history.

Carinthia VI

WILLY WINKLER

1972

- **Alain Colas** wins OSTAR in trimaran *Pen Duick IV* and becomes a national hero. Distance racing will become dominated by multi-hulls.
- Naval architect **Uffa Fox** dies.
- **L. Francis Herreshoff** dies.
- The last Trumpy Yacht, *Sirius* delivers.

Uffa Fox

BEKEN OF COWES LTD.

❦ *Breaking the Mold* ❦

NEVER SAY NEVER

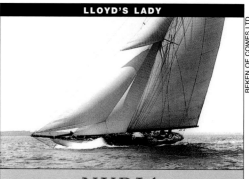

LLOYD'S LADY

T HE WORD UNIQUE IS OFTEN MISAPPLIED IN YACHTING CIRCLES, BUT when *Never Say Never* appeared as Oceanfast's first yacht in 1985, it was a sure bet no one had ever seen anything like her before. This collaborative effort between Jon Bannenberg and Phil Curran showcased their ideas for exciting looking yachts with performance to match. The light, 108-foot aluminum yacht hit a top speed of 30 knots with a pair of 12V396TB93s driving high-performance props. Now called *Apocalypse,* she was lengthened in 1996. In 1988 her near sister, 118-foot *Antipodean,* introduced KaMeWa waterjets as Oceanfast's propulsion of choice.

OCEANFAST YACHTS/ARMADA

NYRIA

 N 1906 *Nyria* was the first racing yacht to be built to Lloyd's Register rules, paving the way for structurally sound sailing yachts and the gradual introduction of scantling rules for racing yachts on both sides of the Atlantic. *Nyria* was the vehicle for another of C. E. Nicholson's other firsts when in 1921 the designer re-equipped her with the first Bermuda rig ever fitted to a large sailing yacht. Her racing career continued through the inter-war years and she was eventually broken up in Italy in the 1950s.

SPEED MERCHANT

ONNE VAN DER WAL

OCTOPUSSY

 UILT TO TOP *FORTUNA'S* 52-knot record, *Octopussy's* speed requirement was stipulated in owner John Staluppi's contract. Thus both designer Frank Mulder and builder Heesen Shipyard had more than reputations at stake. In 1988 *Octopussy's* demonstration of 54-knot top speed and excellent reliability led to the wider adoption of triple engine waterjet propulsion in high speed yacht building. The extreme speed achieved for her size (132 feet) and accommodations (four staterooms and a full skylounge) remains outstanding. *Octopussy's* concept and styling inspired many of the large fast yachts that followed, including sistership *El Corsario, Blue Velvet* (Baglietto), and *Moonraker* (Norship). Stretched to 143 feet, painted blue and powered down for second owner Abe Gossman, *Octopussy* is still exciting at 42 knots.

1973

NORDLUND BOAT COMPANY

- *Shadowfax* is the first Airex foam-cored boat built in the Pacific Northwest. This **Ed Monk** design was built at Nordlund Boat Company.
- The first Whitbread Round the World Race begins
  - Broward Marine's 87' *Evon* is the first yacht with twin turbine engines.
  - Abeking & Rasmussen delivers world's fastest diesel yacht, 46-knot *Kalamoun,* for the Aga Khan.
  - **Fratelli Benetti** celebrates its 100th anniversary of yacht building with the launch of five yachts.

1974

- Kevlar goes into sailcloth for the first time — aboard 12-Meter *Courageous. Courageous,* skippered by Ted Hood with Dennis Conner as starting helmsman, defeats *Southern Cross.*

Shadowfax

1975

- Jongert, now guided by **Herbert Dahm,** installs the first bow thruster in a sailing yacht aboard 22M *Black Molly II.*

MARILYN MOWER

Courageous debuts Kevlar sails

PIONEER

ITH ONLY THREE SUBSTANTIAL steam yachts behind him, C. E. Nicholson designed *Pioneer* as his first large diesel-powered motor yacht. Launched only months before the outbreak of World War I, the aptly named yacht set the tone for powered yachts of the inter-war period. Not only was steam on its way out – the last large steam yachts were launched in 1930 — but with the introduction of diesel power came a new aesthetic. Indeed, Nicholson, who had been ill at ease with the dated clipper bow and counter stern, introduced the cruiser stern and more modern bow profiles that have dominated displacement-yacht design since. Looks apart, the great success of this yacht stemmed from the reduction in size, and therefore cost, of her new propulsion system.

PEN DUICK IV

HE LATE, great French singlehander Eric Tabarly built the high-tech, high-strung 67-foot aluminum trimaran *Pen Duick IV* in 1964 to continue his adventures at sea and, and now seems clear, to inspire generations of French sailors to similar feats in other-worldly sailboats competing at the sport's extremes. During the 1968 Observer Singlehanded Transatlantic Race (OSTAR), *Pen Duick IV* rammed a freighter and had other problems. But later that year Tabarly sailed her from the Canaries to Barbados at an average of 11 knots, beating the transatlantic speed posted by the great schooner *Atlantic* (10.4 knots) in 1905. Of course, the 260-mile days Tabarly recorded in the '60s seem positively prehistoric in the era of *PlayStation's* 400-milers.

❋ *Fit for a King* ❋

PHILANTE

LTHOUGH LAUNCHED IN 1937, this 263-footer remains the largest privately owned motor yacht ever built in Britain (See 100 Largest Yachts.) Commissioned by Sir T. O.M. Sopwith, she escorted his J-Class *Endeavour II* on her unsuccessful bid for the America's Cup. After service with the British Royal Navy during World War II, *Philante* was acquired by a syndicate of Norwegians who had her refitted by her builder, Camper & Nicholsons, and gave her to their sovereign in tribute to his steadfast devo-

tion to independence throughout the Nazi occupation. As *Norge* she remains in service as the Norwegian royal yacht. The Sopwith family continued building yachts at a rapid pace: 131-foot *Philante IX* was launched from Brooke Yachts in 1991.

BEKEN MARITIME SERVICES

PRINCESS ALICE II

IKE MANY IN MONACO'S RULing Grimaldi family, Prince Albert I was keen on the sea. The prince was fascinated with marine animals and plants and the environment. His yachts became his research platform. His first schooner *Hirondelle* soon proved to small. Her steam-powered replacement, *Princess Alice I,* took the Prince on six expeditions. Excited by the prospect of exploring Arctic waters, in 1898 he commissioned 1,400-ton 245-foot *Princess Alice II*. Strengthened for ice and bristling with oceanographic equipment, she carried her royal scientist on 11 remarkable expeditions including three among icebergs. Albert I and his yachts pioneered oceanography, contributing a catalogue of species and the first bathymetric map of the Mediterranean Sea.

1976

- **Alain Colas** races OSTAR in 236' *Club Mediterranee*, setting a record for the largest boat ever sailed solo. He finished second and the rules were changed to prevent future such attempts.

Club Mediterranee

AJAX NEWS AND FEATURE SERVICE

1977

- New Zealander **Naomi James** becomes the first woman to circumnavigate alone. She and her 56' cutter *Express Crusader* made two stops.
- Florida builder Huckins begins using Airex as a hull core material
- The **Rust Brothers** buy West Shipyard and begin building fiberglass motor yachts

Express Crusader

Naomi James

THE SUPER J

RANGER

THE LARGEST OF THE Universal Rule class, the J-Boats of the 1930s were already at the top of sailing's food chain when Harold Vanderbilt's *Ranger* came along. Designed in 1936 in a collaboration between Starling Burgess and Olin Stephens, *Ranger* was 135 feet overall and carried 7,546 square feet of sail. She was the culmination of seven years of J-Class technology. Unlike the bronze-on-steel construction of her forebears, she was flush-riveted steel. Among her features was the snub-nose bow that allowed her to effectively lengthen her waterline when heeled. The plan had been for Vanderbilt to split her cost with the NYYC, but the club couldn't raise the funds and Vanderbilt shelled out the balance. Had this super-J not been built, Sopwith's formidable *Endeavour II* would likely have won the 1937 America's Cup. As it was, *Ranger,* controversial bow and all, won 32 of 34 races she sailed in her first season.

❧ *Western Wood* ❧

PRINCIPIA

WHILE JOHN TRUMPY WAS CARVING a niche with shallow draft inland waterways houseboats, the Lake Union Dry Dock Company in Seattle was making history in the opposite direction. Building mostly in sturdy old-growth Douglas fir, Lake Union boats were deep-draft, ocean-going yachts more narrow of beam than their East Coast counterparts. While the largest yacht to come down the ways was 135-foot *Stranger* designed by Ted Geary, the most famous is undoubtedly 96-foot *Principia* launched in 1928. At one time belonging to singer John Davidson, she now belongs to the Philadelphia Independence Seaport Museum and is used for charter.

AMERICA'S CUP MONSTER

RELIANCE

AT THE BEGINNING OF THE CENTURY, WHEN Nat Herreshoff was the cleverest yacht designer in the world, foreign challengers for the America's Cup had to get to the light-weather race course off Sandy Hook by crossing the rough Atlantic on their own bottoms. Had Herreshoff's *Reliance* been asked to take the same crossing, she likely would have failed. In contrast to Sir Thomas Lipton's third *Shamrock*, the 1903 Herreshoff-designed *Reliance* was a relatively delicate 143-foot, 8-inch skimming dish with more sail on a single mast that any vessel in history — 16,159 square feet — and the first below decks winches. Her mainsheet was 1,000 feet long, and it took 60 men to race her. Her sharply cut away forefoot was the precursor to today's fin keel. She was designed for one series of races on one course, and she was sailed by the masterful Charlie Barr. *Shamrock III* never had a chance.

1978

- Real Estate developer **Dave Christensen** opens a GRP yacht-building facility in Vancouver, Washington.

Dave Christensen

A Fastnet Race victim is laid to rest.

1979

- INMARSAT established with 26 signatory nations to organize satellite communications traffic
- Wooden boat designer and builder **Joel White** dies. The son of E.B., he combined the Herreshoff look with modern underbodies
- Fastnet Race claims 15 lives, forces revision of offshore sailing rules

RARE AS A STRAUSS OPERA

ROSENKAVLIER

NEVER OUT OF COMMISSION, THE former *Haida* and *USS Argus* is one of the best known yachts afloat. Designed by Cox & Stevens and launched from the Krupp yard in 1929, *Rosenkavalier* still retains her original twin Krupp-built diesel engines. As a U.S. Navy patrol boat, 217-foot *Rosenkavalier* briefly lost her elegant demeanor. Happily, this was restored and has

been maintained by a series of post-war owners who have included brewer Lowell Guiness and film producer Robert Stigwood, as well as her current owner Andreas Liveras, who lavished still another refit on her. As an active charter yacht, she serves as a graceful reminder of the days when yachting was an activity for gentlemen and ladies of leisure.

⊰ *Career Launcher* ⊱

RIO RITA

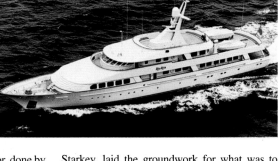

THE YACHT THAT defines an era. The 170-foot (52M) deVries-built *Rio Rita* launched in 1984 is considered by many to be the most lovely transom-stern motor yacht ever built. The styling and naval architecture blending contemporary and classic looks by DIANA Yacht Design's co-founder, Joost Beekman, brought that company to the forefront of the industry. The dramatic, muraled interior, done by then-colleagues Terence Disdale and Donald Starkey, laid the groundwork for what was to become a pair of dazzling careers.

CARLO'S CONQUEST

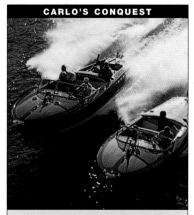

RIVA AQUARAMA

"ROLLS ROYCE OF THE Sea," and "Stradivarius of Boating" are just some of the phrases that have been used to describe the Riva Aquarama. Although Carlo Riva designed many boats, it is for the 26-foot Aquarama he will forever be worshipped. In 1962, Riva redesigned his top-selling Tritone into the Lipicar, a boat perfectly adapted for family water sports. Fortunately, Riva's PR and export manager Gerard Kouwenhoven suggested the name Aquarama instead. The Jet Set quickly made the boat Europe's status symbol. Power options were a pair of 185-hp Chris-Craft engines or 220-hp Riva V8s. Had you been clever enough to buy one in 1963, it would have cost $17,800. When the last Aquarama Special rolled out in 1996 the price was $387,000. Hull number 1 is currently being restored by Bernd Fritz.

1981

- Moonen Shipyard opens. First project is *Cassiopea S*

1980

- The outrigger *Crossbow* sets a new sailing speed record at 36 knots
- *Itaska*, a 175' sea tug built in 1961 begins the yacht conversion craze. She would be significantly enhanced in 1994 for owner **William Simon's** historic traverse of the Northwest Passage.

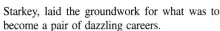

Crossbow

1982

- Original Perini Engineering Company is founded in Italy to build captive winches for **Fabio Perini's** personal sailing yacht

Perini's captive winches

- Camper & Nicholsons shipyard celebrates 200th anniversary
- *ShowBoats International* begins publishing as a brokerage-only quarterly magazine
- The UN creates INMARSAT to offer commercial access to satellite communication.
- INMARSAT leases its first satellite from COMSAT

SAPPHIRE

CONSIDERED by contemporary experts to be amongst the finest yachts designed by the celebrated G. L. Watson & Co., 1,412-ton *Sapphire* was extolled for her looks and seaworthiness. (See photo page 49). Commissioned by the Duke of Bedford and built on the Clyde by J. Brown, *Sapphire* was extensively used by the Duchess from 1912 until the outbreak of World War I. In the inter-war period she was briefly owned by Lord Furness before passing into the ownership of celebrated civil engineer Urban Broughton, whose extensive itineraries brought her to the forefront of yachting. All *Sapphire's* owners commented on her great comfort but this is scarcely surprising given that within her 285 feet she offered accommodation for a guest party of only seven.

❧ *The Pasha's Palace* ❧

SAVARONA

WITH AN ON-DECK length of 408 feet, Emily Cadwalader's third *Savarona* has only lately been usurped as the largest non-state yacht ever built. (See 100 Largest Yachts.) The heiress' money came from the development of the steel cable for suspension bridges, which had made her Depression-proof. *Savarona* was launched in Hamburg, Germany, in 1931, but her career did not live up to the splendor of her specifications. She made only two cruises before being acquired for peanuts by the Turkish government for Kemal Ataturk, Mrs. Cadwalader's rumored paramour. The leader's death in 1938 saw *Savarona* relegated to training ship sta-

tus and eventually mothballed. On lease from the Turkish government, she was restored for service as a charter yacht in 1992 in a lavish refit directed by Don Starkey. A Turkish bath and a small collection of the former president's personal effects are among her many enticements.

RUNNING TIDE

PERHAPS OLIN STEPHENS' MOST FAVORITE design and a yacht that best demonstrated her builder's skill, *Running Tide* was built in aluminum in 1970 by the Royal Huisman Shipyard. Beneath her clean flush deck were pipe berths and other spartan accommodations for a racing crew. Jakob Isbrandtsen sailed her to class honors in the 1970 Bermuda Race and overall honors the next winter on the Southern Ocean Racing Circuit. Second owner Al Van Metre brought her further victories, including the 1973 Miami-Palm Beach Race, the Nassau Cup in 1974 and first overall in the 1976 Bermuda Race.

John Bertrand accepts his trophy

1983

• **John Bertrand**, Alan Bond and *Australia II* win the America's Cup beating Dennis Conner's *Liberty.* The cup leaves the NYYC for the first time in 132 years.

Naval architect Ben Lexcen and the *Australia II* keel

1984

• Danish builder Helsinger Vaerft delivers the world's largest yacht, 482' *Abdul Aziz*, for **King Fahd.** Constuction price was reportedly $109 million. His previous yacht, 269' *Al Yamamah*, was from the same yard.
• **Fabio Perini** takes delivery of a 40-meter schooner christened *Perini Navi* built by Ortona Navi but equipped with his winches. Later in the same year he forms a boat-building company in Viareggio, Italy
• Huisman Shipyard receives its "Royal" designation
• **Franz Heesen** opens his shipyard in Oss, Holland
• Delta Marine launches its first yacht, *Zopilote*
• Benetti Yard reorganizes

Zopilote

SHENANDOAH

 NE OF THE LAST REMAINING SCHOONER YACHTS from the turn of the century, *Shenandoah* was designed by T.E. Ferris and launched in 1902 by Townsend & Downey Shipbuilding on Newark Bay in New York Harbor. Named for an Indian chief, this 145-foot steel schooner was launched for banker Gibson Fahnestock, who sailed her to Europe in 1905. Since 1912 this lucky yacht has had a succession of European owners — German, English, Italian, Danish, French, Monegasque. She was rescued from oblivion in the early 1970s by Baron Marcel Bich, the purse and personality behind four French challenges for the America's Cup. The Baron restored her in 1972, and her current owner lavished another significant refit on her at New Zealands' McMullen & Wing in 1996.

⚹ *Biggest Gift* ⚹

SEA CLOUD

 A BRIGHT BERMUDA day in 1931, Mrs. E.F. Hutton, the former Marjorie Merriweather Post, caught her first glimpse of the 353-foot four-mast bark that her husband had bought for her birthday. Built during 1930-31 by Krupp's Germaniawerft shipyard, *Hussar*, soon to be named *Sea Cloud*, was truly ship-size, and the largest sailing yacht in the world. The cereal heiress and founder of General Foods enjoyed this unprecedented yacht for 24 years before *Sea Cloud* went to other owners and, finally, to a $7-million restoration at the end of the 1970s. With 34 guest staterooms and a crew of 60, *Sea Cloud* sails the world these days as a cruise ship.

SEQUOIA

 HILADELPHIA BANKER RICHard Cadwalader christened his second *Sequoia* in 1925. She was a 110-foot yellow pine, mahogany and teak houseboat motor yacht designed by John Trumpy and built by Mathis Yacht of Camden, New Jersey. She was a successor to the 84-foot Mathis Cadwalader had christened the year before. In 1931 he sold her to the government, which used her to trap rumrunners on the Mississippi River. One of the largest of these uniquely American yacht types that later simply became known as Trumpys, *Sequoia* was destined to serve eight U.S. presidents from Herbert Hoover to Gerald Ford. Designed for comfort, Trumpy gave his boats more headroom and wider passageways than similar boats of the time and the owner's choice of a piano or a fireplace. He also prided himself on efficient galleys and engine rooms. Alas, President Jimmy Carter considered her an unseemly indulgence and sold her. Now completely restored, she is the property of Norfolk Shipbuilding & Drydock, which took title in lieu of payment for her refit.

1985

- Oceanfast delivers its first yacht, 112' *Never Say Never* designed by **Phil Curran** and **Jon Bannenberg**.
- Cantieri di Pisa begins offering *Akhirs* in fiberglass.
- **Sonny Levi** develops the Levi unit incorporating surface props for Virgin Atlantic Challenger.

Never Say Never

1986

- Intermarine SpA of Sarzana, Italy, forms a partnership with a military shipyard on Georgia's Savannah River to build a fleet of GRP minehunters.
- Royal Huisman delivers *Whirlwind XII*, **Ron Holland's** first cruising yacht over 100'.

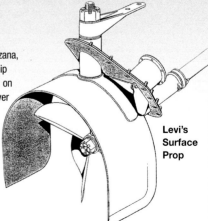

Levi's Surface Prop

❧ *The Sportfishermen* ❧

DEVELOPING THE FISHING MACHINE

Today's convertibles owe much to Wheeler and Rybovich

FAST IS FUN

SHERGAR

WHEN THE Aga Khan wanted a fast yacht for the Med, he sought out the best European talent. The resulting yacht was designed by Gerhard Gilenast, with an engine room by Don Shead. *Shergar*, delivered in summer 1983, is a 153-foot semi-planing rocket ship. To meet a 42-knot contract speed, Lürssen built her with light aluminum scantlings and foam-cored furnishings, and propelled her using two 1,480-hp MTU wing diesels driving KaMeWa water jets plus two 6,100-hp Allison gas turbines coupled to a single centerline jet. Without strict noise control, she would have sounded like the Nice Airport. Lürssen delivered interior sound levels to 65dB(A) at her full speed of 45.5 knots, which also exceeded expectations.

Hemingway's 38-foot Wheeler, Pilar

PAPA'S PASSION

IN THE SPRING OF 1934, Ernest Hemingway borrowed $3,300 from *Esquire* magazine's Arnold Gingrich to make a down payment on a 38-foot Wheeler trunk-cabin cruiser. His collateral was the promise of future articles. *Pilar* served as Hemingway's fishing machine in Havana and Bimini from 1934 to 1961, and is the only survivor from the years when modern sportfishing was in its infancy. Tired of sharks getting the best of his giant tunas, Hemingway invented the practice of backing down on a fish, becoming the first sporting angler to bring a whole tuna into Bimini. Papa outfitted his boat with expandable, 300-gallon fuel tanks and one of the first livewells. Soon,

everyone followed suit. Hemingway, along with William Gregory, Van Campen Heilner, Francesca LaMonte and Michael Lerner founded the International Game Fish Association in 1939. Today, *Pilar* is enshrined at Finca Vigia, the author's retreat east of Havana.

SEMINAL SPORTFISHERMAN

JOHN AND TOMMY RYBOVICH ARE generally credited with many of the most important fishing boat innovations of the

Rybovich Hull #2, Legend

post-war years, especially the raised deck profile and improvements in vee-hull design. This was a break with the flush-deck, trunk-cabin profiles of previous boats, and became the model for most the 30- to 80-foot sportfishermen that have come along since. He invented the transom door and in 1932 turned Zane Grey's chair-on-a-mast idea into the first tuna tower for *Miss Chevy IV.* Buddy Merritt took the tower a step farther by adding steering controls. While vertical bamboo outriggers had been used on both coasts, it was John Rybovich who thought to make them out of aluminum and sweep them back from the cockpit.

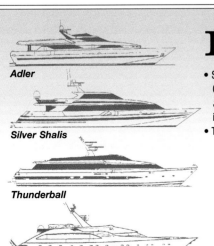

Adler

Silver Shalis

Thunderball

Time

1987

- Sailing for the San Diego Yacht Club, **Dennis Conner** aboard *Stars & Stripes* returns the America's Cup to the U.S.
- The Year of the Jetboat:
  — Baglietto 35-kt *Adler*
  — A&R 32-kt *Silver Shalis*
  — Denison 46-kt *Thunderball,*
  — PJ 31-kt *Time*

1988

Mismatch of the century. **Dennis Conner's** 60-foot catamaran *Stars & Stripes* defeats **Michael Fay's** 90-foot monohull *Kiwi Magic* for the America's Cup.

- Australian **Kay Cottee** becomes the first woman to circumnavigate non-stop alone.
- Oceanco opens for business in South Africa
- Jongert debuts in-mast ventilation on 34-meter *Conny Fever*
- Cheoy lee delivers its first 100' yacht *Ivory Lady*

Dennis Conner

ROCKET GIRL

TIME

ESPITE A NUMBER of successful motor yacht launches over the years, (see also *Fortuna*) Palmer Johnson had always been considered one of the world's pre-eminent builders of sailing yachts. In 1987, however, the 125-foot (38m) Tom Fexas-designed jet boat *Time* made PJ a contender in the megayacht segment. The boat's futuristic styling, displacement yacht-style comforts, innovative waterjet propulsion and exemplary performance helped to propel the company to its current place as the leading builder of large custom aluminum motor yachts in America.

❦ *First to Finish* ❦

TICONDEROGA

SHEILA HILL

FRANCIS HERRESHOFF DESIGNED THE 72-foot ketch *Ticonderoga* to be a fast day boat for Harry Noyes and his family. But he designed her with flowing lines below the water and breathtaking clipper-yacht aesthetics above. *Big Ti*, as she was known, startled everyone with her speed on all points of sail. Racing her soon took center stage. Many yachting connoisseurs consider her the most beautiful ocean racer ever built. Since she was launched in 1936 as *Tioga II*, she has recorded more ocean-racing victories, especially first-overall honors, than any yacht in history. She has been refitted as a luxurious cruising boat, but her current owner frequently races.

THE JOY OF CARBON

CRAIG DAVIS

STEALTH

WO DECADES OF THE DEVELOPMENT OF ULTRALIGHT DISplacement sailing yachts, beginning with Bill Lee's famous downwind sled *Merlin* and the development of water-ballasted racing yachts, reached their zenith with the 1996 launch of *Stealth*. Designed by German Frers and built at Green Marine in England, this 92-footer built for Giovanni Agnelli is a carbon fiber masterpiece, including her carbon fiber sails. Those associated with the yacht are sworn to secrecy. However, at press time, *Stealth* was in New York City awaiting a weather window for a run at the transatlantic monohull passage record currently held by *Mari Cha III*.

JUST ENOUGH

THE HIGHLANDER

ALCOLM FORBES, who once said, "Too much is just enough," applied this principle to the fifth of the family-and–business yachts he named *The High-*lander. A Feadship like her predecessor, this 150-foot hunter-green vessel was designed by Frits de Voogt, styled by Jon Bannenberg. Although there are four guest staterooms below, along with a huge owner's stateroom, *The Highlander's* main deck spaces get the most use in Forbes-magazine schmoozathons hosting as many as 100 guests at a time.

1989

- Perini Navi takes over the Picchiotti yard in Viareggio, Italy, and adds full in-house design, systems and finishing capability.
- Lurssen Werft establishes a separate yacht division
- CRN in Ancona delivers the dramatic 150' *Azzurra* designed by Gerhard Gilgenast and Paola Smith.
- Hatteras enters the custom megayacht era with 92' *Arrivederci*
- *Gentry Eagle* sets new transatlantic record: 62 hours, 7 minutes

PERINI NAVI

Perini's Malizia built for Prince Rainier

1990

- **Louis Hamming** opens Vitters shipyard in Zwartzluis, Holland
- Picchiotti delivers its final boat, *Ginni Lou*

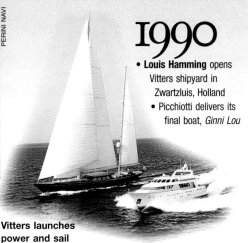

Vitters launches power and sail

SHE'S GOT CLASS

TIGRE D'OR

AN EFFORT to deliver safer, more fireproof yachts, a British agency first called the Marine Safety Agency, later the Maritime and Coastguard Agency, foisted a complex set of rules on the big-yacht world in 1996. British-registered yachts wishing to charter would have to comply or obtain an exemption. In the tempest following, 164-foot *Tigre d'Or* became the first yacht to receive certification when she delivered in 1997. Incidentally, her engineering team was part of the group that designed the regs. She proved that certification might stand in the way of reason, but not beauty.

FASHION FORWARD

T.M. BLUE ONE

HEN FASHION DESIGNER VALENtino ordered a boat in the mid-1980s, one would imagine that form, rather than function, would have been uppermost on the agenda. Yet, Valentino wanted a boat on which he could escape, one with long range and plenty of quiet. He hired Gerhard Gilgenast for the styling, 200-year-old Picchiotti for construction and Peter Marino of New York for the simple blue-and-white interior. The design team created a 152-foot yacht with 7,000 mile range at 14 knots on a simple pair of 775-hp Caterpillars and some rather innovative, vibration-abating skewed propellers.

❧ *Blast from the Past* ❧

TOY GEORGE

KEN & DONNA CHESLER

No WHERE WAS EXCESS manifested more exuberantly than in yacht interiors of the late 1980s. A number of interior designers helped owners create outrageous escape machines but the top of this genre has to be *Toy George,* a stretched Hatteras for movie producer George Barrie. Jeff Smith of First Impressions in Miami was responsible for this totally disco package that relied heavily on etched glass, pink and black leather, neon, and pin-point lights twinkling to the music. Ye gads! As if this wasn't enough, Roy Scalaren unveiled *Night Crossing* the following year, gilding the lily even further with fiber optic carpet.

1991

- The Lazzara Brothers re-enter boatbuilding with Lazzara Yachts in Tampa, Florida.
- Lurssen delivers 40m *Be Mine* as the first boat from its yacht division and wins two awards.

LURSSEN

Be Mine

1993

- Wally Yachts formed by **Luca Bassani** to design and build light, simple boats.
- Sportfishing pioneer **John Rybovich** dies.

John Rybovich

1994

- Hinckley parts with tradition and debuts its jet drive Picnic Boat. Unsure of the market, **Bob Hinckley** and **Shep McKinney** say they hope to sell a dozen. By 1999 148 have been sold.

❧ *This is Fishing!* ❧

VIKING

THE BIGGEST YACHTFISHERMAN EVER, *Viking* took her first owner, George T. Baker, Jr., far from the party crowd on nearly year-round cruises in the pursuit of gamefish – summers in New England and the Canadian Maritimes, winters in the West Indies or the Pacific Coast of South America. *Viking* was a self-sufficient village within her 272-foot length on a 36-foot beam. Her steam-turbines maxed at 2,600 horsepower with two turbo-electric drives giving her a top speed of 16.5 knots. She was designed by Theodore Wells with classic clipper-yacht lines, and

launched in 1929 by Newport News Shipbuilding and Dry Dock. From 1938 to 1940 she was owned by Norman Woolworth, but like so many of her sisters she did not survive the war. As the *USS St. Augustine*, she sank following a collision in early 1944.

© MYSTIC SEAPORT/ROSENFELD COLLECTION

GARY JOHNSON NORMAN

RADICAL CHIC

WALLY GATOR

THOSE WHO THOUGHT Luca Bassani was only interested in speed missed the point. The ideas that crystallized in *Wally Gator* sought solutions to safe and simple family cruising in a yacht fast enough to keep sailing fun. Bassani and designer Luca Brenta borrowed concepts and materials from the race course to create a yacht that was stable, quick, spacious, and oh so pretty, too. This 105-foot award winner still wins trophies when she's not cruising her owner around the Med.

CRUISING THE FAST LANE

BOATPIX

VOLADOR

LAUNCHED IN LATE 1983, *VOLADOR* WAS THE first Royal Huisman yacht to take advantage of new plasma cutter technology for cutting hull plate by computer. She also debuted the yard's facility at building veneered, foam-cored interiors and the latest generation of Huisman's hydraulic furling gear to facilitate short-handed cruising. Designed by German Frers, who was then drawing mostly racing boats, the timeless 81-foot ketch was basically a moderate-displacement Maxi.

1995

- Half of America's great Sparkman & Stephens naval architecture team, **Rod Stephens**, dies
- MTU and Detroit Diesel annouce they wil join forces on new engine series
  - Azimut debuts the *Jumbo,* its first 100-footer
  - H North perfects molded 3D sails

Rod Stephens

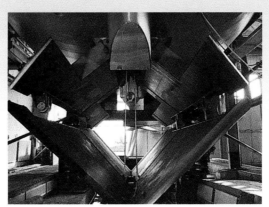

Folding keel

1996

- Naval architect **Jack Hargrave** dies. His last design — 117' *Escape*
- Allloy Yacht's 121' *Atlanta* designed by **Ed Dubois** and **Glade Johnson** is largest sailing yacht launched to date in New Zealand
- Jongert debuts its folding keel on 27-meter *Movesita*

❦ *Oh, That Bruce King* ❦

WHITEHAWK

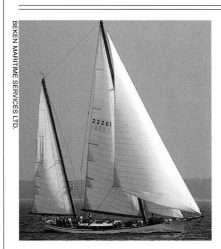

BEKEN MARITIME SERVICES LTD.

WHEN SHE WAS LAUNCHED IN THE FALL of 1979, *Whitehawk* at 92 feet was the largest object ever built using the WEST system of cold-molded epoxy-laminated wood. Her owner's intent was for her to be the fastest monohull yacht in existence and this was quite possibly true, at least in the right conditions. Reaching in the trades, she has recorded 16 knots more than once. It's not for her speed, however, that *Whitehawk* makes this list of the 100 Most Significant Yachts of the Century. Conceived as a larger version of *Ticonderoga*, *Whitehawk* opened the door on retro-styled yachts and in so doing launched the career of her designer, Bruce King. She was quickly followed by *Whitefin* and then even larger boats such as *Signe*, *Alexandra* and the just-launched *Antonisa*. Built in Maine by O. Lie-Nielsen, she was owned only briefly by her original owner Phil Long.

NOT A DIRECTION, A DESTINATION

Although N.G. Herreshoff's 1910 schooner *Westward* was designed for New York resident Alexander Cochran, she spent virtually all of her racing career in Europe. Sailing yachts of the time were not powered, so *Westward* (96' LWL) held a robust tug in her davits. She spent most of her life in British ownership. A stalwart in the 1920s revival of Big Class racing, *Westward* with a crew of 31 competed frequently against King George V's *Britannia* and later the Js.

WESTWARD

BEKEN OF COWES LTD.

Unbeatable in heavy air and off the wind, some of the newcomers to the Big Class resented "Number 5." But with eccentric owner T. B. Davis at the helm, she had become a great racing institution that no rating rule could debar. In his will, Davis followed George V's example and *Westward*, like *Britannia*, was scuttled in 1947. All is not lost, however, Dutch classic yacht aficionado Ed Kastelein is building a replica to be launched by the Dutch yard Van der Graafin in 2001 and christened *Eleonora*.

ROYAL HUISMAN SHIPYARD

WHIRLWIND XII

THE FATHER OF modern performance-oriented luxury sailing yachts is Ron Holland, whose first yacht over 100 feet was the 1986 *Whirlwind XII* designed for circumnavigator Noel Lister and built by Royal Huisman. It was a huge step at the time to consider a moderate displacement fin-keeled sloop with IOR lineage for such a role, but Holland had invested in CAD in 1983 and with then-partner Butch Dalrymple-Smith began working out a new formula for yachts of 100 feet and 100 tons displacement that could be sailed by a crew of four. The pilothouse deck salon also debuted on *Whirlwind XII*.

1997

- Germany's Blohm & Voss celebrates its 100th anniversary
- Amels' *Tigre d'Or* is the first yacht delivered to MCA rules

BILL MUNCKE

La Baronessa

1998

- Palmer Johnson launches 195-foot *La Baronessa*, the largest U.S. built yacht since the Great Depression and the largest all-aluminum yacht ever.

THE SPORT UTILITY VESSEL

NEIL RABINOWITZ

ZOPILOTE

N THE MID-1980S, BRUCE Kessler's quest for an ultimate sportfishing boat led him to Seattle's Delta Marine, then known as a builder of Gulf of Alaska commercial fishing vessels. The result was *Zopilote*, a 70-foot fiberglass bruiser of a boat co-designed by Kessler, Steve Seaton, and John Schubert as a full-comfort yacht in an imposing commercial-vessel envelope. *Zopilote* boated a striped marlin on her maiden voyage from Seattle to San Diego. After that, she fished her way around the world.

❧ *The Duke's Delight* ❧

WILD GOOSE

John Wayne

OT EVERY MOVIE star loved glitz. John Wayne had a love affair with the sea. To his admiring public, The Duke seemed at home on the range, but his captain, Bert Mitchell, says Wayne was more comfortable aboard his yacht, *Wild Goose*. It was fitting that the Hollywood hero's boat was a converted mine sweeper that saw service in the final months of WW II. Built in 1943 by Ballard Marine Railway Company in Seattle, she was constructed of one-inch fir planking and powered by twin eight-cylinder Cleveland GMC diesels. (Cousteau's *Calypso* was a sistership.) Wayne purchased her in 1962 after her yacht conversion. To keep from banging his head, he added a stateroom to the upper deck and expanded the salon. She is currently in service as a dinner cruise boat in Newport Beach, California.

PHOTOS BY CAPT. BERT MINSHALL

BEACH BOAT

WINDWARD PASSAGE

PREBIN NYELAND

INDWARD PASSAGE I, DE-signed by Alan Gurney, was the forerunner for all IOR-maxis. Built for Robert F. Johnson, construction started in November 1967 under a tent in an empty sand lot in Freeport, Grand Bahama. The 72-foot boat was designed with the sole purpose to beat all the records. A year later she won the Miami-to-Palm Beach event, which she also did in 1969, as well as winning the Miami-Nassau race and setting a new record in the Los Angeles to Honolulu Transpac race. The yacht was so good at out-performing her handicap that all of racing's "rock stars" wanted to be in her crew. She improved her time in 1971 and held the record until 1977. *Windward Passage I* could be called the grandmother of the spectacular ICAYA maxi circuit, which reached its peak in the late 1980s. The yacht has been updated numerous times. In 1988 she was refitted with new hull timbers, a new deck, keel and mast, and given a cruising interior.

1999

• The end of the SOS era, the IMO stopped monitoring radio frequencies for Morse code in February. Globe Wireless, the last U.S. network of coastal radio stations using the code, ceased transmission in July. The first telegraph message was sent in 1844.

• Benetti delivers its second largest yacht, 70-meter *Seventy.*

• In July, Oceanco delivers *Constellation,* at 262' the largest yacht yet built in Holland and follows it up with 312-foot *Trick One.*

• Lürssen marks its 125th year with the delivery of 140m (459') *Mipos,* the largest private yacht ever built.

• Trinity delivers 126' *Marlena,* world's largest convertible sportfisherman.

ROY OWEN ROBERTS

Trick One

Mipos

Totally custom dinner service created expressively for the *CORINNE IV*

Dining in Style

With selections from the best English and European craftsmen,
Dahlgren Duck & Associates offers custom-designed china, crystal, silver,
linen, and gift items that bespeak substance and express distinctive style.

DAHLGREN DUCK & ASSOCIATES

Custom appointments for the world's finest yachts, private aircraft,
boardrooms, and residences.

2554 Tarpley Road • Suite 110 • Carrolton, Texas 75006
Telephone 972.478.5991 • Fax 972.478.5996 • www.dahlgrenduck.com

francisdesign.com

FRANCIS & FRANCIS S.A.R.L.
B.P. 072, 2980 Route des Cretes 06902, Sophia Antipolis, Cedex, FRANCE
tel. (33) (0) 493 958 510 fax. (33) (0) 493 958 507 e-mail: francis@francisdesign.com internet: http://www.francisdesign.com

Riva Aquarama

PRECISION

Design for the Future

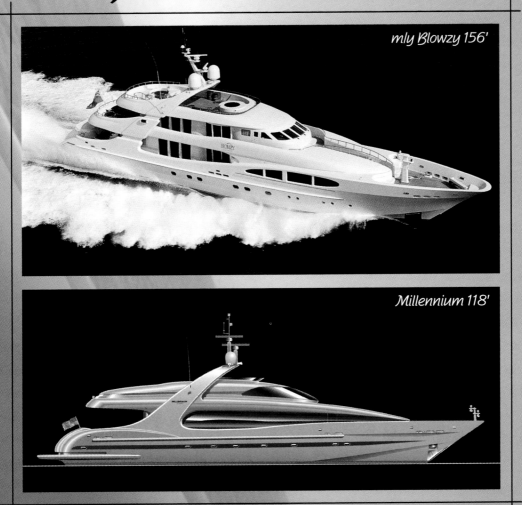

mly Blowzy 156'

Millennium 118'

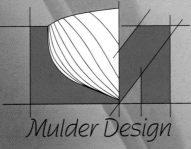

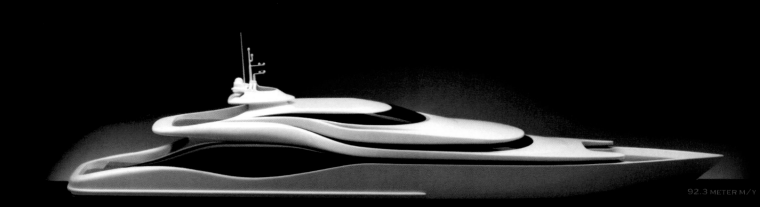

92.3 METER M/Y

DESIGN

INNOVATION

TECHNOLOGY

EXTERIORS • INTERIORS • PROJECT MANAGEMENT

MARBLE CRAFTSMANSHIP

The art of stone has been with us for most of man's civilized history. Over the past century it has made its way into the maritime industry from the elegant Luxury liners of days past to the private yachts and cruise ships of today. Over the past decade, technological advances have made the possibilities endless. The introduction of natural stone composite products has changed the face of the industry. Marbles and semi precious stones, once impossible to work, are now available cut as thin as 4mm.

Proprietary techniques in the impregnation of marble blocks, (Epoxy) has allowed 100% yield of block of raw stone. It can then be cut in various thicknesses. Thin material (4mm) for veneers, walls floors and cladding. With matching thick material for use as sea rails, tub decks, jambs, columns, sinks and more. This allows a marble mason to emulate a monolithic look, yet at a fraction of the overall weight.

Autocad and water jet technology has also made an impact. Once laborious expensive inlay work has become relatively affordable, curved cutting, some of which is impossible by any other means is now an everyday occurrence. Computerized saws now allow a project to be cut directly from a designers drawings. Semi precious stones, mother of pearl, abalone, gold, stainless steel, bronze, and various other materials are now being inlaid along with marble using these techniques. Mosaics that were once difficult to accomplish are now more easily achieved with today's technology.

While all of today's technologies have enhanced our ability to accomplish a task, there will always be a need for an artisans hand work. The idea, sketch, design, block selection, layout and sculpture of a project will never be replaced by a machine. The placement of each individual stone will always be in the hands of one of these master craftsmen.

With each launch, the yachting world continues to raise the standard of magnificence and design, and in doing so, has created new challenges for the marble industry throughout the world.

J · HOMCHICK
CLASSIC STONEWORK

605 South 93rd Bldg. E, Unit P, Seattle, Washington 98108 Phone: 206.762.3933 Fax: 206.762.3974 Cell: 206.947.9756

FRETTE®

FRETTE CRUISES INTO THE YACHT SCENE
The ultimate in fine linens is now available for **Special Orders**.

Since 1860 **FRETTE** has supplied luxurious linens to the most refined clientele worldwide, continuing to be the preferred choice today adorning the suites of the most elegant hotels, fine restaurants, cruise lines and private homes.

Through our newly created **Special Order Service**, we can now provide not only the **FRETTE** renowned quality, but offer the opportunity for an exclusive personalized product, thus creating the perfect complement to any interior, be it a home, yacht or a private plane.

Using the most precious raw material, from the finest 100% Egyptian cottons, to Irish linens and Italian silks, we can provide you with products that best match your color schemes.
Any of our items can also be enhanced by custom color embroideries, as well as by reproduction of family crests and logos.
To add the perfect finishing touch to already top of the line ensembles, we can provide you with sumptuous cashmere blankets and lavish throws.

Thanks to the **FRETTE Special Order Service** you will now be able to enjoy the ultimate in luxurious linens, while enhancing your interiors with a personal touch and an exclusive unique look.

For more information, please contact Ms. Elena Vigano' at:
FRETTE - 799 Madison Avenue, New York, NY 10021
Tel: +1-212-988-5221 - Fax: +1-212-988-5257

Terence Disdale Design
Creators of distinguished yachts

Sussurro

Mipos (140m), Montkaj (75m), Boadicea (70.5m), Awal (65m), Il Vagabondo (64m), Pegasus IV (63m), Cacique (57m), Varmar Ve (55m), Sea Sedan (55m), Wedge One (53m), Rio Rita (52m), Leocrie III (52m), Destiny (52m), Tommy (50m), Sahab IV (50m), Tigre D'Or (50m), Queen M (50m), Sussurro (50m), Thunder Gulch (50m), Tricat (47m), Maupiti (46m), Rima (45m), Joalmi (45m), Princess Magna (45m), Amorazur (45m), Sea Jewel (44m), Shenandoah (43m), Paraffin (43m), Faribana (42m), Lady Suffolk(42m), Matanthar (42m), Sea Sedan (42m), Sahab III (39m), Libra Star (39m), Taramber (36m), Azimut 118 (36m), Yankee Too (35m), Kiring (34m), Quest (32m), Azimut 96 (30m), Azimut 100 (30m), La Masquerade (30m), Vagrant (28m), Alize (28m)

3 Portland Terrace, The Green, Richmond, Surrey TW9 1QQ
Telephone: +44 (0) 181 940 1452 Fax: +44 (0) 181 940 5964
E-mail: terencedisdale@dial.pipex.com

"Performance and comfort or comfort and performance, choose which suits your personality!"

"Superyacht S
Design Awe

Each design of our custombuilt sailing and power yachts is unique, and destined to bear the stamp of the owner's personality.

Our ultimate goal is a combination of performance, comfort and technology which define the quality of our designs.

PHILIPPE BRIAND
Yacht Architecture

41, Avenue Marillac - La Ville en Bois - 17000 La Rochelle - France
TEL 33 5 46 50 57 44 - Fax 33 5 46 50 57 94 - 100445 , 1543 @ COMPUSERVE.COM

DONALD
STARKEY
DESIGNS

YACHT INTERIORS
AND
CONSULTANTS

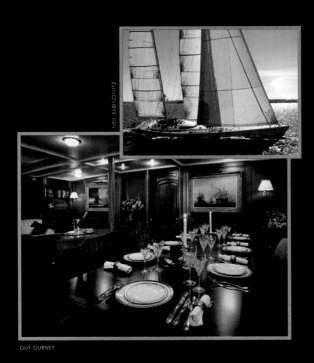

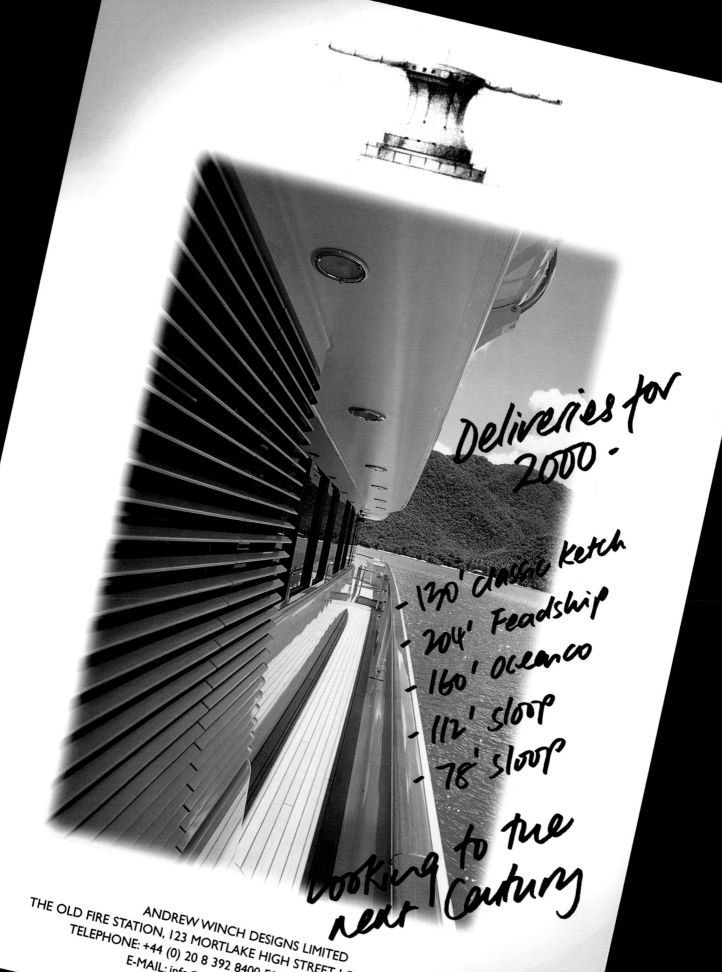

Deliveries for 2000.

- 130' classic ketch
- 204' Feadship
- 160' oceanco
- 112' sloop
- 78' sloop

Looking to the next Century

ANDREW WINCH DESIGNS LIMITED
THE OLD FIRE STATION, 123 MORTLAKE HIGH STREET, LONDON SW14 8SN
TELEPHONE: +44 (0) 20 8 392 8400 FAX: +44 (0) 20 8 392 8401
E-MAIL: info@andrew-winch-designs.co.uk

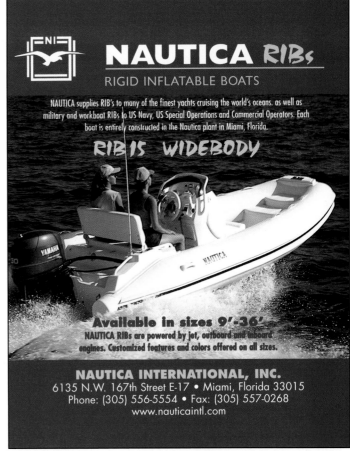
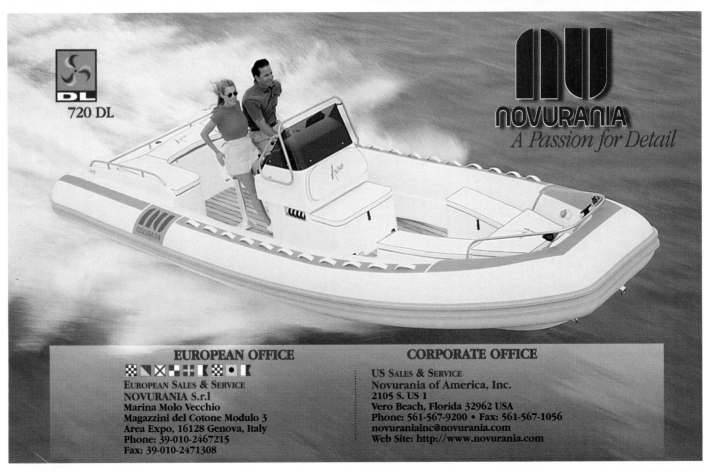

BUILDERS *of*

A Special Advertising Section Featuring Some of the World's Important Shipyards

the CENTURY

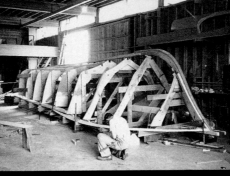

PHOTOS CLOCKWISE FROM TOP LEFT BY RUSS BRYANT, PAUL NURNBERG, NORDLUND BOAT CO., ROY ROBERTS/OWEN AGENCY, BENETTI SHIPYARD STORY

The AMERICAN FABRIC

Building Boats of Quality in America's Heartland

*I*N PREPARATION FOR A SPEECH AT MYSTIC SEAPORT'S recent Yachting History Symposium, David Ross, president & CEO of Burger Boat Company and his wife Katie, laboriously plied company records and the archives of the Wisconsin Maritime Museum. Ross and his business partner, Jim Ruffolo, purchased Burger Boat Company out of bankruptcy in 1993 and had spent the next few years shoulder-to-the-wheel rebuilding a business. Ross began his speech saying that the excavation of facts had become a humbling experience. "I am in awe of the accomplishments of this company and honored to be a part of it. Burger is not just a place where people come to build boats;

In 1888, Burger and Burger Shipyard launched this 80-foot commercial schooner *Lizzie Metzner.* Built of blue oak, she cost the princely sum of $2,000.

Burger is part of the fabric of the American yachting experience."

Indeed, Burger Boat Company is the story of the American Dream as dreamt by Simon and Margaretta Brauberger, who bundled up their children and left Deutschland in 1846 for the United States. Arriving in New York, the family modified its name to Burger and joined the growing number of Germanic Europeans who migrated to the Midwest.

In 1857, the youngest child, 18-year-old Henry B. Burger, began honing his skills at Milwaukee's Wolf and Davidson Shipyards. He soon became a master shipbuilder and married Mary Esslinger, the daughter of a prominent businessman from Manitowoc, Wisconsin. In the South and East, the country was in the grip of the Civil War. But in rural Wisconsin, there was a lake teeming with fish and fishermen eager for boats.

The Henry B. Burger Boat Company opened for business in 1863 producing 20- to 30-foot Mackinaw commercial fishing boats

The Henry B. Burger Boat Company opened its doors when Abraham Lincoln was President of the United States. Building boats – the time-honored name for freshwater vessels – is a proud Great Lakes tradition. The top photo shows the first yard. In the center, Henry B. Burger Jr., grand nephew of the founder, poses with his wife Mamie and four children, Henry C., George M, Walter and Caroline, who would take over the business upon his death in 1914. The photos of the Burgers above represent 100 years of continuous family boat building. The first Henry B. Burger is shown at left. Henry B., known as Henry Junior is in the center and two of his sons are in the early '50s yard photo at right. While their older brother Henry C., was president, Walter (left) was responsible for machinery and systems and George supervised the hull fabrication.

⪻ *Compiled by* MARILYN MOWER ⪼

Burger had a distinguished military career as well building nine vessels for the Navy in WW I including wooden minesweepers like SC330. The company cut its teeth on motor vessels at the turn of the last century with the 85-foot cruiser *Vernon Jr.,* in 1901 (above). Within 10 years, Burger would be turning out motor yachts to 100 feet. Advancement continued and in 1938 Burger launched the Philip Rhodes-designed ketch *Tamaris.* This 81-footer was the first all-welded steel hull delivered in the U.S. In the photo below, Burger's shed is shown chock-a-block with flush-deck motor yachts in 1959.

and soon attracted commissions for larger vessels, including freight-hauling schooners. In the 1870s, the heyday of wooden sailing ships, Henry B. and Greene Rand consolidated their yards into the Greene Rand Burger Shipyard, which grew to employ as many as 300 workers. Burger's personal life, however, held tragedy – all four of his children died. He and Mary adopted two daughters and in 1886, shortly after Rand's passing, Henry's nephew George B. Burger came to live with the family. Henry soon made him a partner.

The First Burger Yachts

George enjoyed shipbuilding, although he could see that steamships would end the days of the big schooners. At his urging, in 1887 the shipyard purchased the only drydock in Manitowoc. Quickly shifting gears, in 1890 they delivered the 201-foot ferry *Indiana* for the Goodrich Transportation Company. The combination of new construction and ship repair was Burger's formula for success during the 1890s. Sometimes eight or 10 ships lay anchored off the yard.

In 1902 the Burgers sold their yard to the Manitowoc Dry Dock Company owned by Elias Gunnell, John West and William Geer. That company evolved into the Manitowoc Company, the world's largest builder of cranes, and into

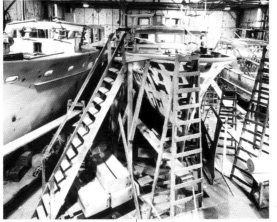

Bay Shipbuilding of Sturgeon Bay and Toledo, Ohio. This was not the end of the family's boat building business, however, for George's son, also named Henry B. Burger, (and usually called "Junior" to avoid confusion) had in 1892 opened his own shipyard across the river from his uncle.

Henry B. Jr., was a visionary builder who recognized the potential of the gasoline engine. When the Kahlenberg Brothers of Two Rivers, Wisconsin, began producing them, Henry Jr., installed them in his launches, the first of which was the 85-foot cruiser *Vernon Jr.,* launched in 1901. Within 10 years, the company had launched many wooden motor yachts of 80 to 100 feet and gained a reputation for high-quality craft.

Henry B. Jr., died suddenly in 1914 and his wife Mamie and four children, Henry C., George M, Walter and Caroline took over the yard. In 1915 they incorporated as Burger Boat Company. In addition to yachts and fishing boats, the Navy kept the yard busy until 1920 with orders for two wooden minesweepers and seven other vessels. Burger also built 13 90-foot tugs for the U.S. Emergency Corps and a fleet of subchasers. The Navy would be back with many more orders for non-magnetic ships during WWII and the Korean War.

The Transition to Steel

The years following WWI saw many larger luxurious wooden cruisers for the recreational market roll down Burger's ways. Technological developments again spurred innovation. With the advent of arc welding, Burger developed techniques for welding steel hulls. While their competitors called the boats "tin cans," consumers quickly realized the benefits of metal. In 1938 Burger launched the first all-welded steel ketch in the U.S., the Philip Rhodes-designed 81-foot *Tamaris*. This was followed by the launch 1941 of Pilgrim, a trend-setting 65-foot flush-deck motor yacht.

The next great innovation occurred in 1952 when Reynolds Metals approached the builder for an experimental hull utilizing aluminum alloy. The collaboration produced America's first all-welded aluminum cruiser, 36-foot *Virginia*. In 1957 the yard delivered a 58-foot centerboard yawl designed by Sparkman and Stephens. Not only did she disprove the myth that 53 feet was the extreme limit for aluminum hulls, but *Dyna* was the first Great Lakes yacht to win the 635-mile Newport to Bermuda race. She weighed 8,600 pounds less than a comparable wood hull and 10,000 pounds less than steel.

Dyna was the first all-aluminum sailing yacht built by Burger.

In 1959 Henry C. turned over the reins of the company to son Henry E. Burger as president and Elias Gunnell II as vice president. Steel boat construction ended during the '60s and the company focused on the design and construction of luxury aluminum motor yachts. Henry E., who had worked at the yard full time since leaving high school, was proud of the fact that he had learned sales and marketing from the ground up. When Henry E. joined the yard, 50 percent of the production was in custom vessels, "one-of-a-kind," he called them. While he understood that there would always be customers for spe-

While *Dyna* was built for racing, *Tamaris* was a luxury cruiser with an interior to match.

1. Burger survived the Depression Era largely by building steel gill net fishing boats. As the economy improved the yard began experimenting with a new design idea, flush deck cruisers. The first to launch was 65-foot steel-hulled *Pilgrim* in 1940. She is still cruising Lake Michigan. Note the sailing dinghy in her davits. 2. The style was further defined as the years passed as in the sleek *Serano* and the characteristic curved deck rails. The 1950s brought the innovation of aluminum and Burger partnered with Reynolds Metals to bring the alloy to boat building. The new material brought a new style, the raised pilothouse motor yacht. Through it all, Burgers kept getting bigger.

cial boats, he was convinced he could grow the business by creating stock designs. At first they were offered in steel at 53, 58, 65, 70 and 80 feet. After 1957, the yard began offering the stock hulls in aluminum.

These were good times for Burger Boat. In 1977 the yard launched 125-foot *Arara,* at that time the largest aluminum yacht built in the U.S. Prosperity continued although there was strife behind the scenes. Elias and Henry E. ran the yard, although they hadn't spoken a word to each other for more than a decade. In 1976 they ended their relationship via a "shotgun" buyout agreement, whereby they drew straws. Elias drew the short straw and named a high price because he wanted the yard. Stubborn Henry exercised his option to pay that sum for Elias's half.

Union and labor problems ensued in the late 1970s and reoccurred in the early '80s. In 1983 Henry lost his beloved daughter and successor Sara Jane to leukemia. Thus in October 1986, beaten down by declining health, a lawsuit, labor problems and lack of a successor, Henry E. sold the company to John McMillian who

While the yard was gaining expertise in aluminum construction, it was its skills at wooden construction that made it popular with the U.S. Navy again during the Korean War. Between 1951-1956 Burger launched seven wooden mine sweepers to 165 feet. 1. With the confict over, however, Burger turned fully to building aluminum motor yachts, voting to discontinue sailboat production in 1959. 2. The 1977 side launch of 125-foot *Arara* set a new benchmark. Built as a corporate yacht for Illinois Tool Works, she was the largest aluminum yacht delivered in the U.S. for a decade. 3. The yard kept busy with commercial work as well such as the fleet of shallow draft sightseeing and excursion boats for the Wisconsin Dells.

was then building 86-foot *Anna Marie*.

McMillian's heart was not in the Midwest. Rather than run the company long distance, he tried to relocate the yard to his home state, Florida. The community and the workers, many of whom were second-, third- and fourth-generation Burger craftsmen, were outraged. Frustrated, McMillian sold the company in April 1989 to United Shipbuilders of America, a newly created subsidiary of Tacoma Boatbuilding, itself freshly out of Chapter 11.

The company's plan was to get out of debt by supplementing military construction with building pleasure boats. The timing could not have been worse: Tacoma lost several important Navy contracts just as the U.S. Luxury Tax was imposed. Existing yacht projects at Burger were all that was keeping the company afloat.

Fishing doesn't end on the Great Lakes when winter comes. The yard built dozens of icefishing boats like this 1945 MacDonald icefishing tug.

A Padlocked Shipyard

"We knew things were in a bad way when all our parts and supplies began coming C.O.D.," said Romy Gaetdke, who has been hull shop leader for at least 100 Burgers. On Friday, Nov. 30, 1990, just 20 minutes before end of their shift, instead of wages, the 167 employees received a fax from the Tacoma office. They were told to take their tools and not report to work until further notice. "I'd never had

unemployment before and it didn't feel good," Gaetdke said.

After the shock wore off, the employees formed an association called Former Burger Workers, or FBWs, for the purpose of organizing redress from the Tacoma owners. They found a strong ally in the Manitowoc Mayor Kevin Crawford. Rick Auth, who had worked under Henry E. Burger and headed yard operations under McMillian, was appointed receiver of Burger Boat to keep the former owners from disassembling the facility bit by bit. "Building boats goes back to our roots. For the people of the Great Lakes, it's our heritage," Auth said.

For Auth and the FBWs, the next year showed their measure of determination. Between threats of lawsuits and howling creditors, these skilled tradesmen put down their tools, put on neckties and, wearing their hope on their sleeves, meet with potential buyers.

An integral part of Wisconsin life, *White Swan,* shown at her christening, diverted from her regular cargo schedule to bring a load of Canadian Christmas trees each year to Manitowoc.

"Most of them weren't sincere," Auth said. "Then David Ross and Jim Ruffolo entered the picture. Mayor Crawford set up the meeting. There were no secrets. It was a very good meeting."

Auth and the FBWs had no reservations about the fact that Ross and Ruffalo were not boat builders. "Heck," he said, "we figured we knew enough about building boats. What we needed was somebody who could sell boats and knew how to run a company."

Twenty-six months after the gates closed, Ross, Rufallo, Gov. Tommy Thompson, Mayor Crawford and the FBWs joyously reopened them. One hundred forty-five of the former work force returned after agreeing to work for less than their previous union wages. After all, one long-timer said, "The union didn't help us when the last owners shut us out." Under the new arrangement, as the yard dug itself out of disaster, the company would share its success by raising wages as fast as it could.

What Burger needed next was a yacht contract. Enter Ted and Dulce Fuller with a request for a 91 footer. "Mr. Fuller was our angel," said Auth. He wanted the best kind of boat, the kind and size of boat Burger wanted to build. The launch of *Windrush* in 1994 stated the case eloquently. Burger was back building the high-quality yachts that first earned the company a place in U.S. maritime history.

Building on Traditions

Seven years later, leaning back in a big leather chair with two computer screens blinking away, David Ross is the picture of contentment. It is late Friday afternoon and most of the workforce has departed. Captains and project managers of the boats under construction pop in to deliver a report or say goodbye. Despite the waning light, Ross is still raring to go. In the next room, Ruffolo is on the phone, talking to suppliers, checking equipment lists and plowing ahead. Finally, Ross reaches for one of his famous cigars and grows philosophical.

"This is my life," said the man who could have just as easily retired after selling his large Chicago-based photo/graphic arts company. "To be able to be at the helm of this wonderful company and continue to build its highly respected brand name along with our very talented craftsmen is more fun than anything I can think of."

In Ross's office hangs a copy of a statement made in 1891 by Collis P. Huntington, then owner of the Newport News shipyard: "We shall build good ships here, at a profit if we can, at a loss if we must, but always, good ships."

"I try to live by that," says Ross. "Our first goal was to build very high-quality boats and the workers have been delivering that. Our current goal is to become very efficient and build four boats a year. For several years we have been laying a keel every 120 days. Next year will be our first four-boat year."

Burger Boat has been improving its infrastructure at the same rate it has been improving the systems and operating features of its yachts. A new seawall and launching area, four new building sheds and new equipment spike the historic site. For a company once burdened with debt, it is telling to note that Burger operates completely in the black with no debt. Where the original Burger Boat Company built every kind of boat, the new Burger Boat Company has chosen a very narrow niche – high-quality aluminum motor yachts of 80 to 130 feet. And where Henry B. Burger Jr., had forged a reputation for innovation, Ross and Ruffalo have made it their business to explore innovations in every shipboard system.

"I'd like to think that if a knowledgeable yachtsman is considering building a new motor yacht within our range, we'd be among their top choices," Ross said. Judging by the seven yacht pennants flying from the Burger flagpole, many people agree. ✦

Since the bankruptcy in 1990 and the reformation of Burger Boat Company in 1992, the yard has been building motor yachts designed by naval architect Don O'Keeffe. 1. The first launch of the new company was the 91-foot *Windrush* launched in 1994. The second *Windrush* for the same owners was delivered in 1998. 2. While maintaining a classic and conservative look, note the updates to the famous flush-deck styling in *Simaron* launched in 1999 and 3. The crisp angularity of *Lady Grace Marie* launched in 1998.

INNOVATION
down the
DECADES

Versatility and adaptation have been the keys to this remarkable success story

FROM ITS HEADQUARTERS IN STURGEON BAY, Wisconsin, Palmer Johnson has quietly emerged as one of the most skilled and innovative custom yacht builders in the world. While the company has been regarded as a pioneer in the design and manufacturing of luxury sail and motor yachts throughout most of the 20th century, Palmer Johnson recently garnered worldwide acclaim with the christening of its 195-foot displacement motor yacht (59m) *La Baronessa*.

PHOTOS COURTESY OF PALMER JOHNSON

Pat Haggerty's 44-foot *Bay Bea* heralded the era of aluminum ocean racers.

Heralded as "The boat of the century" by *Lakeland Boating*, this lavish globetrotting cruiser is a masterful blend of classic design and cutting-edge technology. As the world's largest aluminum yacht, and the largest U.S. build for a private owner since 1930, *La Baronessa* has proven to be, in the words of *ShowBoats International* magazine, "an American milestone." For the builder she is the centerpiece of a legacy defined by superior engineering, meticulous craftsmanship, and a deep-rooted commitment to excellence spanning 80 years.

How the Midwest was Won

Founded in 1918 to build and repair wooden fishing vessels and boats for the booming Great Lakes commercial fleets, the company earned its sterling reputation in the 1930s when Palmer Johnson, the founder's son, began crafting exquisite custom motor and sailing yachts for a small stable of clients. Following the end of World War II, the business prospered by servicing the needs of rapidly expand-

Palmer Johnson's construction facility was honored by the governor of Wisconsin in 1998 on the delivery of *La Baronessa*, the largest yacht constructed in the U.S. since 1930. The contrasts between the Johnson 36 Express Fisherman of 1957 and 195-foot *La Baronessa* mirror the changing face of luxury yachts as well as the builder's chosen path for growth.

Compiled by JOE HANSEN

Door County, Wisconsin, has long been known as a boat and ship building center on the Great Lakes. 1. During World War II, Palmer Johnson's skills in wooden boat building were pressed into service for the military. 3. When company turned from commercial boats to family cruisers, *Bess Emily* (left) was one of the first. 2. Through the years PJ has turned out boats in planked, flat panel and cold-molded wood, steel, aluminum and even fiberglass.

ing global interest in offshore sailboat racing.

One such racing yachtsman was Pat Haggerty, founder of Texas Instruments, whose boats were serviced and moored in Palmer Johnson's yard. A fierce competitor, Haggerty sailed to win. In pursuit of his passion for building the fastest sailing yacht afloat, he purchased the company in 1961 and appointed son-in-law Mike Kelsey to run his new venture. The Texas industrialist's deep pockets and sharp business acumen enabled Kelsey to investigate and refine a relatively new construction technology: welded aluminum. A new era in yachting was about to set sail.

One of the first persons brought on board to assist Kelsey was Bill Parsons, a young CPA just finishing a tour with the Navy and returning to his father's accounting firm. He was assigned the Palmer Johnson account in 1963.

"Bill Parsons and I became fast friends and ultimately partners in 1968," said Kelsey. "After nearly forty years in business together we almost communicate by telepathy. He is now president and I am chairman of the company."

Aluminum Construction Races Ahead

The convergence of new welding techniques with a new series of aluminum alloys that proved extremely resistant to corrosion enabled Kelsey to fully embrace the properties of this new building technology. A hull constructed from aluminum has roughly 10 times the impact-absorbing capacity while weighing 67 percent less than an equivalent tensile strength steel hull. Palmer Johnson and a flock of enterprising naval architects exploited these factors for the rough

and tumble world of offshore ocean racing. As *Bay Bea*, the first aluminum racing yacht designed for Haggerty, breezed past her competitors, orders for similar boats began to flow in. By the end of the 1960s, the company had earned an international reputation for its fast, tough, aluminum sailing yachts.

A string of world-class winners followed, including the 62-foot

PHOTO COURTESY OF PALMER JOHNSON

Mike Kelsey (above) and Bill Parsons have been partners in the yard since 1968. Their skills as sailors helped shape such famous ocean racers as Ted Turner's *Tenacious* (left), winner of the dangerous 1979 Fastnet Race.

Tenacious, 79-foot *Kialoa III*, 62-foot *Congere*, and a string of boats named *Scaramouche* and *Merrythought* among them, some of whom still hold records in the Fastnet, Sydney-Hobart, Bermuda, China Sea and numerous other regattas. Over its history, Palmer Johnson has launched more than 350 vessels while displaying its acumen in materials as diverse as cold-molded wood and fiberglass — used for several strings of small production sailboats – as well as steel.

Palmer Johnson also applied the versatility of aluminum and its own leading-edge construction techniques to a plethora of large cruising yachts and even a convertible sport fisherman or two.

Launched in 1989, *Galileo*, a 124-footer, helped usher in the current trend in large sailing yachts.

"The racing sailboat scene was becoming more and more esoteric in the Seventies and Eighties," says Kelsey. "Ultimately, the boats became dubious in structure and almost single-season throw-aways due to design and rule changes." Interest in long distance offshore racing declined sharply in favor of buoy racing as the boats became faster and yet less comfortable. "These kinds of boats did not fit with our eighty year ocean-proven ethic. We decided that the product focus could change, but not the philosophy behind the boat building."

Ironically, it was Palmer Johnson's success with fast, light ocean racing sailing yachts that won it its first international acclaim in the motor yacht arena. The builder's construction techniques had not gone unnoticed by British fast motor yacht specialist Don Shead. In 1979, Palmer Johnson launched Shead's design *Fortuna*. This 100-foot jewel was presented to King Juan Carlos of Spain (also an accomplished sailor) as a gift from then Crown Prince Fahd of Saudi Arabia. Sporting a state-of-the-art propulsion system combining a gas turbine-powered waterjet with wing diesels for lower-speed maneuvering, *Fortuna* set a world-speed record in its class. At 52 knots, it ranked as the fastest luxury yacht in the world for a decade, firmly entrenching Palmer Johnson as an innovator specializing in one-of-a-kind vessels built to exceptional standards.

Palmer Johnson also helped usher in the era of the mega-sailing yacht by winning a number of exciting contracts for custom, heavy-displacement cruising sailboats, including eight beyond 100 feet in length. The first of these was the 105-foot sloop *Ondine* in 1983, followed by the 124-foot ketch *Galileo* in 1989.

Engineers Who Think Like Artists

Each custom build presents a unique set of demands requiring unique solutions. Rather than confining ideas to designs that have been used in the past, Palmer Johnson's approach involves thinking "outside the box" by giving careful consideration to new ideas, new products, and new techniques. Exceptional performance in every respect – and uncompromising quality in every detail – is the primary focus. As a result, the company's ethos reflects a highly flexible attitude that is not hidebound to history. Walk the yard, and you'll

PHOTOS COURTESY OF PALMER JOHNSON

In the late 1970s, Palmer Johnson once more began getting orders for motor yachts. **1.** Its reputation for strong, lightweight construction led to the high-profile commission for *Fortuna*, an early turbine-powered yacht launched in 1979 to a design by Don Shead. **2.** A need for speed drove the market in the 1980s. PJ launched the Tom Fexas-designed jet boat *Time* in 1987 and *Force of Habit* in 1988. **3.** In the 1990s, Palmer Johnson expanded its business with a first-class service and repair facility in Savannah, Georgia, that also serves as a wintertime commissioning yard for some of its new construction projects.

find a refreshing, highly creative atmosphere that has served as a driving force behind Palmer Johnson's ascension onto the world stage as the premier superyacht builder in the United States.

It's no coincidence that a significant portion of the company's work force, which currently exceeds 500, has family roots within the company dating back several decades. Each generation has built upon its predecessor's strong Midwestern work ethic, discipline and precision craftsmanship – qualities that comprise the foundation of Palmer Johnson's rich heritage. There is a passion and an artistry at work among our craftsmen, leading *Boote Exclusiv*, the respected German journal, to comment in a recent article, "As with Mercedes-Benz, [Palmer Johnson] employees do not just work somewhere, but work for a brand name instead." To meet the demands of its upscale clientele, the company has steadily expanded its construction capacity while extending its presence beyond the Wisconsin-based facility to include sales offices in Europe, Asia Pacific, and Fort Lauderdale, Florida.

Indeed, a Palmer Johnson yacht is a very special breed, created by and for individuals who love the sea… and truly appreciate both the art and the science of fine shipbuilding.

Perhaps no vessels epitomize Palmer Johnson's philosophies and capabilities quite like 151-foot *Turmoil* and 195-foot *La Baronessa*. Both of these yachts, the first an expedition-type world cruiser and the second a long-range displacement yacht, might seem to defy the common thinking about aluminum for their hull choice. Yet for this builder, the material is only part of the equation. Working with naval architects who also think outside the box, Dick Boon for *Turmoil* and Sparkman & Stephens for *La Baronessa*, the team delivered precisely the yachts their owners — both repeat customers — desired.

Timoneer, from the boards of Sparkman & Stephens was launched in 1992.

Aluminum construction allowed both teams of naval architects to forge shapes offering more efficient hydrodynamics while, at the same time, providing a structural integrity and seaworthiness capable of withstanding severe open-ocean weather. The lighter hull weight and increased tank volume also allowed for greater range (10,000 miles in both cases) and reduced power requirements for their determined top speeds.

"*Turmoil's* owner had already completed a circumnavigation in one of our sailboats and was looking to do it again, but this time in a large motor yacht. Since her launching in 1997, *Turmoil* has cruised more than 100,000 miles including two cruises to Siberia. Antarctica is in the long-range plans," Kelsey said.

The Nuts and Bolts of Building a Dream

Going from "the dream to the drawing board" is a process that involved a monumental amount of coordination over the typical

1. Between its construction yard, top, and its interior fabrication shop, Palmer Johnson is among Sturgeon Bay's largest employers. The photo at top was made on the occasion of the yard's 75th anniversary in 1993.
2. The builder pioneered the use of aluminum as a hull material for displacement motor yachts with 151-foot *Turmoil* in 1996 designed by Dick Boon. This expedition-type yacht has logged more than 100,000 miles and made two trips to Siberia. 3. High-quality interiors are constructed in modules at the joinery facility and installed fully finished. This is the salon of *La Baronessa*, designed by Nuvolari and Lenard.

two-year construction period. Here again, Palmer Johnson's custom-build background has spawned project management teams that are among the industry's best at keeping designers, architects and craftsmen on schedule and on budget. For all critical areas, Palmer Johnson can build full scale interior mock ups in its own nearby facility. Often this step is necessary and comforting for owners who have difficulty imagining a three-dimensional space from a two-dimensional

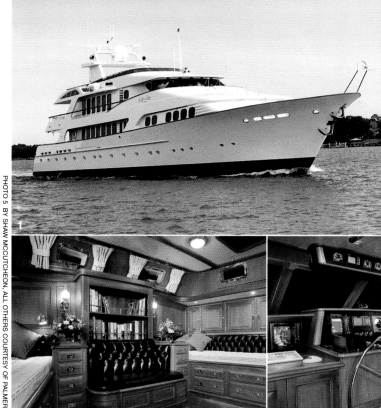

Among the yard's recent semi-displacement motor yacht projects are; 1. 141-foot *Lady Jenn* and 2. 110-foot *Mostro* from its new semi-custom Corniche series. 3. A classic interior aboard the 107-foot sailing yacht *Nazenin III* showcases joinery skills. 4. *Nazenin's* compact wheelhouse of puts everything at the helmsman's fingertips. 5. This C. Ray Hunt-designed 98-footer *Twisted Pair* is an example of the other semi-custom series currently offered by the builder.

plan. A life-size mock-up of the engine room is also often constructed, allowing the captain to make important decisions early on. Once finished, each interior module is taken apart and re-assembled on-board. Utilizing parallel construction in such a manner, Palmer Johnson can reduce build times by as much as half a year. A less tangible, but no less rewarding aspect of Palmer Johnson's experience is the ability to maintain an enjoyable creative process – one that establishes solid relationships between owners, captains and artisans and ensures that the journey is part of the reward.

At your service

A cursory scan of the Yachting Registry will reveal a lot of companies that build yachts. But very few display a genuine passion for it. And while this passion manifests itself in quality workmanship during the construction phase, an equally important litmus test is the passion for service a company displays after the sale. Which explains why, in addition to its reputation for building world-class yachts, Palmer Johnson has established the largest yacht service and refit yard in the Western Hemisphere. Conveniently located on the Intracoastal Waterway in Savannah, Geor-

gia, tucked safely about 10 miles inland Palmer Johnson's 35-acre complex features a 29,000-square-foot Interior Fabrication Facility, a 1,160-ton Synchrolift, a 205-foot (60m) undercover capacity, and the largest tabletop in North America.

Palmer Johnson's Marine Supply division takes customer commitment even further by extending its global network of marine equipment and supplies sourcing agents to the owner of any yacht. From French stoves to German hinges and everything in-between, PJ service technicians will insure *exactly* the right part is drop-shipped *anywhere* in the world.

Palmer Johnson represents a standard for excellence and a set of values that are rare in business today.

"Looking ahead," said Kelsey, "our mission isn't merely to sell the finest yachts money can buy. We're driven to support our clients by adding a range of services that enhance their lifestyle. In short, we want to create a lifetime ownership experience that is both richly rewarding and vastly superior to anything else currently offered. In this regard, Palmer Johnson will continue to build upon its eighty-year heritage … and expand upon its pioneering ways." ✠

EXPERIENCE *that* COUNTS

Three families determined to succeed established a yacht-building dynasty

From these humble but typically tidy beginnings, the DeVries ship-yard grew. This is the yard circa 1931.

With her proudly flaired bow, teak cap rail and deck house, *Capri* was the queen of the 1953 New York Show.

PHOTOS COURTESY OF FEADSHIP

WITH HALF A CENTURY OF GROUNDBREAKING achievement, Feadship looks back proudly on its own Golden Age. Yet the visionary builders who formed Feadship in 1949 can hardly have expected that 50 years later the name would be synonymous with excellence.

Today there are three parties in Feadship, each with a distinguished history. The first is De Voogt Design, a company formed in 1913. Second and third are two shipyards — Van Lent on Kaag Island and De Vries at Aalsmeer — whose roots date back to 1849 and 1903 respectively. Yet the rich heritage of yacht building in the Netherlands goes back much further still.

Simply put, the Dutch have boats in their blood. In the 17th century, over half of Europe's trade was carried in some 10,000 Dutch ships. Pleasure sailing, with boats made for that purpose, actually began in the Netherlands a century before, a time when the Dutch name for a yacht *jacht* first entered into common use. The word stems from *jagen* ("making haste") and referred to boats that were — thanks to their construction, rigging and sails —faster than others of their kind. Although Holland went on to export yachts to many European countries, commercial vessels dominated its shipbuilding industry until the start of this century.

ALL IN THE FAMILY: Learning the business from Cees Van Lent were a young Jan and Kees, Jr. in the 1950s.

The early 1900s saw a new generation of builders and designers appear. Van Lent, De Vries and Henri De Voogt (father of Frits) achieved international renown with such classics as *Bruinvisch II, Tjimanouk, Ramsar, Iduna* and the royal yachts *Chahsevar* and *Piet Hein.* All would surely have succeeded independently of each other if the horrors of war had not intervened in 1939.

The Launch of Feadship

Looking back, it was a pivotal moment in the history of yacht building, although those involved in Feadship's launch in 1949 remember it as a difficult time. World War II had left the market for this previously successful industry in ruins. And despite four years of peace, little money or inclination existed in Europe for ordering yachts. Encouraged by the Dutch government's export incentives, Van Lent, De Vries and four other yards thus decided to cooperate in the thriving American market under the Feadship banner (the First Export Association of Dutch Shipbuilders), with De Voogt responsible for the designs.

This fledgling organization made an instant impression at the New York Boat Show of 1951, with several yachts shipped in expressly for display. Americans were amazed at Feadship's use of steel, almost unheard of at this time stateside. *Wasp II* had the distinction of being the first custom-order yacht. Her double-planked mahogany hull and galvanized steel frames gave a foretaste of how Feadship would adapt to specific American tastes.

Crowned "Queen of the 1953 International Motor Boat Show"

1. Henri de Voogt designed the Dutch royal yacht *Piet Hein* for Queen Wihelmina. 2. Among the Americans who lived like royalty was Henry Ford II. He commissioned 107-foot *Santa Maria* in 1961. Her interior paneling was distressed with beer to achieve an old world ambience. 3. Little *Wasp II* has the distinction of being the first Feadship built to order. She was mahogany on steel. 4. *Coronet's* interior, circa 1954, showed Feadship's commitment to luxurious interiors.

in New York, *Capri* was the first Feadship to achieve international acclaim. Some 100,000 visitors marveled that such a beautifully constructed and finished boat was available at such a reasonable price. One journalist described her as "a palace that has sprung out of the water ...a wonderful example of Dutch workmanship." The same award was won next year with *Coronet,* putting the Feadship name truly on the map.

Other significant landmarks in the 1950s included two yachts built simultaneously, *Ventura* and *Olga II* . Equipped with automatic pilots ("You no longer have to leave your bed if you change your mind about your course" enthused a Dutch newspaper), air-conditioning (a first), central heating and many other new technologies, these yachts redefined the meaning of state-of-the-art. *Souris II* set a precedent of a different kind in 1955 as the last wooden yacht built by Feadship.

Making a Name

Forty years ago there were far greater differences in culture and business methods between Europe and the States than are evident today. A ten-minute transatlantic phone call, for example, cost the equivalent of a month's wage for a skilled worker. Feadship adopted a more streamlined approach to business in 1960 with the formation of a cooperative structure and, by 1966, a combination of factors left the three strongest components — the De Vries and Van Lent yards and De Voogt Design — piloting the Feadship course together .

This decade was marked by steady growth in the organization's reputation, facilities and the size of the vessels it built as well as higher quality standards and technological improvements. Well-known figures turning to Feadship included Henry Ford II, who commissioned *Santa Maria* in 1961. Although luxuriously fitted, Ford wanted her to be "a place like home." Interior decorator Jacques Frank created an "old chateau" effect using beer as the magical ingredient for partially stripping the painted panels.

Other major launchings of the 1960s included a second *The Highlander* for Malcolm Forbes, *Blackhawk* for Arthur Wirtz, *Prosit* for Dieter Holterbosch and *Westlake,* the first Feadship with a fully raised wheelhouse. The dedicated involvement of owners played a key role. While a Feadship was still strictly a yacht sold to Americans at this time, in retrospect the members' activities and experiences in other areas of the world made an equally vital contribution to the Feadship story.

For example, contacts with Italian yacht builder Carlo Riva resulted in important developments at De Vries and De Voogt. The Caravelle series was a great success in sales terms. When one was displayed at the 1962 HISWA fair in Amsterdam, visitors thronged to see the largest, heaviest yacht ever shown in Europe. Van Lent was also active in building yachts for various European countries, especially the UK. Immense press coverage was generated by the yard, taking the largest (and most expensive) boats to London's Earls Court Boat Show.

Bigger and Better

Feadship's popularity in the United States continued to soar in the 1970s with several yachts being launched each year. Many took advantage of Feadship's almost unique offer — to design and build a completely customized yacht, one with proven performance. James Ryder typified a trend for repeat orders from satisfied owners. Delighted with his first yacht, *Jardell,* delivered in 1970, Ryder immediately commissioned a larger Feadship, the appropriately named *Big R.*

At the launching of *Meduse* in 1997, the entire De Vries workforce climbed aboard.

In 1977, Feadship established a U.S. sales and service office. Don Kenniston was Feadship America's first general manager, a position he still holds today. The new office had an auspicious beginning, signing its first contract a day after opening. A superb example of the classic Feadship look prominent in the '60s and '70s, *Enterprise II* was the first of three new Feadship yachts that would be built for the Amway Corporation.

The Middle East market also increased in importance. In 1978, the largest Feadship of all time — and still one of the world's largest luxury yachts — slipped into the waters off Kaag Island. She was 64.64m (212'1") overall, her name was *Al Riyadh,* and she was a floating fantasy. Having passed the 50-meter barrier three years earlier with *Ogina Bereton, Al Riyadh* also proved that Feadship could build quantity and quality in equal measure.

One year later, the launching of *Daria* set precedents of a different kind. Packed with innovations in the field of noise and vibration attenuation, she was the first Feadship to have a satellite communication system — heralding a revolution in the way yachts would be used. While yachts such as *The Highlander* and *Gallant Lady* already served as floating business cards for their astute owners, satcom opened up huge opportunities for owners wishing to work onboard.

In fact, the multiple uses for Feadships have led to many fascinating developments. Yachts such as the *Carmacs* and the *Excellences* were aimed at chartering, while others — such as *Double Haven* and *New Horizon L* — were designed strictly for private world cruising. As diving and watersports increased in popularity, so did the demands of owners to adapt their Feadships to the facilities required. Fead-

1. *Al Riyadh* from Van Lent at 212 feet is the largest Feadship to date. 2. Jon Bannenberg's *Cedar Sea* set new standards in design complexity in 1986. 3. Taking the high road was *Alpha Alpha III,* en route from the De Vries yard to the sea. 4. De Vries' *Sussuro* is Feadship's first turbine powered yacht. A second is underway for delivery to Roger Penske.

ship also began working with other yachting luminaries during the 1980s: From Jon Bannenberg's styling work on *Azteca* and *Paraiso* to Susan Puleo's stunning glass interior on *Circus II,* fresh ideas and influences were constantly assimilated.

Global Visions

By 1984 the yachts truly had become world cruisers. So with the

Together the de Vries and Van Lent yards have delivered more than 200 yachts of great diversity up to 212 feet. With the turn of the century, a third yard in Papendrecht will come on line to deliver even larger vessels than 1. *Solemates* and 2. *Gallant Lady* pictured here after launching at de Vries. 3. The Van Lent yard on Kaag Island will deliver the first Feadship of 2000, the 170-foot *Blue Moon.*

Feadship name established as a corporate identity in its own right on one side of the world, De Vries, Van Lent and De Voogt decided to formally extend their cooperation on a global scale. Feadship opened a sales office in Antibes in 1985 and began a coherent world-wide marketing strategy.

The ingenuity and vision of Feadship owners has helped power the relentless pursuit of innovation. The awesome complexity of yachts such as *Cedar Sea* in 1986 and *Siran* six years later pushed the boundaries of the possible, and other owners have taken this as their cue for still more innovation. Distinctive style and design preferences were also a driver for change. For example, the lowered windows on *Confidante,* launched in 1987, offered unprecedented views from the main lounge. And while the much-admired *Virginian* (1990) was an archetypal classic yacht, she set new standards with four full decks.

The success of Feadship's global strategy can be seen from the diverse destinations of its yachts — *Yemoja* to Africa, *White Rabbit* to the Far East, *Claire* to Brunei, *Ulysses* to New Zealand. No place is too remote, as *Méduse* and *Charade* proved with their epic two-month voyage up the Amazon River in 1997. Meanwhile, *Battered Bull* is complet-

Above, Feadship's current management team: L-R Hein Velema, Dick Van Lent, Henk de Vries III and Hugo van Wieringen. At right is Feadship's guiding designer Frits de Voogt.

ing its second circumnavigation.

These and other achievements can be partially attributed to Feadship's continuous R&D programs. A bulbous bow was first placed on *Mylin IV* in 1992, while *Sussurro* recently became the first Feadship to benefit from jet propulsion. Quality control has also remained a top priority. And in 1998, DeVries launched *Solemates* — the first Feadship to be fully MCA-compliant.

With over 200 Feadships now gracing the world's oceans, experience can truly be said to count. The designs may be different, the range of onboard facilities diverse, yet all these yachts have one factor in common — an inherent quality that is instantly, unmistakably and uniquely Feadship. ✣

This article is adapted from "Experience Counts." Richly illustrated, this limited-edition, 248-page book was created by a special editorial committee. Having spent more than two years trawling through the archives, the result is a truly unique insight into "The Feadship Story." Priced at £75 (incl. P&H), you can order your personal copy from TRP Publishers in London - Tel: +44 171 610 3663. Fax: +44 171 610 1055. E-Mail: trpmagazinesltd@BTInternet.com.

POLISHING *the* DIAMOND

Cutting its teeth on naval vessels, Intermarine is moving into yachts in a big way.

TIMING IS EVERYTHING. SEIZING UNIQUE BUSINESS opportunities, this new-old yard is gearing up for exciting expansion and new fields of endeavor.

As Thom Conboy and a group of Fortune 500 investors culminated the marine deal of the decade in 1998 for ownership of Intermarine, they analyzed the reasons why some boat builders run into financial trouble. They made another list identifying the potential of the company, including the physical site and the skills of the employees. By looking at both lists simultaneously, a unique business plan crystallized, one that develops boat building skills to their fullest and then prospers by applying those skills in other profitable ways. In following that plan, Intermarine's executives believe they are pioneering the future for shipyards in the 21st century. It is a bold concept, but well designed to withstand the vicissitudes of the boat building industry and a fluctuating economy.

Conboy, who serves as Intermarine's chief operating officer, is

a 20-year veteran of the boat building business. He has forgotten more about what makes a boat go than most people know. Yet he's reached the stage where he's comfortable pointing out the industry's warts and swapping fantasy for reality.

"Building custom yachts the way it is generally done is

RUSS BRYANT

The composite shed is capable of holding six hundred-foot-plus yachts simultaneously in various stages of hull completion.

largely a social exercise, and I've learned that is not the way to keep meeting a payroll. Another thing that seemed inappropriate is the separation that most yards maintain between new construction and repair and service," said Conboy. "I think we've come up with a better business plan. Regardless of the economy and the demand for luxury yachts, we will be working."

Welcome to the new Intermarine.

One of the keys to Intermarine's new directions is cross train-

PHOTOS COURTESY OF INTERMARINE SAVANNAH

It's a scale issue. It wasn't the cash flow or the pedigree that attracted Intermarine's new owners in 1998; it was the potential offered by the facility's sheer size. As the century draws to a close, the job is one of polishing a diamond in the rough. For a sense of scale, the facility, shown in the 1960s at top, encompasses 25 acres; the mine hunter does not nearly fill the 535-foot graving dock and, the deck being turned belongs to a 188-foot fiberglass mine hunter under construction.

⊰ Compiled by H. SHAW McCUTCHEON

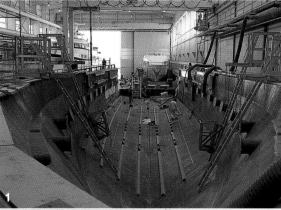

1. The expandable hull mold will serve Intermarine's new construction products. Refits and repairs are expected to become a significantly larger segment of the yard's business. 2. Among recent yachts in for maintenance was 191-foot *Izanami* and 3. 180-foot *Calixe.* Painting can be accomplished in either of two covered facilities, one accommodating yachts up to 360 feet. 4. Intermarine's riverfront has 1,000 feet of pier berthing, 700 feet of enclosed docks, and a 1,000-ton marine railway augmented by mobile cranes to 300 tons.

ing its employees. Shortly after Intermarine changed ownership early in 1998, a group of its fiberglass workers began gathering together after work. Leading this unusual assembly was a Belgian named Andre Coquyt who had been hired by Intermarine to fine-tune its GRP systems and techniques. While long on experience in building boats such as Osprey-class mine hunters for the U.S. Navy, constructing yachts required a much finer touch and more streamlined and integrated production process.

Intermarine's workers, though highly skilled, were each limited to their own specialties. Cross-training, he decided, was crucial to bringing the company's staff into the mainstream of modern composite yacht construction. Yet more to the point, cross training would create a workforce capable of shifting to all manner of construction projects, and composite fabrication is a key element of Intermarine's business plan.

For the next six months, utilizing a delicate 48-foot catamaran as "class project," Coquyt trained the hand-picked group in all aspects of building composite yachts, from reading blueprints to creating molds to finding and fixing problems. Just as he anticipated, as the team's proficiency improved, the num-

ber of problems on the main floor diminished dramatically.

However, an unanticipated benefit came in the form of an infectious team spirit that spread throughout the plant. Coquyt was also pleasantly surprised at how quickly the workers' craftsmanship was honed. For shipwrights who had seen jobs come and go on the whims of Navy contracts won or lost, learning skills that could be applied to boxcars or windmill blades or all manner of composite components that Intermarine might manufacture engendered a genuine enthusiasm in the work force.

Historic Yard in a Historic City

While the shipyard is, in fact, new to yacht construction, its origins date back to 1912 as the Forest City Machine and Foundry, specializing in ship repair and castings. Just before World War II the company, renamed Savannah Machine and Foundry, built a 535-foot graving dry dock in which it constructed more than two dozen mine sweepers for the U.S. and British Navies.

After the war, the yard focused on ship repair and conversions. Among other projects it transformed Liberty ships into missile transporters for the Military Sealift Command. In 1986 Compart, an Italian conglomerate, purchased the

PHOTOS 1, 3 & 4 BY PAUL NURNBERG PHOTOGRAPHY, 2 BY RUSS BRYANT

yard, and its marine division, Intermarine SpA, won a Navy contract to build the GRP-hull Osprey-class mine hunters. When that project began to wind down in the early 1990s, Compart made the sage decision to undertake yacht construction. First forays consisted of helping to build several boats that were started in Savannah and finished in Italy. Only one, 111-foot *Lady A* delivered in 1995, was built start to finish at the Savannah yard.

In 1999 Intermarine displayed its first completed product, the 136-foot tri-deck motor yacht *Mia Elise.* With its rich Marc-Michaels interior, a classic profile jointly drawn by Paragon Design and Luis de Basto, and thorough engineering in the vessel's oversize, well-fitted engine room, the yacht became the hit of the Miami International Boat Show.

It would be incorrect, however, to describe *Mia Elise* as an overnight success. In fact, Intermarine's ultimate arrival in the market represents a winding path. In May, 1999, while *Mia Elise* was underway, the yard was sold for $14 million to Conboy and a group of astute North American investors.

What they purchased was a premier facility on the bank of the Savannah River that included the enormous dry dock, a 1,000-ton marine railway, 700 feet of docks, a 160,000-square-foot composite construction shed capable of housing over a half-dozen 100-foot-plus hulls, and 45,000 square feet of fabrication shops for systems and finish work. To build such a facility from scratch in 1999 dollars would easily cost $45 million. To the existing structures, Intermarine has invested $2 million in a 360-foot rolling cover over the graving dock and a fixed shed over the 200-foot wet slip to create shelter for painting and exterior repairs.

Shifting to Semi-Production Construction

Recasting the company from a commercial, heavily government-oriented operation into a first-rate yacht construction yard was the first significant issue facing the new owners. Basing its decision in part on the yard's enormous physical resources as well as its analysis of current market trends, Intermarine's new team decided to modify the earlier strategy of building completely custom yachts. Instead, the company embarked on a plan to build semi-custom ABS-classed, 20-knot semi-displacement vessels between 105 and 142 feet.

"The customer has changed in the past few years," says Conboy. "Most buyers don't want to wait a long time, six months or a year, maybe. If they can get their boat right now, they're happy." *Mia Elise*, an intensive custom project, isn't representative of the yard's future, he adds. "The quality will continue. Where *Mia Elise* got expensive was in the changes to the interior finishing. Our idea is to build a boat to the level of *Mia Elise* from the outset ."

To insure quality, delivery time and a business-like approach to the production schedule, Intermarine's yachts will be offered completely finished or at a 70-percent-complete stage to allow for cosmetic interior changes. Two hull molds (one with a 23-foot beam, the other a 28-foot) will be used to build all models. Seven boats, most begun by Compart and now owned by Intermarine, are presently under construction.

With its building program organized, Intermarine has turned its attention to repair and refit work. Blessed with an excellent Atlantic Seaboard location, the yard's massive dry dock can handle any megayacht afloat today. The marine railway is specially fitted so the keels and centerboards of mega-sailboats can protrude beneath the carriage bed for easier on-land repairs. And another 8-10 nearby acres are slated for more paint and repair sheds as demand increases. Ulti-

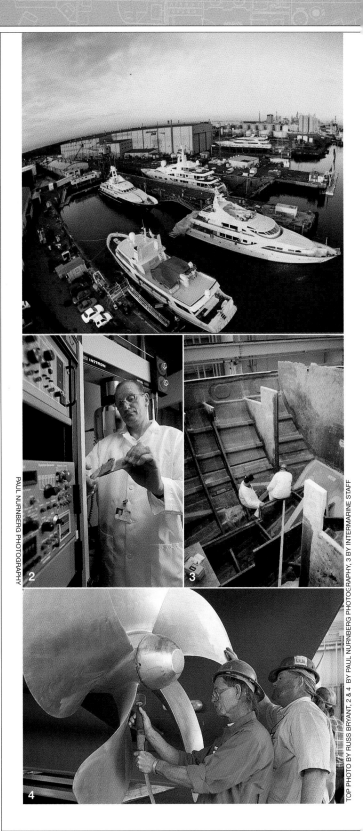

1. Since opening its repair and refit facilities, Intermarine has attracted top luxury yachts from builders around the world. The workforce is interchangable between new construction and repairs. 2-3. Andre Coquyt has brought scientific method to the yard's composite capabilities. 4. Intermarine's fabrication shop comprises 45,000 square feet.

PAUL NURNBERG PHOTOGRAPHY

RUSS BRYANT

1. *Mia Elise* is Intermarine's 136-foot flagship. The yard's well-thought-out business plan steers away from custom construction and toward spec yachts that will be at least 70 percent completed prior to sale. The first yacht in this program, 105-foot *Waving Girl* was completed in fall 1999.
2. The expandable mold will provide hulls from 105 to 142 feet. Building to military specification honed the yard's composite construction techniques.

mately, Intermarine hopes to expand across the river. "By 2001, repair, refit and service will be sixty to seventy percent of our business," said Conboy. "The labor force will be capable of working on either new construction or refits. These guys are used to working on ships. If a 250-footer pulls in here, they won't be nervous."

As with any builder, the company's reputation depends on its craftsmen, so Intermarine brought in experienced managers to help in the transition from a military to a yachting mindset. It hasn't always been easy. Garland Bennett, who began working at the yard over three decades ago when it was converting Liberty ships, says, "It's a lot different than anything I'd ever done. The fit and finish of a yacht – I'd never had to go into that much detail before. The first one was a big surprise, but now I've become accustomed to it."

RUSS BRYANT

For veteran joiner Dave Lewellyn, who runs the woodworking group, the problem was finding true craftsmen. "Woodworking is a dying trade," he says, "and it's tough to find people who can excel in yachts." Savannah has many fine furniture makers but local unem-

ployment is so low that the pool of available talent is very limited. Subsequently Lewellyn convinced local trade schools to incorporate the craft into their programs. In several years the forward-thinking Lewellyn hopes to lure graduates into an apprenticeship program that will sustain the yard far into the future. In the meantime, Intermarine has built excellent relationships with the cadre of woodworking subcontractors who count luxury home builders and other yacht yards among their clients.

As Intermarine completes its transition to the demanding world of yacht construction and repair, all signs are that it will succeed. The decision to build semi-production yachts should appeal to owners who prefer not to wait years for a boat. In fact the first such offering, a 105-foot raised pilothouse motor yacht called *Waving Girl,* will be available this fall. Yachts are already lining up for repairs and paint. Certainly the facility is one of the best in the North American continent, and the workforce is rapidly learning the exacting art of yacht finishing. The industry will be hearing a lot more from this young, energetic company. ✠

MASTERY
of
BUILDING

125 Years of Shipbuilding Mastery

O N JANUARY 25, 1918, FRIEDRICH LÜRSSEN WERFT burned to the ground. Nearly all its 20 buildings — and within them many vessels, including torpedo boats for the German Imperial Navy — were destroyed. This sprawling, accomplished shipyard in Aumund, down the River Weser from Bremen, succumbed not to the Great War but to a mere electrical short circuit. So intense was the fire that even the adjacent home of the yard's second-generation owner, Otto Lürssen, was badly damaged; he and his wife Frieda, and their two young sons Gert and Fritz-Otto (the three of whom would later share the yard's ownership after Otto's death), were forced to move in with relatives. But the fire would become a turning point in Lürssen's history, for out of the devastation it would be reborn into a more sophisticated, more capable shipyard than before.

These slim, plumb-bow beauties were typical of the Lürssen yachts of the early 1920s. In the center is *Rhenama* flanked on the left by the family's demonstrator, 17-meter *Onkel Fidi* and on the right by 20-meter *Yvonne*.

Fr. Lürssen Werft was founded in 1875 by Otto's father Friedrich, who in his 24th year set up shop in Aumund to build rudimentary wooden craft, using the typical tools of the 19th-century artisan — adz, plane, auger, and handsaw. Instilled with the same industrious spirit of many other local shipwrights, Friedrich Lürssen slowly mechanized his operation by installing steam-driven saws and began to build jewel-like, lightweight sporting craft — rowing boats, shells, canoes, kayaks, and small sloops — plus a few steam-driven launches for commercial usage.

Yet despite his simple beginnings, Friedrich Lürssen was ever-attuned to the swift progress of science and technology in the world beyond his modest boatyard. Indeed, with the proven viability of the internal combustion engine, in 1886 he accepted an invitation to collaborate with another giant of innovation, Gottlieb Daimler, to produce the world's first internal-combustion motorboat: a six-meter launch powered by a 1.5-horsepower gasoline

Just 24 years old, Friedrich Lürssen (far left above) opened a boat yard in the small Aumund house at the top of this page. The original and only 1875 photo of the shop was damaged. In the 1940s the yard's former naval architect and artist Alfred Bunje reconstructed the right-hand side of the picture. The shipyard grew quickly as a result of innovations, including internal combustion engines developed in collaboration with Gottlieb Daimler, to employ the 180 workers posed here (center) in 1907. In the portrait gallery above of the first three generations of Lürssen shipbuilders, Friedrich is followed by Otto, who took over the yard in 1912. Frieda, Otto's widow ran the yard from 1932 until her younger son Gert finished school in 1943. Her oldest son, Fritz-Otto joined the business after military service in 1949.

Compiled by JACK SOMER

1. *Donnerwetter,* c.1908, was one of Otto Lürssen's most important racing boats, its speed record of 35 knots proved his round-bilge hullform design. 2. In the early 1950s, the yard delivered numerous small runabouts marketed under the "Olympic" brand. 3. Among the most important of the early yachts, 90-foot *Oheka II,* built for the president of the Metropolitan Opera, established the builder in the U.S. Powered by three 550hp Maybach engines, she cruised at 34 knots. Her hull would become the model for the wartime *schnellboot.*

engine. Over the next decade, Daimler, his ingenious colleague Wilhelm Maybach and Friedrich Lürssen further advanced the engineering and hull form of the motorboat, which gained quick public acceptance. In the early 1900s Daimler, Maybach and other inventive makers co-produced a number of ever-faster, high-profile Lürssen racing motorboats, many of them driven to record-setting speeds by Otto Lürssen.

During World War I the shipyard built a small number of torpedo boats and remote-controlled drones to aid the German war effort. After the war and the 1918 fire, the shipyard was resurrected on new land in the nearby villages of Vegesack and, later, Lemwerder. Forbidden to build military boats under the strict terms of the Treaty of Versailles, Lürssen returned to building wooden pleasure craft.

Otto Lurssen reshapes the product line

But soon, with Otto Lürssen at its helm — and a new generation of university-trained naval architects like himself in the design office — the shipyard evolved a distinctive motor yacht style: with plumb bow, raised foredeck, canoe stern, trim beam, and soft bilges. The style naturally attracted European yachtsmen. But through a discerning New York sales agent, a number of American moguls took advantage of a reasonable exchange rate and ordered Lürssen motor yachts for speedy, comfortable commuting from their country estates to their city offices. In fact, through 1931, Lürssen built more than 25 yachts as large as 30 meters for Americans, among them

the comely 23-meter *Charming Polly,* the first vessel built in a composite of laminated wood skins mounted over Duralumin frames (a system still used in some mine-warfare vessels), and the 22-meter *Oheka II,* a 33-knot commuter built for New York tycoon Otto Kahn.

When Otto Lürssen died in 1932, his wife Frieda took the yard's

The Vegesack shipyard spread along the river front. Shown here in 1953, the yard's production was almost entirely commercial new construction or repair.

helm and ran it capably until her sons Gert and Fritz-Otto completed their education. Even as the Depression held the yard's civilian order book down, at the behest of the German Navy Lürssen began work to perfect a new type of attack craft, the *Schnellboot* (German for "fast boat"). In the 1940s this torpedo-firing craft became an important instrument for Germany's seaborne offensives, attaining high performance by virtue of Lürssen's round-bilge semi-planing hull and the imposing power of three diesel engines (which by then replaced dangerous gasoline-powered machines). The *Schnellboot* proved seaworthy in rough weather, and was a steady platform for military action.

The Fortunes and Misfortunes of War

During World War II, Gert Lürssen ran the shipyard while Fritz-Otto served as an officer in the German submarine corps. With the Allied victory, Lürssen was again prohibited from building fast craft, so it built a fleet of sail-rigged fishing cutters to help feed its hungry neighbors and employees. In time, however, Lürssen was encouraged to build cargo vessels, and between 1949 and 1984 it delivered nearly 83 freighters, tankers, and other commercial vessels for mostly German, Scandinavian, and Asian clients. Although these ships were marginally profitable, they still enabled Gert and Fritz-Otto Lürssen (now jointly running the yard) to expand and upgrade the facilities.

As Germany gained economic strength and earned re-entry into the world community, Lürssen was once more called upon — this time by NATO, nations of Asia and the Middle East, as well as Germany — to build a new generation of fast military craft, quickly re-securing its leadership in the field. As business improved, Fritz-Otto and Gert Lürssen systematically expanded, modernized, and consolidated the yard, while progressively adding to their repertoire a variety of commercial vessels and specialized craft for domestic and export use, such as customs and rescue boats. In cooperation with the German government, Lürssen also experimented briefly with hydrofoils in the 1950s and 1960s, increased its efforts in ship and yacht repair, and, to keep workers busy during slack times, it diversified into pre-fabricated housing.

The 1970s and early 1980s were dominated by military orders. But as the Cold War wound down, the future of military shipbuilding looked increasingly doubtful. Lürssen's management saw a critical need to shift away from dependence upon naval work and to develop new business strategies, including increased yacht production. By its own admission, in fact, Lürssen had not focused on the remarkable postwar luxury-yacht boom: Between 1951 and 1987 it had built barely a dozen yachts, though among them were three remarkable vessels: *Carinthia VI* designed by Jon Bannenberg, *Shergar* by Don Shead, and *Falco* by Gerhard Gilgenast.

Lurssen refocuses with a Yacht Division

To alter that situation, Lürssen began exhibiting at boat shows in Düsseldorf, Tokyo, and Genoa. In 1989 it created a separate Yacht Division of naval architects and marketing experts dedicated exclusively to satisfying the megayacht market. The decision paid off quickly and handsomely. At the end of 1989 Lürssen was contracted for a 40-meter displacement motor-yacht (unusual for a yard with a reputation for speed, but a fortuitous marketing turn), and delivered the yacht *Be Mine* in mid-1991. At the 1992 Fort Lauderdale boat show she received the Superyacht Society's notable "Design Award" after winning the "Best Interior" ShowBoats Award at the magzine's annual conclave in Monaco.

As military business indeed slacked off, it was replaced by

PHOTOS COURTESY OF FR. LÜRSSEN WERFT

Between the end of WW II and 1987 only a dozen yachts had been launched by the yard, the largest of them **(6)** 233-foot *Carinthia VI*. In 1989 a new generation of Lürssen's — cousins Freidrich **(2)** and Peter **(3)** — focused on yacht construction once again with creation of an exclusive Yacht Division. The first project from the division was **(1)** the handsome 131-foot *Be Mine*. Obviously, the focus was on custom yachts for no yard has ever launched such a diverse fleet of yachts in a decade as the Ron Holland-designed ketch *Twirlybird* **(5)**, the high-speed semi-displacement *Izanami* **(4)**, and the luxurious full-displacement yacht *Coral Island* **(7)**.

1. Lürssen's focus has also been on very large, very private yachts such as 315-foot *Limitless.* Her styling is derivative of *Carinthia VI,* but her complex folding transom and her diesel electric propulsion are on the cutting edge. Both *Limitless* and 3. *Xenia* have won ShowBoats Awards for their design and construction. 2. Today, the Lürssen yard has facilities on the River Weser in both Lemwerder and Vegesack and its construction is both military and recreational. In September 1999, the yard began sea trialing the yacht that is Number 3 on the list of the 100 largest yachts of the century.

more distinguished — and distinctive — megayachts, beginning with the second *Falco,* a 46-meter Gerhard Gilgenast design, delivered in 1992. She was followed in 1993 by an arresting 58-meter motor yacht, *Izanami,* a melding of a Gilgenast semi-planing patrol-boat hull with an aggressive superstructure and chaste interior by Sir Norman Foster, England's preeminent (non-naval) architect. The next was Ron Holland's 40-meter *Twirlybird,* a rare Lürssen sailing ketch, also delivered in 1993.

The highlight of 1994 was the delivery of Bannenberg-designed *Coral Island,* a 73-meter yacht with great volume and greater originality. Then the yard completed the 41-meter *Xenia. Xenia* was named the "Best Semi-Displacement Motor Yacht" of 1996 by the Superyacht Society in Fort Lauderdale, having already won the ShowBoats Award in Monaco for best yacht in class. The yacht division further enhanced its validity when in 1997 it delivered the 96-meter Jon Bannenberg/Tim Heywood-designed *Limitless.* Conceived 10 years earlier, and growing steadily along the way, *Limitless* demonstrated Lürssen's capacity to handle the sheer size, finish, engineering, and detail of a true superyacht. A project of imposing complexity, she, too, garnered awards. In September 1999 Lürssen delivered yet another superyacht, and achieved another milestone with its largest launch to date. Known as the *Mipos* Project, at 140 meters in length, the yacht had to be subcontracted to HDW, a commercial shipyard in Kiel, which built her under Lürssen supervision.

With its yachtbuilding ascendance re-established, Fr. Lürssen Werft continues to explore other avenues to secure its place in the new Millennium. In early 1987 it created a new sister company, Lürssen Logistics, to expand, manage, and better deliver after-sales service and spare parts for clients of its military craft and yachts, and to train their crews. And out of a long-term relationship with Indonesia, in 1998/99 Lürssen delivered five fast inter-island passenger ferries and 10 striking, 16-meter wave-piercing customs craft guaranteed to deliver 50-knot speed.

Today, Fr. Lürssen Werft sits astride the River Weser. With offices in Vegesack, design and construction facilities in Lemwerder, Lürssen continues to build the finest vessels of their kind. Indeed, Lürssen has consistently responded to commercial, military, and yacht marketplace demands with solid architecture, technical innovation, and uncompromised craftsmanship. In its 125 years Lürssen has witnessed the shift in its operations from Friedrich Lürssen's humble front yard to a more than 225,000-square-meter facility; it has seen its materials change from elementary wood to Finite-Element endorsed scantlings in steel, aluminum, and exotics; it has seen its tools change from 19th-century handsaws and hammers to 21st-century numerically controlled laser cutters and welding machines.

Through those 125 years this shipyard has borne only one name, Lürssen, and has been owned and operated only by members of the Lürssen family. Today it is steered by Friedrich and Peter Lürssen, great-grandsons of the yard's founder, and sons, respectively, of Gert and Fritz-Otto Lürssen. Like their forbears, these energetic young leaders face the future secure in the knowledge that whatever the Millennium brings, familial tradition and modern technology will always be available to meet the challenge of tomorrow. ✠

SOUND THINKING

Conservative innovation ties Nordlund Boat Company's future to its past

THERE IS A LOT OF TRUTH TO THE EXPRESSION THAT first impressions are the longest lasting.

In the case of the Nordlund Boat Company, a number of things come to mind as a first-time visitor walks among the buildings and boats, talking to the workers and to their employers, Paul and Gary Nordlund. It seems that life in this clean, orderly place goes on smoothly, not too fast, but not at all slow. There is also a distinct sense of purpose, the legacy left by the company's founder, the late Norm Nordlund.

The boating community in Tacoma, Washington, became familiar with the Nordlund name over 40 years ago. Now one of the most successful yachtbuilding companies in the Pacific Northwest, the Nordlund Boat Company enjoys a worldwide reputation for high-quality composite construction.

"A family business is everything, your entire world," Paul explains. "It's all you know, and, for the most part, all you do.

"We all worked here . . . after school, weekends, summers. Mom ran the business side. In fact, without Phyllis Nordlund, my dad would never have been a success. She still works here. . . and our sister Karen worked here until she became a teacher after college."

There is no doubt that Norm Nordlund's guiding principle — an honest day's work for an honest day's pay — has paid off, for the success of this small but prosperous company. Founded by Norm and partner Walt Silva in 1958, the company, then called Nordlund-Silva Boat Company, built 26-foot plywood boats known as SoundCraft. In those days, marketing consisted of showing the boats at the Puyallup Fair each summer and by placing classified ads in the Sunday newspaper year 'round.

"We'd have to stay home on Sundays, because that's when people would call in on the ads," said Gary, recalling the routine the children followed each weekend.

1. The early 1960s were an interesting time for the Nordlund family's young business. Equipment was simple, then, and the company truck served more than one purpose, being enlisted at times to move rather large boats around the yard. 2. Wood was still the construction material, but the methods changed as the company moved from plywood construction to plank-on-frame. 3. On occasion, the Nordlunds took time to relax and enjoy the water with a customer. Gary, Paul, Karen, Phyllis and Norm aboard *Shadowfax*.

Compiled by MARK T. MASCIAROTTE

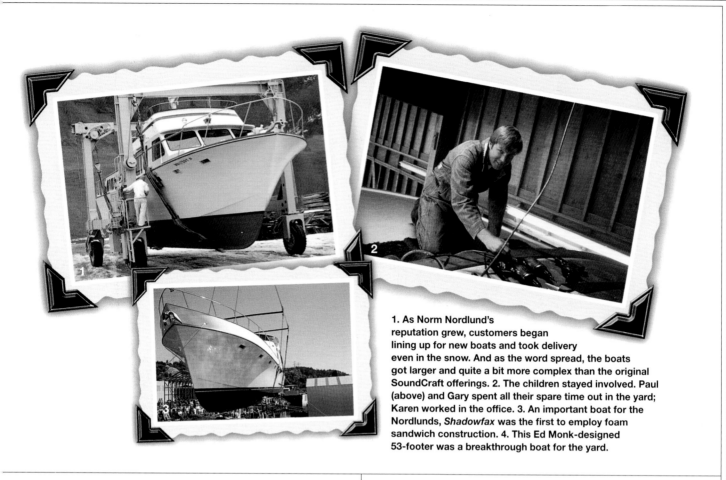

1. As Norm Nordlund's reputation grew, customers began lining up for new boats and took delivery even in the snow. And as the word spread, the boats got larger and quite a bit more complex than the original SoundCraft offerings. 2. The children stayed involved. Paul (above) and Gary spent all their spare time out in the yard; Karen worked in the office. 3. An important boat for the Nordlunds, *Shadowfax* was the first to employ foam sandwich construction. 4. This Ed Monk-designed 53-footer was a breakthrough boat for the yard.

But loss of freedom never bothered Nordlund senior, who, much to the dismay of his young family, considered painting the house or struggling to erect a cabin on the beach fine ways to spend vacation time.

By 1966, Nordlund owned the company outright and was building some highly successful boats for the tuna and salmon trade on the Washington coast, as well as a number of recreational craft. Shortly thereafter, a hull mold was taken off what designer Ed Monk describes as a revolutionary 53-footer, a breakthrough because of Monk's and colleague Ed Hagemann's success at reducing wave-making drag.

The 53's reception in the marketplace was good, and by the early '70s, the Nordlunds had made the daring transition from wood to fiberglass. Much of the early work was done with developable fiberglass panels. These were laid up on what might well have been the Pacific Northwest's first flat stock tables, the prototypes of which were built using large sheets of plate glass.

In 1973, Norm received an order from a prominent local businessman for what was then a large pleasure boat, 105-feet. The project was revolutionary inasmuch as it the was the first motor yacht in the Pacific Northwest to be built using Airex foam in the hull's lamination schedule.

Tom Johanssen, then the North American representative for Airex, had been instrumental in introducing structural core materials to the boatbuilding industry. He remembers the boat well.

"Ed [Monk, Sr.] had proposed using Airex to the client who, in turn, mentioned it to Norm. Norm was having none of it, telling the client, 'I'm not interested in any of that fancy stuff.'

"But the client said that he could see that there were a lot of advantages to foam coring, and after talking to a number of people and following up on all the details, he told Norm he really wanted it," Johanssen said.

That boat, *Shadowfax*, was a great success, and after many years working together, Norm Nordlund and Tom Johanssen became good friends. The builder often reminded him of the rocky start, quipping, "I fought you like mad, Johanssen, and then I could never sell another boat without it."

The transition was both necessary and timely, says Paul Nordlund, who adds, "We were not pioneers. But there were a lot of wooden boatbuilders who didn't make the change to fiberglass, and they're gone."

Cored hulls have become the company standard, and over time, other construction methods changed as well. Gone are the days of stick-built superstructures and flat-panel hulls. Today the company strives to use large molded parts, many of which are laid up on throw-away tooling; other details and systems have become more and more sophisticated.

Ed Monk, Jr., has fond memories of his relationship with the Nordlunds, who have built many of his designs.

"Norm was like a second father to me," he recalls. "He had a presence, you know? He didn't talk all that much, but when he said something, everyone listened . . . and he was usually right."

But it was not only the man that Monk admired. He also has a fondness for the place he left behind. "This is my favorite yard. We work well together, and the customers are always pleased with the results."

Judging from the list of repeat clients, that statement is indisputable, and both Paul and Gary say that beyond the work ethic instilled in them by their parents, there are several things that have made their company successful. One is the company's workforce, many of whom have been in the yard as long as Paul and Gary can remember.

The 67 foot *El Vato* underway.

There's one fellow, a man named Bonnie, who signed on to help Norm build his first fiberglass boat mold. It was supposed to be a one-year job. That was nearly 30 years ago, and Bonnie still clocks in every day.

"He's retired, well, at least three times," says Paul, "but he keeps coming back. These days, I guess you could say he's half-retired."

"Yeah," Gary adds, grinning, "half-retired. Now he only works 50 hours a week."

Like the IBM of Watson years, Norm Nordlund's yard was a place where workers were rarely fired. Norm believed strongly that he hired people to have a secure job, not to use them as a commodity. Firing employees, he believed, was "the easy way" to deal with someone who was not performing as expected. Instead, Nordlund would move them to another job, perhaps retrain them. But the main emphasis was to keep that employee in the fold. With only rare exceptions, Paul and Gary carry on that tradition.

Gary recalls the overall philosophy. "My father used to say that if we had a

The Nordlunds today: Paul (left) and Gary with their mother Phyllis.

business where customers wanted to come to have a boat built and where people wanted to come to work building boats, then the rest — all the details — would fall in place."

PHOTOS BY NEIL RABINOWITZ

Norm Nordlund believed in loyalty. The close relationships that developed between the Nordlunds and their vendors have lasted for years. One of the closest is with designer Ed Monk, who with colleagues Ed Hagemann and Tim Nolan has designed all of the composite yachts for Nordlund Boat Company. Shown above are: 1. *Aerie* (100'), 2. *John's Rendezvous* (67'), 3. *Jacana* (76'), 4. *Alexa C* (74') and 5. *Happy Doc* (84'). Yachts, however, are not the only product to be launched from the Tacoma yard. It is not uncommon to see a workboat come down the ways on occasion. Recently, the company delivered a 75-foot pilot boat to be used by the Puget Sound Pilot Association. Propelled by a pair of Hamilton waterjets, the boat makes 28 knots.

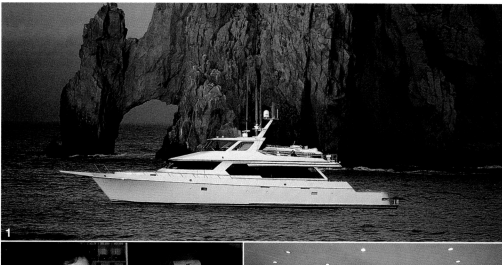

PHOTOS BY NEIL RABINOWITZ

Nordlund yachts such as the 100-foot *Southern Way* have come to represent a style that has proven popular among yachtsmen who not only use their boats for cruising but also for fishing and diving. 2. Much of the work that goes into each boat is done in the Nordlund yard by Nordlund craftsmen, many of whose parents worked for Norm and Phyllis in years past. In addition to the beautifully executed composite construction, metalwork and joinery is of the highest quality. Unlike some yards in the Pacific Northwest, however, Paul and Gary Nordlund believe in using subcontractors for specialty work, ensuring that such work is carried out by experts. 3. The results speak for themselves, as can be seen in the image of *Southern Way's* interior, designed by John Pokela. 4. The high standards bring customers back time and again, as it did for the owner of the lovely 100-foot *Shadowfax II*.

It would seem that customers agree with that way of thinking. Over the years, fewer than a dozen have requested signed contracts to build their boats. The rest have been handshake deals. It is an impressive statistic, especially considering that the company has built nearly 100 boats to date.

Another thing that customers and colleagues enjoy is the family's sense of humor, considered by the Nordlund brothers to be an important ingredient in the mix that defines their company and their lives. They genuinely enjoy a good laugh, even if it sometimes comes at their own expense.

The workers, too, like the atmosphere. Many have worked for the company for more than 15 years. There are husband-and-wife pairs among the employees, as well as fathers and sons and a pair or two of brothers. The high quality of the Nordlund product is a direct result of this ongoing loyalty and of the history that surrounds some of these talented individuals. For example, many of company's retired employees, themselves the children of immigrants, were apprenticed as youngsters in skilled trades such as violin-making, trades that prepared them well to produce the fine detail and finish required of a yachtbuilder's joinery shop. They, in turn, have taught the present generation.

These are people who are very proud of what they do and who

they work for. When asked by a competitor's workman whether Norm Nordlund was "hard to work for," a long-time Nordlund shipwright replied, "Nope. I just do everything right!"

"My dad had an interesting way of looking at this business," Paul Nordlund says. "This company was not started with money as a motive. It was built as a place to create things, to do new projects."

Gary sits at the table smiling at something only he can see, then adds, "Dad sure had a different perspective on business. You know, when someone, even a prospective client, would ask him how many boats he built a year, he'd look them in the eye and answer, 'As few as possible.'"

As this is written, there are four boats under construction and one a day away from delivery. Although there is capacity at the yard for more, four is a number that the Nordlunds consider to be ideal for them, their workers and their customers.

While it is true that first impressions are lasting, so are the last. At Nordlund Boat Company, Gary walks his visitor to the door. There's no hype, no platitudes, no last-minute sales pitch. Just a smile, a simple handshake, and a sincere statement: "It was nice getting to know you better." Indeed it was. ✠

LINKING *two* DESTINIES

Merging the talents of two yards makes business and boat building sense

HE STORY OF A BOAT YARD IS THE STORY OF THE boats it has built and the promise of boats yet to be.

The story of Queenship and Admiral — two Pacific Northwest builders who joined forces in the spring of 1999, is also one of similarities and differences, the least of which is that Queenship is a Canadian builder, Admiral American.

But it is the similarities that make this alliance strong with promise, the most crucial of which is an unwavering commitment to building the very best boats possible. Between them, Queenship and Admiral have been building better boats for almost a century in composites, steel, aluminum and wood.

Queenship has its roots in a long-established boatyard based in Maple Ridge, just up the Fraser River from Vancouver, British Columbia. Starting in 1969, the yard built several thousand pleasure sail and powerboats. By the late 1980s it had made a name for itself as an ambitious, quality-conscious builder, having successfully produced not only ever-larger boats but also a whole generation of highly skilled craftsmen. When its mainstay market declined and the company foundered in the early 1990s, this irreplaceable body of knowledge might have been lost but for Dan Fritz, a Seattle-born bush pilot-turned-developer of high-end urban real estate in Vancouver.

Fritz first refocused the yard on larger custom-built motor yachts, such as the *Mary J.* (98'), *Glory* (98'), *Reminisce* (97') and *Mary J. II* (112'). He combined the calculated risk-taking of a bush pilot and the organizational skills of a successful businessman to introduce an entirely new way of building luxury yachts. Queenship offers custom-finished interiors with exquisite joinery within production hulls incorporating some of the industry's most extensive use of advanced composites. The result is lighter, stronger, longer-lasting yachts.

Celebrated yacht designer Juan Carlos Espinosa put it this way: "Dan understands as few others do the delicate balance between art, engineering and the bottom line. He makes it possible to allow clients to express themselves in the interior design of their yachts and to combine extremely high-quality custom work within the benefits of production hulls and superstructures."

The company now offers three series of motor yachts in pilot-

After founding Admiral Marine in 1947 in Seattle, Earle Wakefield brought the yard's first two boats completed on spec to the Seattle Boat Show in 1948. Wakefield, leaning on the rail of a 30-foot sedan cruiser designed by Ed Monk Sr., successfully sold both boats at the show.

PHOTOS 1 & 2 BY NEIL RABINOWITZ

1. A member of Queenship's Berretta Series, which includes six different models ranging from 70 to 75 feet, 70-foot *Stargazer* features a widebody design with slightly-raised pilothouse. 2. In 1992 Queenship's president Dan Fritz, bought the company, which had been building both sail and power yachts since 1969, and refocused its efforts towards building large and mid-sized luxury motor yachts throughout the '90s.

Compiled by PATRICK COTTER

1. Located in Maple Ridge, just up the Fraser River from Vancouver, British Columbia, Queenship expanded its production abilities in June of 1999 by acquiring Admiral Marine Works of Port Angeles, Washington. The result combines "old world" joinery and advanced technology with expanded yacht building, refit and repair capacity. 2. Admiral's Daryl Wakefield, left, and Earle Wakefield shake hands with Fritz, center, on the sale of Admiral to Queenship. 3. Queenship's ability to feature exquisite joinery work and custom-finished interiors within their advanced-composite production hulls is demonstrated onboard 112-foot *Mary J. II*, below.

house, sport cruiser and sport fisherman styles: *Admiralty* (57'-70'); *Berretta* (70' to 75'); and *Caribe* (72' to 99'). In addition to custom yachts to 130', the company also crafts classic displacement vessels based on modified trawler designs.

"We like giving owners the chance to get involved in the building process to see their dreams being realized," says Fritz. "No two of our owners ever have quite the same requirements. So it turns out no two Queenships are quite alike, except in the way we engineer our boats and try to make the layout, fit and finish of each yacht perfectly match each owner's needs."

With its semi-custom series, Queenship has helped redefine what a luxury yacht can and should be. Proof of the yard's ability to meld custom craftsmanship with production techniques can be seen in the number of yards attempting to duplicate Queenship's achievement. Although imitation is the sincerest form of flattery, Queenship has opened up a commanding lead in marrying highly polished custom craftsmanship with forward-thinking technology and production techniques.

A marriage of a different sort took place when Queenship Yacht Works and Admiral Marine Works joined forces. To Admiral's brilliant record of producing innovative, award-winning vessels, Queenship has brought proven business discipline and market-based research to open a new chapter in yacht building in the Pacific Northwest.

A New Beginning for Admiral

Earle Wakefield launched Admiral Boat Works in Seattle in 1947. Over the ensuing 30 years, Wakefield's reputation as both a boat builder and a teacher of boat building gained legendary status. It is said that if you were involved in boating in the Pacific Northwest, you had either worked for Earle, been taught by him, or bought a boat from him.

In 1978, Admiral Boat Works moved to Port Townsend, Washington, and became Admiral Marine Works, with Wakefield's son, Daryl, eventually leading the yard to the summit of custom yacht building. Each of the vessels Admiral built over the last two decades in some way advanced the technology and materials used in boat building, whether working in wood or composites. Admiral's expertise was such that it provided Boeing Aircraft with carbon-fiber/FRP tooling and components. Each of the following Admiral launches represents a step in the evolution of one of the industry's premier builders.

For the 88-foot Jack Sarin-designed yachtfisher *Crazy Horse* (now known as *Peppermint*), Admiral created the hull entirely without structural wood. All stringers and bulkheads are fiberglass sandwich construction, a pioneering breakthrough in the mid-1980s.

Hawkeye III, a 95-foot long-range cruiser built of foam-cored fiberglass and an aluminum pilothouse, was one of the first yachts to feature a bulbous bow to increase hull speed while reducing pitching and lowering fuel consumption to as little as one gallon of fuel per hour at 10 knots.

At the time of her launch, 161-foot *Evviva* was the largest fiberglass yacht ever built in North America. In order to create a fiberglass hull that was to be neither filled nor painted, Admiral developed a process to develop fully detailed one-off female molds. To decrease weight, it also developed a resin blend that was 10 percent lighter than normal. Laying up decks with a combination of Kevlar and fiberglass cloth yielded an additional 30 percent weight savings. Nomex interior panels totally replaced solid wood, even in furniture and as a base for marble counter tops. *Evviva* so impressed the industry that she won the International SuperYacht Society Design Award and the *ShowBoats International* Award for Semi-Displacement Motor Yacht for Admiral in 1993.

Award-winning *Evviva* built by Admiral Boat Works, was the largest fiberglass yacht ever constructed in North America at the time of her launch.

For *Sensei*, a 124-foot refit, Admiral raised the headroom three inches by rebuilding the original deck beams. Additions included a garage for watersports equipment and two Harley Davidson motorcycles and a transom Jacuzzi. The rebuild and a near-total overhaul (including mechanical, acoustical, electronic, décor, water making and generators) was accomplished in just 10 months and earned Admiral *ShowBoats International's* Refit of the Year Award in 1995.

The 74-foot *Plumduff* brought additional accolades in 1997 including yet another *ShowBoats International* Award for Best Motor Yacht Interior, acknowledging that Admiral's finishing is as accomplished as its technical innovation. The exterior is no less stunning. *Plumduff's* hull is three layers of mahogany plywood heavily sheathed in fiberglass and epoxy, while the superstructure is the reverse, fiberglass sheathed in mahogany. In an article in *ShowBoats International,* the yacht was described as, "foot for foot, pound for pound … *Plumduff* … might very well be the … most finely engineered and mostly artfully designed yacht ever built." *Plumduff's* designer, Michael Peters, credits Admiral with perfectly translating the vision of the boat into reality. "She looks as good as we envisioned, no misinterpretation," he said.

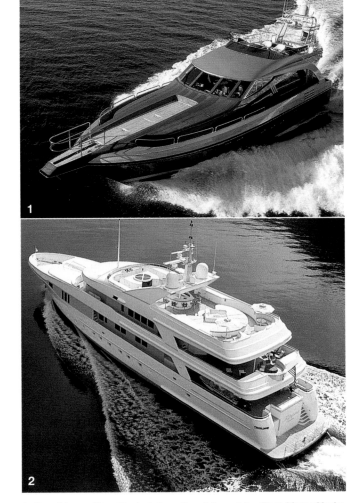

1. Receiving a ShowBoats International Award for Best Motor Yacht Interior, 74-foot *Plumduff* acknowledged Admiral's finishing capabilities. Designed by Michael Peters, *Plumduff's* stunning black hull features three layers of mahogany plywood sheathed in fiberglass and epoxy. 2. The first yacht to be launched after Admiral's move from Port Townsend to Port Angeles was 154-foot *Roxana*. Her 6'6" draft allows cruising in the shallow Bahamian waters.

Admiral was commissioned to build 154-foot *Roxana* after the prospective clients spent a night on *Evviva*. They were won over by quality of the workmanship as well as by the yard's expertise with lightweight materials, which allowed *Roxana* a shallow draft of just six feet, six inches, ideal for diving in their favorite Bahamian cruising grounds. The twin-screw yacht was built to ABS Classification and A1 Yachting Service AMS Standards.

Queenship's Admiralty Sport Cruiser, 68-foot *Titan*, features an extended aft deck which allows plenty of space below for a separate lazarette area.

English yacht designer Donald Starkey was involved in creating *Evviva* and *Roxana,* as well as eight of the other largest yachts made in the U.S. Having worked with other U.S.

Queenship's most recent debut is its Caribe series. With styling by Juan Carlos Espinosa, the Caribe series features five different models ranging in length from 70 to 96 feet. Every Caribe arrangement plan is designed to meet a particular owner's needs, and will typically include three to four staterooms and crew quarters aft. 1. *Mary P* is the first Sportfisherman Convertible to launch. The 89-foot yacht provides an large cockpit to accommodate fighting chairs and bait/tackle storage, and is also available in an open flybridge model as well as the closed version pictured here. 2. The Caribe Raised Pilothouse Motor Yacht, 86-foot *Oregon Mist*, features side decks and a beautiful interior by Zoe Luyendijk. A wide-body model is available as well.

RENDERINGS COURTESY OF QUEENSHIP/ADMIRAL

yards, Starkey declares, "In terms of quality, Admiral beat them hands down." He also rates Admiral highly in comparison with leading European yards, noting it is one of the few yards anywhere to really do GRP properly."

Roxana was the first launch after Admiral moved from Port Townsend to its new yard in Port Angeles. The site features a specially designed 60,000-square-foot refit facility as well as a new 330-ton Travelift, the largest on the West Coast. These facilities complement the ongoing expansion of Queenship's operation, which includes 1,400 feet of dedicated water frontage and a new purpose-built, 100,000-square-foot facility that will enable the yard to significantly expand the number of vessels it can build, as well as the efficiency with which it can build them.

The right facilities can set the stage for new accomplishments. While Admiral is best known for its motor yachts, it has also pro-duced stellar work in sail. The first time the yard used the process was on a Pedrick 75, with hull, deck and internals SCRIMP-molded at Port Angeles. Typically, Admiral executed it flawlessly – and even managed to produce the second-largest part ever molded using the process. Designer David Pedrick says he and his client "are thrilled with how the boat turned out."

If the past is prologue, then the future is bright for both Queenship and Admiral. The two yards' complementary strengths allow the new combined operation to take on yacht-building challenges in both power and sail from 60 feet to 160 feet that are simply beyond the technical and/or creative reach of other yards.

"Every yacht is a beginning and an end," says Fritz. "At Queenship and Admiral, we take the best from each boat we build and add it to our quality benchmark. It's a constant process of improving our engineering and craftsmanship. We are always looking to find better ways to deliver better quality." ✛

VISION
of the
FUTURE

Yachtsman and entrepreneur Luca Bassani's vision for a fast, safe cruising yacht redefined the genre

AFTER ONLY SEVEN YEARS IN BUSINESS, IT IS DIFficult to imagine the contemporary luxury yacht sailing scene without Wally Yachts. In its short but meteoric history, Wally Yachts has helped change not simply the look and feel of large cruising sailing yachts, but has forever altered the very construction, systems and engineering that define the genre.

The Wally Yachts story begins with its founder, Luca Bassani, a passionate 42-year-old sailor who in his career has cut a wide swath through European racing circuits. In 1972, Bassani won both the IOR Mediterranean Championship and the Two Ton Cup. His string of thoroughbred racing yachts include *Phantom,* the very first Maxi-rater. In 1979, Bassani introduced the J24 class to Europe. Also active in the Six-Meter class, Bassani won two European Six-Meter Championships in 1986 and 1990, placing third at the 1983 World Championships. In 1997, he started racing in the Mumm 30 class, placing second in the European Championships and winning the World Championship the following year.

Bassani, who hails from one of the world's premier yachting families, is also Treasurer of ICAYA, the Maxi owners' association, and is a founder of the One Hundred Division, the ICAYA class for large cruising yachts.

Apart from his sailing exploits, Bassani is also a family man with young children. Bassani found that while there were no shortages of lively and competitive racing yachts in the world, fast, safe and comfortable cruising yachts were non-existent. More specifically, Bassani wanted a stable but speedy yacht with wide, uncluttered decks and featuring sailing systems that would allow him to cruise safely but with a minimum of crew.

His search for such a yacht began in the late 1980s and led him to designer Luca Brenta, who readily agreed to begin work on an 83-foot carbon fiber-and-wood composite yacht, which he named *Wallygator* after a big yellow cartoon alligator. As the Brenta/Bassani collaboration progressed, their enthusiasm produced a concept for an even more sophisticated yacht, a 105-footer incorporating a

After years of contracting with some of the world's top boat-building facilities, Wally Yachts brought its design, engineering and production management teams under one roof in Fano, Italy. 2. Built at Pendennis Shipyard in England, the 107-foot *Wally B* is the evolutionary sistership to *Wallygator,* the first Wally Yacht's conception. 3. Recipient of a 1999 ShowBoats Award for Best Sailing Yacht, *Wally B* had a powerful impact on the industry with her dramatic architectural, minimalist interior and superior sailing capabilities.

GUY GURNEY

MATTEO PIAZZA

❧ Compiled by CRAIG DAVIS *❧*

Wally engineers employ the most advanced composite construction techniques achieving a reduction in weight, increased safety and superior sailing performance. 1. This engineer applies a vacuum system in a custom hatch lamination process. 2. Wally's approach to deck layout features open uncluttered space for ease of movement and a surplus of sunning areas as is obvious here onboard *Kauris II.*

wide range of novel solutions to age-old sailing and construction challenges. In 1992, work began on the second *Wallygator.* Before long, the passion for this project spilled over into a plan to bring to market the extraordinary new ideas Bassani was conceiving for the new boat. Thanks to a sensational marketing campaign orchestrated by the company even before this yacht's launch in 1994, Wally Yachts was well on its way to becoming a household name. The sailing and racing worlds watched in eager anticipation to see how this revolutionary new yacht would perform.

They were not disappointed.

Launched that summer at Concordia Custom Yachts in Massachusetts and sea-trialed off Newport, Rhode Island, the carbon fiber-and-Kevlar flyer matched or exceeded nearly every performance expectation. In addition, her advanced engineering included thruster-style auxiliary and docking propulsion, diesel-electric and electric-hydraulic systems, bomb bay-style anchoring, fully automatic sail handling and advanced touch-screen yacht management and control. *Wallygator's* instant acceptance included several awards, including a ShowBoats Award as the most innovative yacht of 1994.

Even the company was revolutionary. Rather than a business selling man-hours and production facilities, Wally Yachts was conceived as an intellectually-driven firm, selling design, engineering and supervision of projects contracted at the very best facilities around the world.

The formula clicked almost instantly. Even before the 105-foot *Wallygator's* launch, Wally Yachts signed up a contract to produce 60-foot and 65-foot IMS raters built of advanced composites at Yachting Development in New Zealand.

In 1994 Wally Yachts started an 80-footer that would usher in the second revolutionary step. Called *Genie of the Lamp,* this lovely yacht featured a number of technical and engineering breakthroughs and refinements in weight control and construction quality.

The next three years saw the signing and launch of six new yachts, including 107-foot *Wally B* built at Pendennis Shipyard in England. A highly refined sistership to *Wallygator,* now called-*Nariida, Wally B* established her own aura, thanks to her dramatic, highly architectural minimalist interior which used the polished inner carbon fiber skin of the hull layup as a design element.

Wally B also won accolades, including a 1998 Best Sailing Yacht Award from *ShowBoats International* magazine.

Having redefined the genre of fast cruising yachts with its first five projects, Wally Yachts began a metamorphosis of its own. Up to then, the company had employed six different shipyards in four different countries to build its yachts. As more orders piled in, coordination and communication became more problematic. Moreover, all of Wally Yachts' contracts called for highly sophisticated composites, materials that require strict production controls. Bassani began thinking it was time to develop proprietary facilities for his company to deliver timely, consistently high quality.

Thus the next stage of development for Wally Yachts included bringing in house the entire design team, including the various structural and systems engineering firms that previously had worked on a subcontract basis.

This stage of development included developing a sophisticated computer network to fully integrate and coordinate design, engineering and project management functions.

To ensure smooth delivery, Wally Yachts has entered into exclusive participation-based relationships with key suppliers: C.N.B. shipyard in Fano, which has begun five hulls as of fall 1999; WWW Woodcraft, which supplies the high-tech interior joinery for the company's yachts; MedTech, which supplies electrical system design and hardware and software controls for the electrical and hydraulic systems; Cariboni, which provides the proprietary Magic Trim hydraulic ram responsible for automatic sail control on Wally Yachts; and, W Service in Savona, which services the Wally fleet.

Over the years, practically every system and function has been scrutinized carefully by the Wally design team. As with *Wallygator* and *Genie of the Lamp,* 88-foot *Tiketitan,* launched in 1998, have been the company's most important test-beds for new ideas. For example, the bomb bay anchor-delivery system in the bow of *Wallygator* evolved on *Tiketitan* into a anchor that deftly integrates itself into the bow below the water level, thus eliminating the two doors in the hull.

Tiketitan also introduced the latest technical innovation from Wally Yachts, a canting keel. While this system has been used previously on racing sail alone, this is the first developed for a cruising boat. Since this required a sophisticated hydraulics installation, Wally engineers decided to move the yacht's entire mechanical installation to the center of the boat directly above the keel. This provided the company with the opportunity to design an aft salon, opening up to what Wally Yachts refers to as its "terrace on the sea," a large open space almost at water level. The company also used *Tiketitan* to introduce new furling systems for the main, jib and gennaker. In order to keep fumes away from its "terrace," Wally neatly ran engine and generator exhaust lines out the top of the mast.

Never a company to rest on its laurels, Wally Yachts is in the process of developing such revolutionary systems as a lifting keel. Not a centerboard arrangement, it is a true America's Cup-style movable lead bulb that on an 80-foot boat will reduce draft from 13 to 8.5 feet.

Always on the lookout for new ideas, Wally Yachts has cast a wide net for data and information. For example, in order to learn more about the forces at play when a boat slams its way through the waves, Wally is funding a research project to better understand

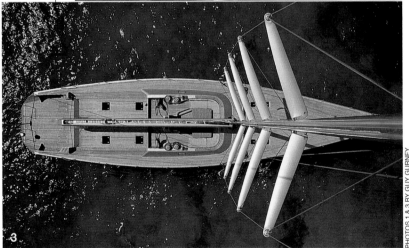

PHOTOS 1 & 3 BY GUY GURNEY

1. Launched in 1998, *Tiketitan* introduced both Wally's canting keel and a new furling system for the main, jib and gennaker. The 88-foot yacht also perfected the company's below-waterline anchor system. 2. The navigation station onboard *Narida*. 3. This bird's-eye view of *Tiketitan* demonstrates Wally's sleek exterior lines and swept-back spreaders.

1. Dual helm stations onboard *Tiketitan.* 2. *Kauris II's* comfortable aft deck seating for outdoor enjoyment. 3. Touch-screen control panel 4. *Nariida* glides through the surf with ease on her carbon sails, which can be managed single-handedly because of Wally's sail plan philosophy. 5. All Wallys feature self-tacking jibs, full-batten mainsails and masts with swept-back spreaders to avoid laborious running backstay management.

the sea and its effect on sailing yachts. Wally also worked closely with North Sails to develop 3DL carbon fiber cruising sails.

"Due to the correct equilibrium we have developed between displacement, sail area and on-board systems," Bassani said, "Wally Yachts offer significantly better performance than any other cruising yachts without compromising interior comfort or maneuverability.

"The deck hardware and sail-handling systems, including our patented Magic Trim, have closed the circle, making it possible for a small crew to sail these large yachts faster and more safely. In essence,"

Bassani continued, "we have created yachts which, because of their larger sail plans, are higher performance, but because of their smaller jib are also more agile and more manageable. In addition, because we use fewer sails, they are less expensive, and because of all these factors they are far safer.

"More and more owners," Bassani concludes, "are demanding these refinements. And thus more and more shipyards are trying to copy the innovations and style of sailing introduced by Wally Yachts. Although the life of our company has been short, its impact on sailing has been great. Without question, the vision

VALUES *of this* FAMILY

Success based on Old World tradition and New World ingenuity

*I*N MAY OF 1959, A YOUNG TOOL AND DIEMAKER by the name of Bernardus Vermeulen emigrated from The Netherlands to western Canada with his wife, Leidy, and hopes for a bright future. He had $52 in his pocket when he landed in Vancouver, Canada.

Over the next several years, Ben Vermeulen worked in the steel business, fabricating and erecting structural components for the Pacific Northwest's burgeoning construction industry. Eventually, he saw an opportunity in the boat building business and set up West Bay Boat Builders, a small operation on the south bank of the Fraser River in Delta, British Columbia. The year was 1967.

Early on, Vermeulan built in wood and steel. It's been all fiberglass since the 1970s.

Even before Vermeulen had finished his first shed, a local contractor named Stan Cassidy walked through the door with a set of drawings from the board of Ed Monk, Sr., and a request for a good boat.

"She was a 42-foot trawler yacht, all-wood construction, carvel planked, wedged seams. We made an agreement and the challenge was on. The boat was named *Aquaknot II* and was delivered in the fall of 1969."

Cassidy enjoyed his West Bay for 27 years until he passed away. *Aquaknot II's* new owners, Bet Oliver and her husband Alan, have renamed the vessel *Longboard,* and she can still be seen cruising the coves and harbors of the Pacific Northwest.

Following the success of *Aquaknot* there were calls for fishing boats, small steel tugs and refurbishing of wooden pleasure boats. "We also built crew boats and water taxis, most of them triple- and quadruple-screw vessels capable of forty to fifty knot speeds. They were scary, especially in Pacific Northwest waters with all the logs

1. Humble beginnings: The small shed that first held the family's entire operation has since grown into a complex that covers more than five acres. 2. Many of the early boats were destined for commercial use and thus were stoutly constructed to withstand the rigors of Northwestern waters, beneath which lurk huge logs known as "deadheads" that float under the surface, poised to hole any but the strongest hull. 3. The building of a shipyard demanded a strong hand and boundless energy. The young Vermeulens, Ben and Leidy, had both.

Compiled by MARK T. MASCIAROTTE

West Bay's operation grew in direct proportion to its reputation. As word spread that Ben Vermeulen built a quality product, the company began to add yachtsmen to its customer list. New designs for recreational use — classic cruisers and swift, stylish fishing boats — began to appear from West Bay's new shed on the Fraser River, and soon the company began its final metamorphosis into large yachtbuilding.

and debris," Vermeulen recalled. Later, the young company would use its expertise with fast crew boats to build law enforcement agency patrol boats.

In the 1970s, fiberglass boats were becoming more and more in demand. Vermeulen soon realized fiberglass was a material ideally suited to the extraordinary demands of Northwest winters. Sensing the importance of this trend, a new phase of construction started at West Bay.

"They'd call me in the winter and say 'We have to go through six to ten inches of ice. Will this fiberglass hull take the punishment?' I'd tell them, 'As long as you can get the bow on top of the ice to break it up you will be okay.' Ice doesn't do too much to fiberglass; the impact is very noisy, though.

"One day, a logger friend called and told me he had dropped his twenty-six–foot wooden crew boat from a crane and broken her back. She was a pretty little lapstrake Turner design, very seaworthy," Vermeulen recalled. "He suggested we make a mold out of her and put the boat into production. Always looking for opportunities, I agreed. This decision heralded the introduction of our first pleasure boat, the Centennial Series. They were great little sea boats and we built about twenty-five of them from twenty-one to twenty-six feet." West Bay's production at this time also included water taxies, log-salvage boats and small salmon trawlers.

In 1976, Vermeulen installed a marine ways to carry out repair work, a move that helped the company weather the recession that had stricken Canada. The new construction drought lasted nearly five dreary years, until West Bay began receiving new orders

thanks to a series of successful crewboat refits.

Today, West Bay encompasses over five acres in Delta, B.C., a far cry from the original roadside yard built more than 30 years ago. There is 54,000 square feet of covered space in six buildings, the largest of which is 200 feet by 65 feet that can easily accommodate vessels up to 160 feet in length. And where only 60 employees labored in 1994, over 345 employees now operate two shifts. An additional staff of 15 builds hulls and decks in the company's leased facility in Bellingham, Washington, under the same roof that once sheltered Uniflyte's original yard.

Each member of the family is involved with the company on a daily basis. Vermeulen's wife, Leidy, is the company's interior designer, assisted by their daughter, Rochelle. Son Wes is vice-president of marketing. The couple's younger son, Bas, is vice president of engineering and production, and son-in-law Danny Kilberg manages the CAD department.

In addition to the factory's sales effort, which is augmented by marketing manager Bruce Taylor, West Bay products are sold through a network of dealers in Washington, California and Florida, as well as in Ontario, Canada and Auckland, New Zealand.

It is interesting to note that the West Bay name has nothing at all to do with the location of the shipyard, despite there being a body of water of that name in the Vancouver area. In fact, the name was coined after the Vermeulens joined the names of their two sons, Wes and Bas and searched for a word or phrase that would employ both. As to the origin of SonShip, which has been adopted as the company's tradename, Ben Vermulen, a deeply religious man, expresses the intent best: "God's signature over all creation is His Son, the Christ. All things are created through him and we are co-creators with him in a never-ending process. That's why we put His name behind our product."

The next keystone for West Bay came from lines laid down by Vermeulen for what was known as the West Bay Lloyd 4500. "She was a forty-five-foot motor yacht named after a family friend and based on the company's successful forty-foot crew-boat hull." Later, some of the 4500s were extended to 52 feet. All in all, 18 of these boats were built. Today, the Lloyd 4500/52 is very sought after because of her seaworthiness and maneuverability.

With this series, West Bay became a major player in the yacht building business. Depending on the propulsion package, the 52 had a top speed of up to 32 knots, which is still great performance for a cruising boat of this size. The success of the 52-footers created the platform for further growth.

In the company's quest to always unite form and function, Howard Apollonio and Glade Johnson were brought in to develop new tooling and styling for what has become the company's best-known boat. The 58-foot SonShip is the final iteration of the original Lloyd 4500 motor yacht. Due to her clean lines, forward-thinking styling, comfortable arrangement and quality finish, the 58 has proved a remarkable success, with West Bay delivering one boat a month to market. Over its production history the series has enjoyed continuous refinement, and to date more than 50 of the handsome boats have been ordered.

A Decade of Exponential Growth

The SonShip 58 continues to be the company's most popular model in terms of units sold. The current line of West Bay SonShip yachts includes the recently introduced 6000 and 7000-series of motor yachts, a group that includes 68-, 78-, and 80-foot models with plans on the drawing board for two 85-foot designs. The company also builds motor yachts of 92, 98 and 103 feet on hulls supplied by Westport Shipyard.

The output from the Delta facility has reached 15 to 18 launches per year, production that makes West Bay SonShip Yachts Canada's biggest yacht manufacturer, according to a recent story in the *Vancouver Sun*. Documenting the wide audience for West Bay yachts, the *Sun* story last summer was illustrated with a photograph of the lift ship *Dock Express II* loaded with four West Bay yachts destined for Fort Lauderdale, about as far away from the yard as is possible in the Northern Hemisphere.

Smaller boats find their way East in an equally interesting fashion. Those under 80 feet are run from the factory to the Pacific Ocean, south to Oregon, then up the Columbia River to the head of navigation on the Snake River in Idaho. There, they are lifted out of the water and trucked to Texas or Wisconsin to be re-launched and delivered to their final destinations. Upon arrival, the boats receive complete factory service. The trip serves as an excellent shakedown cruise and assessment of all equipment and machinery prior to release to the new owner.

West Bay SonShip exudes stability. Careful planning is evident as one walks through the yard. In the best tradition of Dutch ship-building, innovation often takes a back seat to reliability to preserve the value of the product. Second-generation builder Wes Vermeulen explains that although West Bay has developed or refined various pieces of equipment or for on-board systems, the focus in the design office has always been to increase the quality and value of the company's boats incrementally.

1. Today, West Bay SonShip is the most successful yachtbuilding company in Canada. The riverside facility has expanded to include 54,000 square feet of covered space. 2. The same high quality on which the company's reputation is based is evident in each of the trades. Attention to detail can be seen as one visits the various shops and inspects the fiberglass work, metal fabrication and joinery. 3. West Bay's newest building is capable of handling yachts of up to 160 feet in length, while providing easy access to workers and equipment handling machinery. Shops are located on a mezzanine to enhance production, and most tooling can be stored inside within reach of the building's overhead crane. 4. Launch and retrieval of boats is a simple matter, thanks to deep water alongside the company's wharf. The arrangement facilitates repair and testing activities as well as providing a controlled program for the launch of new vessels.

NEIL RABINOWITZ

With its impressive range of boats and plans underway to expand the line, West Bay SonShip continues to offer a size and style to appeal to most any yachtsman. Shown here is the 98-foot *Protocol* leading the fleet through the incomparable waters off British Columbia. Close on her heels are the enclosed flybridge 80-foot *MariAdele,* the 84-foot *Segue,* the 75-foot *Shipshaw* and the 58-foot *Serenité.* Each West Bay yacht is designed to provide the customer with a quality product that will stand up to prolonged use while maintaining its value over time. Indeed, the company's first yacht, *Aquaknot II,* is still in use — and in nearly perfect condition — after 30 years of use. Whether the company will someday build a boat large enough to fill its main construction hall remains to be seen, but West Bay's founder enjoys the prospect and the exciting picture it paints in his mind's eye.

"We've adopted some things over the years that other builders now do as well," he said. "But the goal here is to constantly better the product."

For example, all major components and structures utilize vacuum-bag sandwich construction methods. Hull and house sides consist of fiberglass knits, Corcell foams and isophthalic resin. Rigid decks are achieved with end-grain balsa core and knitted laminates are laid over urethane foam to create the hull stringers.

Interior joinery is crafted in oak and is a available with a variety of finishes. The workmanship is to the finest standard to be found in a semi-custom motor yacht. West Bay prides itself in its ability to do most work in-house.

"It makes for a busy plant," admits Wes Vermeulen, "but we are better able to control quality this way. We have some very talented craftsmen here, which is one of the reasons our customers seek us out."

The Vermeulens are committed to the engineering process. Jack Sarin has been involved with West Bay's hulls since 1992, and each new model is tank tested at BC Research. Glade Johnson continues to provide styling, and an in-house design staff of 14 has access to the latest CAD tools with which to deliver the best possible design and engineering for West Bay boats. The suite of software includes AutoCad 14, AutoShip and MultiSurf, and details are produced for

NEIL RABINOWITZ

Two generations working together: Ben and Leidy (seated) with Wes, Rochelle and Bas (left to right).

all departments, including joinery. Because performance is a critical element in West Bay's boat-building philosophy, the engineering department constantly monitors the weight and balance of each boat through the construction process.

The company's new advertising campaign carries the family message to readers. The first ad in the series shows the Vermeulen boys as youngsters, sitting with their father. The copy talks about tradition while the photos show the company's latest products. As the series progresses, the family grows until, in the latest release, readers meet the third generation of seafaring Vermeulens, as life-jacket-clad two- and three-year-olds, enjoying the scenery through the shiny ring of a hawsehole.

These traditions appeal to customers, many of whom return to West Bay for new boats as their needs have changed. The loyalty is evident in such examples as the sale of the first 7000-series motor yacht, purchased by a previous West Bay customer before the first hull was ever launched.

When asked whether he wants to build even bigger boats in the future, Ben Vermeulen smiles and shrugs slightly.

"Sure," he states. "Someday I'd like to do a 150-footer. Then I can look back and say that I've built everything I've ever wanted to build."

Will he do it? Grinning, he points to a proof of his latest ad. It reads, "The best is yet to come." ✛

BUILDING on STRENGTH

With a strong commercial background, Amels quietly delivers magnificent megayachts

Nearly as large as the shop beside her, a traditional Dutch workboat rests on blocks in Makkum, the home of Amels Shipyard.

N 1661, THE DUTCH ROYAL FAMILY GAVE CHARLES II OF England a small ship to celebrate his restoration to the throne. A small sloop of 52 feet, *Mary* was the first of many *jachten,* or yachts, that would soon establish Holland as the world's foremost yacht-building center.

Mary's design was similar to the type of vessel much used by Holland's then pre-emi-nent navy for ferrying VIPs, dispatches and small stores between larger vessels at sea and from ship to shore. Although often armed with small cannon, these fast, elegant boats were also appointed with comfortable interiors, lavishly gilded and painted by Holland's best craftsmen and artists.

Careful planning and attention to detail are hallmarks of the Amels yachtbuilding organization, founded in 1918.

The Dutch village of Makkum is no stranger to this fine tradition. Men have been building ships here on the northern edge of the Ijsselmeer since the 17th century, and it was here that the Amels shipyard was established in 1918.

Originally located in the center of town, the company first specialized in the construction of small commercial vessels. Its reputation for high quality was soon established, and that legacy has continued through several generations of the Amels family and their employees.

In the early postwar period, expanding activities and inquiries for larger vessels resulted in a move to a new site on land reclaimed from the Zuiderzee. Between 1949 and 1967, 150 vessels were delivered to clients, including container ships, tankers, freighters, special craft for the Royal Dutch Navy, passenger ships, and supply vessels for the offshore oil industry. Indeed, the range of designs built by Amels during this period can only be described as astonishing. It is clear that many of the modern motor yachts produced at Amels during the past two decades owe their strength and quality to this impressive pedigree.

Work aplenty: the shipyard as it appeared in the mid-1960s.

Spectacular side-launches such is this were no longer carried out after the great building hall was erected in 1967.

❧ Compiled by JONATHAN EASTLAND *☙*

Amels is widely known for the extensive range of superb vessels that have been built at the Makkum shipyard. 1. *Maupiti* is a lovely 46-meter expedition yacht with a diesel-electric propulsion system. 2. *Katalina* was the first of many yachts built in collaboration with DIANA Yacht Design. 3. One of the largest in Europe, the enormous building hall boats an area of over 177,000 cubic meters and can easily accommodate separate enclosures that facilitate fairing and painting as well as allowing covered, climate-controlled drydocking for repairs and refits. 4. Deep water surrounds the shipyard, allowing vessels to be moored alongside for dock trials or outfitting.

Several Amels-built commercial vessels are worthy of note for their elegant lines, innovative engineering and performance. Were it not for the fact that they were designed to carry freight, some would, even today, make excellent selections as expeditionary or research yachts.

The hull of the *Geestland* for example, a fruit carrier delivered in 1960, sported a long, elegant sheer and canoe stern surmounted by a classic, three-deck, aft-mounted superstructure. This 300-foot (91.4-meter) vessel was fitted with a single 4,000-hp gas turbine and easily outran *Corantijn,* a newer vessel of similar size, equipped with standard diesel power.

The 196-foot (59 meter) *Spica,* built in the 1970s for the Netherlands Pilotage Authority, was one of three similar special-purpose vessels designed by the Dutch Navy and the pilotage service for work in the southern sectors of the North Sea — a lee shore where, in winter, weather is often appalling. These ships are used as seagoing bases for pilots and for the small "jolly boats" that transfer pilots to and from their assignments. Therefore, special ballast tanks were fitted to the class to enable them to remain on station and to perform their duties in severe rolling conditions. A testament to their good looks is *Altair,* one of three sister-ships, which required only a modernization of her superstructure styling and a cruising interior in her recent conversion to a yacht.

To increase efficiency, improve delivery times and produce an even higher standard of workmanship and finish, Amels management built a remarkable covered building and drydock in 1967, an undertaking that took several years to complete. Today, the huge facility at Makkum comprises a 120-meter (390 foot) building dock enabling the construction of vessels up to 7,500 tons deadweight, well beyond the requirements of the largest megyachts.

The main building hall covering the dock measures 168 by 37 meters and has a height of 28.5 meters. The caisson-type dock door is hinged at the sill and is provided with floodable tanks. A second door may be placed in any position in the dock to prevent flooding where hull assembly is still in progress. Overhead cranes with a lifting capacity of 30 tons can be remotely controlled from any location in the hall or can be operated from the cab. In the first 10 years, some 25 large construction projects were successfully completed in this remarkable facility.

Thanks to the new hall and the critical and commercial success of the 158-foot (48 meter) *Katalina,* its first major yacht project, management decided to concentrate exclusively on new yacht construction and refit. With a highly skilled work force and decades of quality shipbuilding already in place, the transition to luxury motor yacht production progressed easily.

Managing director Sjoerd Veeman recalls that the work force was so proud of its efforts that they often brought their families to the yard over the weekend to show them the projects.

"Our philosophy," he explains, "centers on the business of conventional yacht building, which we believe we do better than anyone else."

Without question, the craftsmen at Amels are among the best in the industry. Most live nearby and serve an apprenticeship during which they are required to master at least two basic crafts applicable to yacht building before they can don the coveted white overalls that symbolize a fully qualified Amels yachtbuilder.

When work began on *Katalina,* Amels worked closely together with DIANA Yacht Design, an association that started a new chapter for both companies and produced a series of safe, seaworthy and luxurious vessels that are now legendary. Those designs, each fully tested at the Netherlands Ship Model Basin at Wageningen, reflect the tradition of commercial successes and what was to soon characterize the Amels yacht. In addition to *Katalina,* the superb *Jamaica Bay, Secret Love* and Jon Bannenberg's *My Gail III* are examples of Amel's classic displacement style.

Launched in 1993, Maupiti is an eye-catching exploration yacht

Amels maintains a staff of design professionals to augment each client's design team.

with true worldwide capability. The rugged, 151-foot (46 meter) vessel is fitted with a helideck and is further distinquished as the only Amels yacht to have diesel-electric propulsion.

"This is an area in which we have quite some experience," remarked Veeman, adding that studies for other motor yachts with diesel-electric propulsion have been completed. "In our view, constant power loading results in better efficiency than conventional diesel propulsion, adding life to the main engines."

In 1997, Amels' 50-meter (164 foot) *Tigre d'Or* became the first yacht in the world to meet the British Maritime Coastguard Agency (MCA) rules established to improve passenger safety in newly constructed yachts. Designer Terence Disdale overcame the problems of aesthetic compatibility with the new rules, and the yacht has proven to be one of the builder's best launches to date, affording her owner a seaworthy vessel of uncompromising luxury and winning a *ShowBoats* Award for Best Motor Yacht Interior. The three projects under construction in the fall of 1999, ranging in size from 51 to 61 meters and due for delivery in 2001, as well as the recently launched 54-meter *Sarafsa,* also meet MCA rules.

In recent years Amels has delivered two of the largest private yachts ever launched in Holland, 75-meter *Monkaj* in 1995 and 71-meter *Boadicea* in 1999.

After being sold by the Amels family to foreign interests in the late 1980s, Amels returned to wholly Dutch ownership in 1991 when it became part of the celebrated Damen Group of shipbuilding and ship-repair companies. As it has since its founding, Amels continues to enjoy a unique position and reputation throughout the world by being able to provide its clients unparalleled support, expert advice and unmatched product quality. ✛

PHOTOS 1, 3 & 4 BY ROY ROBERTS/OWEN AGENCY, 2 BY MARILYN MOWER

1. The Amels shipyard today, one of the world's foremost yacht-building facilities and a member of the renowned Damen Group of shipbuilding companies. 2. Amels latest delivery is 71-meter *Boadicea,* styled inside and out by Terence Disdale. 3-4. Thoughtful design, proud craftsmanship and flawless execution work hand-in-hand to ensure that Amels yachts have a measure of safety and comfort for passengers and crew that continues to be an industry standard. Working with the finest designers, naval architects and engineers, Amels yachtbuilders carry on the tradition of quality construction and finish that have made them famous. As in all successful shipyards, computer-aided design used in concert with centralized billing and inventory enhance project management and coordination as well as providing real-time job tracking. Nevertheless, throughout the construction process, each yacht receives individual attention as, piece by piece, each customer's yacht progresses 4. from concept renderings and models to finished product. 5. The results are always spectacular, as evidenced by the remarkable 75-meter *Montkaj,* shown during trials.

ITALIAN PERFECTION

Originally a builder of small production boats, CRN constructed its megayacht fortunes by looking East.

*W*ITH ONE OF THE LONGER HISTORIES IN THE LUX-
ury yacht market, CRN in 36 years has completed
more than 114 custom yachts of indisputable quality,
including 15 motor yachts over 150 feet.

Unlike many of the country's yachtbuilders, CRN is situ-
ated in the bustling port of Ancona on Italy's Adriatic coast. Nearby,
large fishing fleets and ferries dart back and forth from Greece,
Corfu, Split and Dubrovnik. Ancona has been Italy's main trading
post with the East since Roman times. Alongside the quay, old
traders' warehouses date back to the 15th century. Its shipbuilding
tradition continues with large commercial yards like Fincantieri and
Morini, which now build tankers, fast ferries and bulk carriers.

In 1963, CRN founder Sanzio Nicolini decided to begin building luxury yachts. Securing an old WW II seaplane hangar, and hir-
ing local craftsmen experienced in commercial boats, he began
offering 30-foot steel hulls with wood superstructures. Both his reputation and his clientele soon grew. Moving up to larger motor yachts,
he soon switched to aluminum for the superstructures. Classic CRN
designs, like the 75-foot Super Conero, named after the mountain-
ous cliffs behind Ancona, can still be seen cruising all over the Eastern Mediterranean.

In 1973 Gian Domenico Palmerini, an enthusiastic investor
from Rome, joined the company's management, allowing the creative Nicolini to focus on production. During the 1970s the yard concentrated on a series of 90- to 108-foot semi-displacement steel
yachts designed by Carlo Riva, who worked as consultant naval architect. In 1978, cementing an extraordinary learning curve, the yard
launched its first yacht over 150 feet, *Fathal Khair.*

By the 1980s, the majority of CRN's clients were from the eastern Mediterranean. Greek ship owners and Middle Eastern oil sheiks
recognized the yard's reputation for quality workmanship and dis-
cretion. Ever-larger state yachts were built for the royal families of
Bahrain, Qatar and Saudi Arabia.

However, the fact that 80 percent of CRN's clients were now
concentrated in the Middle East left the company vulnerable to any
downturn in those economies. For stability, during the Gulf War CRN
diversified into refit and commercial work. In 1984 Palmerini
acquired the majority of the yard's shares and moved CRN into a
new shipyard, reorganizing the workforce to rely more on local sub-

Secure behind a man-made breakwater, the huge CRN Ancona facility
has direct access to the Adriatic Sea and an all-important rail link for
delivery of raw materials. The nearly half-million square-foot site
includes 205,387 square feet of construction sheds.

The origin of CRN's distinctive second-chine hull styling can be seen
on this 1973 photo of a 75-foot flush deck Super Conero, the first large
yacht series for the builder.

The 1999 conversion of *Awal* to *Alwaeli* involved a three-meter extension to the yacht's stern.

PHOTOS COURTESY OF CANTIERI RIPARAZIONI NAVALI

Compiled by JASON HOLTOM

1, 3. *Azzurra,* now named *Neninka,* remains one of the yard's best calling cards. Styled by Gerhard Gilgenast with a Paola Smith interior, the 156-foot yacht featured a full-beam skylounge and clearstory windows in the master stateroom. She was built for the yard's first U.S. client. 2. Commercial manager Marcello Maggi (left) and Norberto Feretti, chairman of the Feretti Group, announced plans for a 141-foot CRN spec boat named *Magnifico* in September 1999. The Ancona facility will also be the fitting-out site for Feretti's Custom line of boats to 112 feet. 4. *Sahab IV* equipped with Ulstein Z-drives to reduce vibration, was launched in 1977.

contractors, many of whom work only for the CRN yard.

The yard looked hard for new markets, and in 1986 the turning point came with the contract for the 156-foot *Azzurra* from its first U.S. owner, Ed Sacks. "My decision to build at CRN," says Sacks, "was largely based upon the recommendation of the naval architect Gerhard Gilgenast. It was Gilgenast's view that the Italian yards had been much maligned over the years, in the sense that you went to Italy to build a 'pretty boat,' but that for real engineering one needed to build at a Dutch or German yard. Gerhard, who had already had experience building there, felt that this was a myth, and he and CRN and the rest of us became partners in disproving this public perception."

Azzurra became the watershed vessel for the yard and a defining moment for the design team, which included Paola

Smith for the interior. "While expectations were high," says Sacks, "no one had any way of knowing that the combination of the systems, design, styling, and aesthetics were ahead of their time or that *Azzurra* was destined to become an industry standard." *Azzurra* set another milestone in the industry as the first yacht to charter at over $100,000 per week.

Azzurra was built to American Bureau of Shipping (ABS) classification, although most CRN yachts have been built to Lloyd's 100+A1. The last two yachts built at the yard, 164-foot *Pestifer* and a 210-footer still to be named, were built to British MCA classification. The latter project has classic styling and a rounded transom. She is fitted with two sets of bilge keels developed in the towing tank in Vienna and Berg four-blade variable pitch propellers.

While CRN has worked with many naval architects over the years, the strong in-house design team has allowed the evolution of the characteristic CRN hull shape recognized for stability and seakeeping, typically with reduced draft and greater beam. The double chine of the bow reduces spray and pitching and gives CRN yachts their distinctive look.

Naval architect Paolo Scanu, who has worked on the last four CRN projects, notes the yard's conservative practices are based on long shipbuilding experience. "They sometimes recommend extra steel to my scantlings," says Scanu, "The yachts are built to last. I have also found the yard has a more flexible approach than many Northern European yards when it comes to working out the engine-room and systems designs.

"The CRN workforce has magic in its hands. Cesare the teak-rail man is an artist. He can do anything he wants with teak. He molds it like clay. Sergio the steel work foreman, Enrico the plumber, Maurizio

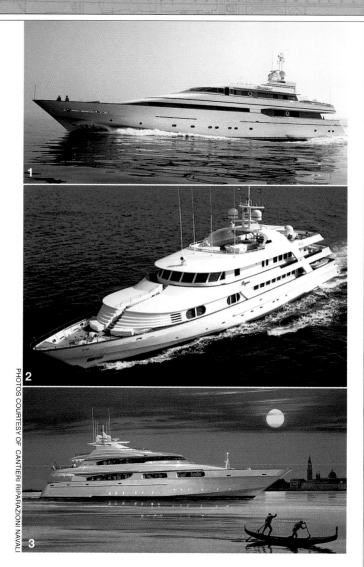

1. CRN's stable includes the sleek 164-foot *Maracunda* launched in 1990 with a steel hull and aluminum superstructure and **2.** classically styled 157-foot *Pegaso* launched in 1996. **3.** *Magnifico,* styled by Nuvolari and Lenard, will incorporate styling features both classical and contemporary, while retaining the yard's characteristic chine element. *Magnifico* will deliver in 2001.

and Moreno in the technical office, Dainiele, who heads design, Alberto in production, Antonio the project manager and Stefano the engineer are all people for whom we have feelings of sincere friendship and appreciation," says Scanu.

CRN's facilities are impressive. With 205,387 square feet of construction sheds, they are capable of building and refitting custom yachts under cover up to 260 feet in length and 1,000 tons in displacement. The yard also has a 280-foot dock for fitting out. Eighty percent of CRN-built yachts come back to the yard for refits and upgrades. This maintains continuity for both the owner, crew and the yacht. It also demonstrates a high level of client trust.

CRN's location has forced the workforce to be more self-sufficient than many builders. The in-house naval architecture team led by Moreno Guerrieri, — who has been with the yard for 25 years —creates its own programs for plasma cutting as well as coordinates all tank-testing and all systems engineering.

Interior designer Terence Disdale, who has had three major projects built at CRN including two over 200 feet, has seen this atmosphere at work. "I enjoy working with CRN,"says Disdale,"There is a creative and positive atmosphere."

A new chapter for CRN opened in September 1999 with the 100-percent acquisition of the shipyard by the Ferretti Group. The Group, with a turnover of $150 million, is aiming to reach $240 million by 2003 with further acquisitions as well as investment in the existing companies, which now include Ferretti, Ferretti Custom Line, Bertram USA, and Pershing. The Group has 10 shipyards in Italy and the U.S. with a total workforce of 600.

Marcello Maggi, commercial manager of CRN, enthusiastically supported the acquisition. "I believe that CRN's entrance into the Ferretti Group is a very important opportunity for future growth. CRN, with its history, prestige, and the quality of its boats, will evolve with Ferretti into a shipyard with an industrial and programmed outlook that can rely upon very strong commercial, financial and organizational resources."

Among the first changes will be the introduction of new production techniques and preparation of space on the Ancona shipyard site for fitting out the Ferretti Custom Line of 94-, 104- and 112-footers as well as the new 85-foot Navetta displacement yacht.

Future Projects

In September 1999 CRN started the construction of the 141-foot Nuvolari Lenard-styled *Magnifica,* a speculative-build boat for delivery in early 2001. Its design was preceded by a six-month period of minute market analysis.

Norberto Feretti, the head of Feretti Group, has conceived the *Magnifica* project as a showcase for CRN's expertise by offering a very complete boat built to the highest CRN standards and MCA compliance. "Functionality and quality rather than economics have been the consideration in developing *Magnifica.* The aim is to level out the flow of production for the yard and offer the owner a much faster turnaround," says Maggi. "Many owners do not want to wait two years for a new build, and we believe that not all owners want to go through the experience of developing a yacht from scratch. *Magnifica* will offer a tested design, not an unknown one-off."

Norbeto Ferretti has served as the imaginary client. Dan Lenard of Nuvolari and Lenard says, "Norbetto has a very special feeling about yachts and life onboard. He was very particular, for example, that we should include a good-size tender in a transom garage.

"Working around the Novurania Equator 600 we have created a garage where all the equipment is in place, including diving bottles and jetskis. We even have made space for a transom crane and a Mercedes Smart Car."

Magnifica's hull styling maintains the CRN family feeling with the military-like chine forward and the angle of the bow that is recognized the world over as the CRN Ancona look. She will no doubt represent both a testament to CRN's distinguished past and an inspired statement for a promising future. ✢

•Royal Huisman•

WOODEN PUNTS
to
MEGAYACHTS

Five generations of boat builders have concentrated on excellence in sailing

ONE THING IS CERTAIN, WHEN YOU DUST OFF YOUR copy of *The Megayacht Century* in 10, 20 or more years' time, the name The Royal Huisman Shipyard will still be synonymous with the world's finest luxury sailing yachts. In 1984 the Huisman Shipyard celebrated its own century in boat building and added "Royal" to its title, an accolade bestowed by Queen Beatrix of Holland in recognition of the status and success of the yard and its export achievements.

As the last days of 1999 slip into history a fresh fleet of Huisman yachts has been commissioned, turning dreams into bluewater realities for the next millennium. But before exploring the possibilities for the future, we should look at how a small family boat-building business in the tiny hamlet of Ronduite, Holland, grew from humble, wooden-shoe beginnings to become the only "Royal" yacht builder in Holland.

It is not surprising that the great maritime nations of the past centuries continue to celebrate their skills by building the world's finest ships and yachts. The maritime history of the Dutch nation is extensively chronicled, but behind the popular images of Old Masters depicting Dutch merchantmen lies a shipbuilding heritage that, in volume, would be awesome even in the mechanised world of today. The exponential advancements in yacht building technology over the last decades of the 20th Century can perhaps best be illustrated by revisiting 1993, when Royal Huisman Shipyard hosted a special event for designers

In 1971 the family moved to Vollenhove to a site that would enable them to launch yachts of deeper draft and wider beam.

and naval architects entitled IDEA. The conference explored the future in yacht building and the techniques and technology that beckoned on the horizon. The assembled audience was enthralled by demonstrations of virtual-reality software, 3-D modeling, talk of composites, carbon fiber and exotic alloys.

The passing of just seven years has seen most of these developments become reality, and in turn spawn even more advancements.

The Ronduit yard was established in 1884 by the second generation of Huismans to build boats. The original yard founded by Jan Peters Huisman in the 1820s was in Blauwe Hand.

WESTERINK FOTOGRAFIE

The fourth and fifth generations of Huismans delivered 151-foot *Hyperion*, the largest sloop of the century in 1999.

JACK SOMER

Walter Huisman, 55 years a boat builder, has seen his company grow from wooden ships to the most exquisite luxury yachts.

⁂ *Compiled by* ROY ROBERTS

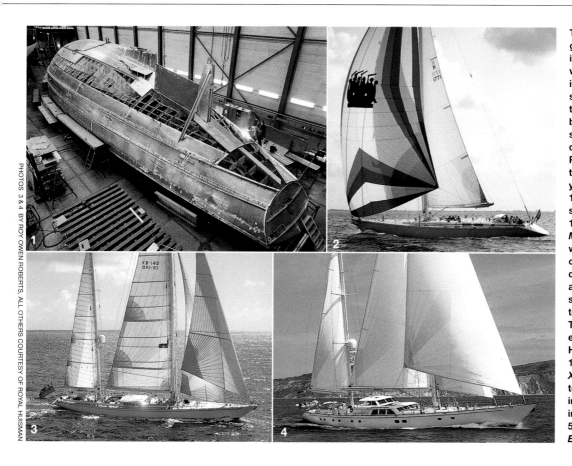

The Huisman shipyard gained its Royal designation in 1984 and switched from wood to steel construction in the early 1950s. It would shift materials again, this time to aluminum, in 1964, beginning with a series of 15 sweet 30-foot racer cruisers designed by van de Stadt. Royal Huisman now builds the largest aluminum sailing yachts in the world.
1. Shown here in her plating stage is Ted Hood designed 133-foot *Surama*. 2. *Metolius,* launched in 1992 was a fast 83-foot racer cruiser. 3. *Cyclos III,* designed by Ron Holland and Andrew Winch, represented a huge leap in technology for the yard. This 139-footer was delivered just six years after Huisman first crossed the 100-foot bar with *Whirlwind XII*. 4. *Juliet* was massive in terms of volume. Launched in 1993, she was the indirect inspiration for *Hyperion*. 5. Royal Huisman refitted *Endeavour* in 1989.

As usual, the Dutch maritime industry has been on the cutting edge. For instance, Huisman's Rondal subsidiary recently made the world's largest one-piece carbon fiber mast for *Hyperion* plus deck hatches and spars of the same material.

In the same way that computers have revolutionized the broader manufacturing industries, the digital revolution has been harnessed to provide on-board networks for yachts, even to producing the operating manuals on CD-ROM, including in-build digital images captured by digital cameras.

The century-long journey of the Royal Huisman Shipyard began in 1884, when Wolter Huisman's grandfather set up shop in Ronduite to build the local style boats. Called "puntas" they were used by farmers to transport cattle, hay and other goods along the maze of canals in central Holland, and by fishermen to work the rich fishing grounds of the salty Zuyder Zee.

By 1928, Wolter's father, Jan, was employing similar designs tested by time and local wind and sea conditions to make sturdy wooden pleasure boats. In 1954, however, Walter — fresh from his Navy experience in rough North Sea conditions aboard rugged steel ships — convinced his father that steel was a much better material for building strong, long-lasting boats.

After some 30 Huisman steel yachts, the 1960s saw new materials such as glass-reinforced plastic and aluminum, become popular for their strength and lightness. In 1964 the Huismans began working with aluminum. By 1971, when Wolter's father retired, the business had moved to its present location in the small town of Vollenhove building exclusively in aluminum. It was a wise decision. The popularity of aluminum hulls has propelled the yard to its current success, with hull number 374 already commissioned.

Aluminum proved to be the ideal building material for racing yachts, and it was a string of highly successful campaigns by yachts like *Pinta 1* (1969), *Running Tide* (1969), *Sabina V* (1976), and *Midnight Sun* (1979), that put Yachtwerf W. Huisman BV in the public domain.

Big boat racing soon became the order of the day with Huisman launching such important yachts as 65-foot *Flyer I* competing in the 1977 Whitbread Round the World race. But soon the word "maxi" — the abbreviation for racing yachts at the maximum length within the RORC rules — began to dominate the talk at the world's yacht clubs. This move into larger boats such as 76-foot *Helisara* brought about a sequence of events that changed the position of the Huisman yard forever.

Cornelious von Rietschoten's maxi-rater *Flyer II* dominated the 1981/82 Whitbread Race, taking line honors on all legs. The publicity *Flyer II* gained for the Huisman Shipyard was global: While racers had long known of the benefits of aluminum construction, *Flyer II* caught the imagination of cruising sailors who also wanted the speed, strength, responsiveness and volume the material provided.

The first of the new breed were *Belle Fontaine* (1981) and *Volodor* (1982) both at 81 feet. In 1984, *Cyclos II* topped the Huisman fleet at 92 feet. Two years later Ron Holland-designed *Whirlwind XII* raised the bar again to an overall length of 103 feet. *Whirlwind* remained the biggest Huisman yacht for only a year when she was eclipsed by the groundbreaking 112-foot *Acharné* (now *Diamond Forever),* with her startling lines by Jon Bannenberg.

Size, they say, is not everything, as Huisman proved in sweet collaborations with the late Henry Scheel *(Hetairos* and *Foftein)* and the S & S designed *Ebb Tide.* Punctuated by the rebuild of 130-foot *Endeavour* in 1989, the next milestone in size was the 139-foot Ron Holland/Andrew Winch collaboration *Cyclos III* in 1990.

The 132-foot twin centerboard Ted Hood ketch *Anakena* was designed with tremendous interior volume. She is shown sailing in photo 3 at right.

Each yacht produced by Huisman generates its own profound influence in yacht design and construction. For example, during the building of *Cyclos III,* another Huisman customer discussing his new yacht added considerably to her length as a result of seeing *Cyclos* taking shape. *Juliet* was launched in 1993, and at 143 feet remains a goliath in her class. *Juliet* set benchmarks both in size and luxury. A hefty book, *Juliet, The Building of a Masterpiece,* now rests in many a private library and has inspired many yachtsmen to pursue the quest for such a yacht.

One such yachtsman was Dr. Jim Clarke who came to the Royal Huisman Shipyard and in the process of building his yacht created a team that would push the boundaries of yacht building and technology to new zeniths of style and systems sophistication.

Gitana VI was part of Baron Edmund de Rothschild's famed racing fleet. Here she is competing for the French Admiral's Cup team. Huisman built many top Admiral's Cuppers before shifting to cruising yachts.

What a fitting way to round off the last days of the Millennium than by launching the world's largest sloop, 151-foot *Hyperion.*

For the Huisman family, the first chapters of the new century are already being written, with new orders such as the second Huisman-built *Borkumriff.* In the coming years ever more clients will enjoy the special Dutch hospitality and culture, admire the close teamwork and spirit unique to the Huisman yard and, in the words of Dr. Jim Clarke, enjoy the process of building "the shape of things to come." ☩

PHOTOS 2-5 BY ROY OWEN ROBERTS

1 & 2. *Borkumriff III* matched a modern roller-furling rig to classic Gloucester schooner lines by Henk Lunstroo. 4. *Surama* under her 9160 sq.ft. of sail. 5. The Vollenhove yard as it looks today. *Surama* dwarfs a classic Dutch leeboarder. 6.The projects under construction as the century draws to a close include (from left) 110-foot *Unfurled* designed by German Frers, 112-foot *Pamina* and 143-foot *Erica VII* from the boards of Ted Hood Design, and 99-foot *Foftein,* also by Frers.

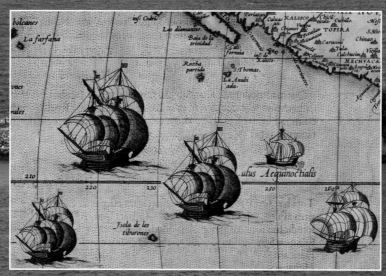

A Continuing Tradition
of Excellence Since 1866

Merrill-Stevens is the oldest continuously owned and operated yacht repair and refit facility in the world. Spanning five generations, Merrill-Stevens Dry Dock has established an extraordinary history of unsurpassed quality and service in the marine field.

The company was founded by James G. Merrill in 1866 and formally incorporated in 1888 by James Eugene Merrill, making Merrill-Stevens Florida's oldest continuously operating company. In the early 1900s, Merrill-Stevens was described as an "immense shipyard and dry docks visited by vessels from practically every port in the world."

Merrill-Stevens Dry Dock of today still maintains the high standards set forth at the company's inception. Located in South Florida with two facilities on the Miami River, Merrill-Stevens has evolved with changes and advances in the marine industry to its position today as the most respected name in marine services, marine products, yacht brokerage and charter services.

Whatever the scope of your yachting needs, contact the professionals at Merrill-Stevens Dry Dock, who stand behind five generations and more than a century of service, quality and customer satisfaction.

James G. Merrill
Founder 1866

James Eugene Merrill
Incorporated 1888

James C. Merrill

James C. Merrill, Jr.

James C. Merrill III

Performance Over Time

"Aussie Rules" captures the spirit of another era, gracing its guests with genuine luxury and beauty. Nineteenth century elegance and twenty first-century technologies blend together on this 142' Feadship. With perfect performance over time, "Aussie Rules" has everything you need for the journey of your dreams.

For more than 125 years, Marsh has evolved in step with the changing world. We have built a reputation for excellence in the development of innovative insurance solutions. Marsh Private Client Services clients can expect the best insurance counseling and advice for their luxury yachts, homes, automobiles, fine art and personal liability.

Performance over time, a measure of ourselves, a promise to our clients.

MARSH

1600 S.E. 17th Street • Suite 410 • Fort Lauderdale, FL 33316
Tel: (954) 763-1777 • Telefax: (954) 763-1668 • 1 (800) YACHT MM • http://www.jhmarshmc.com/pcs

Havelock Chambers • Queens Terrace • Southampton S014 3PP
Tel: +44 1703 318300 • Telefax: +44 1703 318391

YACHT PHOTO BY SHAW McCUTCHEON

EXPERIENCE COUNTS

Circa 1999

Background photo circa 1925

As Ft. Lauderdale developed, so did the need for a waterfront property specialist who knows and loves this tropical paradise. Intercoastal Realty has filled that need with great success for over a quarter century and has built a reputation as the most respected name in land on water.

From cottages to castles, Intercoastal Realty has quietly found homes on these waterways for yachtsmen and water lovers alike, including some very well known personalities.

We are so proud to be a part of this city's history, of watching it grow and growing with it. Fort Lauderdale has become one of the finest small cities in the country and Intercoastal Realty remains Fort Lauderdale's Realtor of choice.

INTERCOASTAL
REALTY, INC.
EXCLUSIVELY WATERFRONT

The Registry   LEADING ESTATES OF THE WORLD

1500 East Las Olas Boulevard
Fort Lauderdale, FL 33301
Office: (954) 467-1448 • Fax: (954) 467-6714
www.intercoastalrealty.com

It's the detail that make yachts unique. The same goes for insurances.

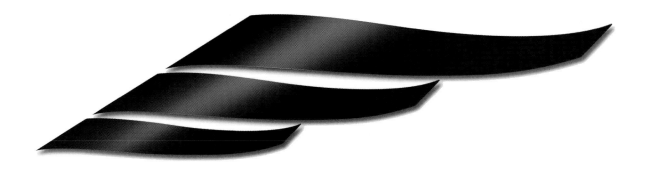

Why are we regarded as one of Europe's leading specialists for super-yacht insurances?

Perhaps because we offer individual cover for different requirements. Or is it because of our comprehensive advisory service which extends internationally far beyond the arrangement of insurances? It could also be because of our first-class in-house claims service with representatives in ports world-wide. But one thing is for sure: we have the same eye for detail in the individual construction of policies that great designers have for yachts.

Our policies are not as impressively beautiful as super yachts, but they are just as valuable.

PANTAENIUS
The Yacht Insurance Broker

D-20457 Hamburg, Postfach 11 07 29, Phone +49-40-37 09 10, Fax +49-40-37 09 11 09
Plymouth, Phone +44-1752-22 36 56, Fax +44-1752-22 36 37 · Monaco, Phone +377-97 98 43 43, Fax +377-97 98 43 40
Skive, Phone +45-97-51 33 88, Fax +45-97-51 33 89 · www.pantaenius.com · E-Mail: info@pantaenius.com

The Dream Yachts

Savarona

Lady Moura

Golden Odyssey

Eco

Blohm+Voss

Builders of exquisit yachts, fast ships and *intelligent*[3] naval vessels

Blohm+Voss GmbH · A company of ThyssenKrupp Industries · P.O.Box 10 07 20 · D-20005 Hamburg · Germany
For further information call Jürgen Engelskirchen: Phone: +49 40 31 19-13 01 · Fax: +49 40 31 19-33 38
E-mail: engelskirchen@blohmvoss.thyssen.com · http://www.blohmvoss.com

If only yachts could talk
this one would tell the grandest story!

m/y "Christina O"

Onassis' private yacht played host to Presidents and
Prime Ministers, Royalty and Film Stars...
Now she is ready to host the world's most discerning charterers.

Length: 325 feet (99.1 metres), completely refurbished and repowered to
accommodate up to 36 guests in 19 state rooms, in full compliance with
SOLAS requirements, pampered by 32 officers/crew.
Entire refurbishment managed/supervised by Titan.

 Titan, Hyde
& Torrance

Worldwide Central Agents

ATHENS: 81 Akti Miaouli, 185-38 Piraeus, Greece, Tel.: +301 428 0889, Fax: +301 418 2834, Telex: 241 988 TITA GR
LONDON: 18 Mansell Street, London E1-8AA, Tel.: +44 171 459 2000, Fax: +44 171 481 2966, Telex: 886 708 HYDE G

Selective list of Mega Yachts available for charter through our personal relationships

243' ECO

200' MYLIN IV

192' OCTOBER ROSE*

180' CLAIRE

175' KISSES

173' DESTINY♦

170' ACCLAIM

170' TOMMY

168' INTREPID II†

163' INDIAN ACHIEVER†

163' JEFFERSON BEACH†

153' QUINTESSENCE*

150' CONTEMPLATION†

149' KISSES*

149' SEA KINGDOM†

Merle Wood & Associates Continues to be the Global Leader in the Sale of the World's Finest Motoryachts

A Small Sampling of the Motoryachts in Excess of 125' Sold Through our Superyacht Division

1988 - 1998*†♦

*Sold Two Times   †Sold Three Times   ♦Sold Previously and Currently Offered for Sale

147' AMBROSIANA*

146' FORTUNATE SUN†

143' ALMAVIVA

142' PARAFIN

142' CAKEWALK

141' LADY DUVERA

141' SEA SEDAN

139' BRIDLEWOOD

139' ASPIRATION

139' LIMITLESS

138' JAMAICA BAY*

135' EL CORSARIO

132' FIFFANELLA*

132' LADY ALICE†♦

132' OCTOPUSSY

132' SEA PUMPKIN†

131' HEADLINES*♦

131' LADY KATHRYN*

131' TULLY

125' KALLISTA†

More and more owners of large yachts choose Koch, Newton and partners.

Sold
108´ Tauro

Sold
108´ Iliki III

Sold
112´ Renalo

Sold
112´ Aschanti

Sold
115´ Basil´s

Sold
118´ Blue Attraction

Sold
118´ Maalana S

Sold
121´ Extasea A

Sold
131´ Be Mine

Sold
135´ Zew

Sold
138´ Limitless

Sold
138´ Da

Sol

&partners
LÜRSSEN YACHTS

The right people
worldwide

From a network of international offices
we offer a comprehensive and interrelated

Building a New Yacht

Our brokers' depth and knowledge across the world's best shipyards is unrivalled. From the start, we work closely with you in establishing your requirements, arranging privileged access to the finest designers and naval architects of our age. From contract negotiation to delivery and sea trials, our service is total. Alternatively, we can use our global database and network to find an existing megayacht that meets your requirements.

Yacht Management

Our business is about customers' pleasure. And because the organisation of yachting can be onerous, we relieve you of the work involved.

Technical support: Refits, modernisation projects, new construction and maintenance.

Operations and Purchasing: Supplies and spare parts can be supplied at the most advantageous price.

Financial Management: We work with you to set realistic budgets and then rigorously apply them. The volume of business we place with insurers means we can guarantee you the best rates.

Crew Selection and Placement: A dedicated crew search and placement service, handling of contracts, insurance and payment. We will take care of all your manning requirements.

Rules and Regulations: Our in-house naval architects provide in-depth technical advice on the MCA Code of Practice.

Charter Management: Chartering out your yacht defrays costs and keeps on-board systems active. Our team of charter managers handle everything from marketing your boat to drawing up charter contracts.

Yachting Vacations

A holiday aboard a Camper & Nicholsons International yacht is the ultimate vacation. Indeed, yacht charters are a speciality of the house. We offer the cream of the world's yachts, including vessels from our own managed fleet, well-positioned to serve the Mediterranean, Caribbean and other cruising areas worldwide. Call for our latest Charter Annual.

Left 74m, 34-knot ECO - A George Nicholson project

Charter... The "Timeless" Vacation!

ROSENKAVALIER

Travel back in time to the 1930's to experience life aboard this 218' traditional yacht. Extensively refit in the 1990's, **ROSENKAVALIER** stands as proud and beautiful as when new. Elegant accommodations for up to 14 guests in 7 staterooms provide all the comforts of "home". Available in the Mediterranean during Summer months and in the Caribbean during the Winter months. Charter rate from $182,000 per week, plus expenses. Available for the Millennium!

PRINCESS TANYA

From the moment you step aboard, you will be impressed by the spaciousness of **PRINCESS TANYA!** This 189' classic yacht is the ultimate charter vessel for up to 18 guests in 9 sumptuous staterooms. To complement an array of activities found on board, there is also a private gymnasium and a beauty salon. Available in the Mediterranean during the Summer months and in the Caribbean during the Winter months Charter rate from $210,000 per week, plus expenses.

GRAND CRU

A blend of antique furnishing and modern fabrics are found on this classic 106' Burger yacht. By chartering **GRAND CRU** you will discover a special pampering enhanced by the European flair of her rich interior. There's even a fireplace in the main salon! Up to 6 guests can be accommodated in 3 private staterooms. Available in the New England area during Summer months and in the Florida/Bahamas area in the Winter months. Charter rate from $28,000 per week, plus expenses. Available for the Millennium!

PRINCESS SOPHIA

This charming yacht has had many "lives" since 1938. In her more recent years she has fulfilled the vacation dreams of charterers in the Mediterranean. **PRINCESS SOPHIA** is a "one of a kind" 100' Camper & Nicholson yacht. She was loving restored to accommodate up to 10 guests in 5 comfortable staterooms. Available for Charter in Greece and Turkey, plus other Mediterranean ports - of - call, year round. Charter rate from $38,000 per week, plus some expenses.

Luxury Yacht Vacations • Charter Marketing • Yacht Brokerage • New Construction

BROKERAGE · CHARTER · NEW CONSTRUCTION · MANAGEMENT

EDMISTON:
THE RIGHT YACHT
IN THE RIGHT PLACE
AT THE RIGHT TIME.

Edmiston is dedicated to providing the very best in yachting. We buy, sell, charter, arrange to build or refit, the finest yachts in the world. Our experience takes in superyachts of every persuasion, from the latest in modern technology to Classics that grace the oceans. Each client and every yacht has a distinct personality and we will find the perfect yacht to charter for a cruise in the Mediterranean, or to purchase for the ultimate in privacy. Only the best yachts stand the test of time and that is why, at Edmiston, we make a point of distinguishing the best from the rest.

edmiston

EDMISTON & COMPANY LIMITED
51 CHARLES STREET
LONDON. W1X 7PA. UK
TELEPHONE: +44 171 495 515
TELEFAX: +44 171 495 515
E-MAIL: edmiston@btintern

EDMISTON & COMPANY
9 AVENUE D'OSTENDE
MONTE CARLO, MONACO
MC 98000
TELEPHONE: +377 93 30 54 44
TELEFAX: +377 93 30 55 33
E-MAIL: edmiston@infonie.f

http://yachtworld.com/edmiston

At Richard Bertram, excellence has been a time honored tradition since 1946.

For over fifty years, Richard Bertram has been catering to the needs of yachtsman around the world. Whether it's purchasing a new or pre-owned yacht, selling your current yacht or undergoing a complete refit or extension, Richard Bertram's standard of excellence is a time honored tradition.

Benetti's new *Classic Series*

   AZIMUT BERTRAM

RICHARD BERTRAM, INC.

Benetti CLASSIC

MIAMI, FL
(305) 633-9761 • Fax (305) 634-9071

FORT LAUDERDALE, FL
(954) 467-8405 • Fax (954) 763-2675

DANIA, FL
(954) 925-9070 • Fax (954) 925-9540

Web Site: www.bertramyacht.com • E-mail: rbi@bertramyacht.com

YACHT BROKERAGE • MARTY A LOWE INTERIORS • YACHT FINANCING AND INSURANCE • FULL SERVICE YARD • CHARTER SERVICES

extravagance you can enjoy.

Or the simplicity.

Freedom of choice for the discerning few on the world's finest luxury yachts. For two decades the Crestar approach to private yacht charter has become synonymous with a service that is second to none ~ an exclusive charter formula tailored for those who demand excellence.

CRESTAR
YACHT CHARTERS

COLETTE COURT 125 SLOANE STREET LONDON SW1X 9AU, ENGLAND.
Tel: +44(0)171 730 2299   Toll Free from USA: 1 800 222 9985   Fax: +44 (0) 171 824 8691   E-mail: crestaryachts@mail.com

CRESTAR YACHTS...DEDICATED TO EXCELLENCE

NIGEL BURGESS

INTERNATIONAL
LARGE YACHT SPECIALISTS

MONACO - FORT LAUDERDALE - LONDON

Le Panorama, 57 rue Grimaldi
MC 98000 Monaco
Telephone: +377 93 50 22 64
Telefax: +377 93 25 15 89
Email: monaco@nigelburgess.com

801 Seabreeze Boulevard, Bahia Mar Yachting Center
Fort Lauderdale, FL 33316, USA
Telephone: +1 954 525 1090
Telefax: +1 954 525 0297
Email: ftlaud@amels.nigelburgess.com

16/17 Pall Mall
London SW1Y 5LU, UK
Telephone: +44 (0) 171 766 4300
Telefax: +44 (0) 171 766 4329
Email: london@nigelburgess.com

THE MEGAYACHT CENTURY SPONSOR

DIRECTORY

CONTRIBUTORS

Cotter

PATRICK COTTER

Patrick Cotter writes about many kinds of boats, from skiffs to supertankers. Besides magazine and commercial writing, he writes children's stories, poetry and cartoons. He lives with his wife, two children, one dog, two cats, and five rabbits in Burnaby, a suburb of Vancouver, B.C.

CRAIG DAVIS

Never far from the sea, Craig Davis is *ShowBoats International's* contributing editor for Southern Europe. As a photo-journalist, he concentrates his lenses and writing on yacht racing and the luxury boat market. Davis lives in the south of France and travels throughout the world, covering events like the America's Cup and the luxury boat centers of the Mediterranean basin.

Davis

JONATHAN EASTLAND

An award-winning British photojournalist and specialist in marine affairs, Jonathan Eastland is *ShowBoats International's* contributing editor for Northern Europe. Author of many books, including *Great Yachts and Their Designers, Camera At Sea, Romance of Tall Ships* and several photographic works, he is an acknowledged expert on Leica cameras. He and his family live aboard a converted British patrol boat.

Eastland

JOSEPH GRIBBONS

Joseph Gribbons has been on board boating publications since 1961. He was the founding editor of *Motorboat* in 1973-74, and in 1977 he launched *Nautical Quarterly* in partnership with Don McGraw and Martin Pedersen. Currently he is the Publications Director at Mystic Seaport in Connecticut.

Gribbons

JASON HOLTOM

With a BA in history, Jason Holtom was lured to sea with the chance to skipper an offshore racing yacht. Eventually he ended up aboard *Lionheart,* Britian's 1980 America's Cup entry. He filled spare moments with regatta reports for *Seahorse* and *Yachting World.* He was editor of *Seahorse* and *Boat International,* and managing editor of *The Superyachts* annual. He now heads a marketing consultancy in London.

Holtom

MARK MASCIAROTTE

A regular contributor to *ShowBoats International,* Mark Masciarotte applauds portable satellite communications, which allow him to stay in touch with clients no matter where he pursues his two favorite pastimes: angling and aviation. A respected consultant on vessel design and construction, Mark writes and coordinates yacht and ship projects from his base in Vancouver, Washington.

Masciarotte

SHAW MCCUTCHEON

For over a quarter-century Shaw McCutcheon was a newspaper and magazine reporter, gradually turning to photography to illustrate his stories. As a New York-based photojournalist, he traveled to 26 countries on assignment for magazines. He served as Senior Editor and chief photographer at *Boating* before moving to Florida to devote his attention full time to writing and nautical photography.

McCutcheon

ROY OWEN ROBERTS

After earning a degree in fine art and a spell playing guitar in a '60s rock band, Roy started The Owen Agency in 1969 and began photographing yachts some 20 years ago. Brought up in a sailing family, it was natural that the agency's client base gravitated to marine accounts.

Roberts

PAUL O'PECKO

Paul O'Pecko is the Library Director at Mystic Seaport in Mystic, Conneticut. He is a member of the editorial board of the Log of Mystic Seaport, as well as its book review editor. He is a frequent contributor of reviews and other publications about maritime history.

O'Pecko

ANDREW ROGERS

Born in Ipswich, England, Andrew Rogers graduated with a degree in history. After seven years teaching school, he moved to Holland for a career in corporate journalism. Under the company name Writewell, Andrew creates copy for various international concerns within and outside the yachting industry.

Rogers

JACK A. SOMER

Jack Somer became a professional sailor in 1970, running ocean racers, private yachts and charter yachts. After contributing many marine articles as a freelancer, he joined Yachting as an associate editor, becoming editor in 1986. Since returning to freelance writing, Somer has authored seven books, including *Juliet: The Creation of a Masterpiece, M/Y Izanami, and Tigonderoga: Tales of an Enchanted Yacht.* He lives in Connecticut.

Somer

IVOR WILKINS

Ivor Wilkins is New Zealand's leading marine journalist and photographer. He has edited a number of marine publications and is a contributing editor for *ShowBoats International.* Apart from a close interest in superyachts, he is also totally immersed in the America's Cup. Wilkins and his wife immigrated from the UK to New Zealand aboard their Sadler 34.

Wilkins

WILLIAM COLLIER

Actively involved in the preservation of the world's yachting heritage, William Collier has been responsible for ensuring the restoration of a number of significant classic yachts. Along with practical involvement in restoration projects, he holds a Ph.D. in the history of yacht design and construction.

SHAW McCUTCHEON

EDITORIAL STAFF

From left to right, Jim Gilbert, Editor-In-Chief; Marilyn Mower, Executive Editor; Lee Barnes, Picture Editor; and Janet Santelices, Art Director.
The Editors gratefully acknowledge the contributions of Stan Grayson and George Fotiadis, as well as the entire staff of *ShowBoats International.*